The Economics of Defense

Members of Congress for Peace Through Law Military Spending Committee

introduction by
Senator Mark O. Hatfield

The Praeger Special Studies program—utilizing the most modern and efficient book production techniques and a selective worldwide distribution network—makes available to the academic, government, and business communities significant, timely research in U.S. and international economic, social, and political development.

The Economics of Defense
A Bipartisan Review of Military Spending

PRAEGER SPECIAL STUDIES IN U.S. ECONOMIC AND SOCIAL DEVELOPMENT

Praeger Publishers   New York   Washington   London

PRAEGER PUBLISHERS
111 Fourth Avenue, New York, N.Y. 10003, U.S.A.
5, Cromwell Place, London S.W.7, England

Published in the United States of America in 1971
by Praeger Publishers, Inc.

© 1971 by Praeger Publishers, Inc.

Library of Congress Catalog Card Number: 76-153393

Printed in the United States of America

As members of the Military Spending Committee of Members of Congress for Peace Through Law and other involved offices, we offer this volume as a bipartisan review of selected U.S. military programs. Obviously, the materials herein are not exhaustive. We feel, however, that these particular issues demand greater public and Congressional attention.

Our examination of the utility and necessity of requested defense funding is made with particular concern for fiscal responsibility and with a deep interest in a proper allocation of national resources. We have concluded that significant military reductions can be made without in any way weakening our national security. Indeed, the improved management and procurement practices we recommend would undoubtedly strengthen the national military posture. A reordering of national priorities, moreover, would help stabilize the economy on which all our federal programs are based and would release funds for the education and basic research on which our future security depends. Although we may not be in complete agreement on every specific point, we are unanimous in our recommendations for adjustments in the Department of Defense budget, including general reductions.

Our recommended retrenchments for FY 1971 ranged from $4.4 to $5.4 billion, excluding manpower. To include manpower figures would roughly double this number. Considering that the projects affected involved long-term funding commitments, these immediate cutback figures understate the long-term savings.

The Committee's previous research was concerned almost exclusively with weapons systems. In the present volume, however, we thought it necessary to also address the question of overseas troop deployments, threat projections, and the impact of defense spending on the economy. In each case, we offer recommendations pinpointing problem areas.

We emphasize that this is only a small part of what should

be a continuing review of military programs by Congress and the public.

We invite the comments and support of the American public and other Members of Congress.

Military Spending Committee
of the
Members of Congress for Peace Through Law

Senator Mark O. Hatfield
Senator William Proxmire, Co-Chairmen

Senator Thomas F. Eagleton
Senator Charles E. Goodell
Senator Mike Gravel
Senator Vance Hartke
Senator Harold E. Hughes
Senator Charles McC. Mathias, Jr.
Senator George S. McGovern
Senator Walter F. Mondale
Senator Gaylord Nelson
Congressman Brock Adams
Congressman Edward P. Boland
Congressman George E. Brown, Jr.
Congressman Jeffery Cohelan
Congressman Donald M. Fraser
Congressman Gilbert Gude
Congressman Lee H. Hamilton
Congressman Robert L. Leggett
Congressman Abner J. Mikva
Congressman William S. Moorhead
Congressman Charles A. Mosher
Congressman F. Bradford Morse
Congressman Lucien N. Nedzi
Congressman Ogden R. Reid
Congressman Henry S. Reuss
Congressman Morris K. Udall

ACKNOWLEDGMENTS

To the small staff of Members of Congress for Peace Through Law, led by its former Executive Director, Joan L. McKinney, fell the burden of assembling and coordinating the original manuscript. Rebecca Rubenstein, executive assistant, spent many long days typing and stylizing that manuscript. George Gilder, formerly of Senator Charles McC. Mathias' staff, struggled intensively with the preliminary chapters, checking for accuracy and consistency. The overall editor of this book is Ronald Tammen. As consultant to the Military Spending Committee, he was responsible for coordinating the work of the Congressional staffs, non-Congressional specialists, and student researchers, as well as furnishing all those talents necessary to complete this study.

This book is dedicated to the many private individuals who so generously gave of their resources in the spirit of world peace through law. Without their moral and financial help, this project never would have been completed.

CONTENTS

LIST OF TABLES

TABLES IN THE APPENDIX

LIST OF ABBREVIATIONS

AA   Anti-Aircraft

ABM   Anti-Ballistic Missile System

ABRES   Advanced Ballistic Re-entry System

AMSA   Advanced Manned Strategic Aircraft (B-1)

ASROC   Anti-Submarine Rocket

ASW   Anti-Submarine Warfare

BDM   Bomber Defense Missile

BMEWS   Ballistic Missile Early Warning Systems

CAINS   Carrier Airborne Inertial Navigation System

CASS   Command Activated Sonobuoy System

CIA   Central Intelligence Agency

CPI   Consumer Price Index

CRAF   Contract Reserve Air Fleet

CVA   Attack Aircraft Carrier

CVS   Anti-Submarine Carrier

DCI   Director of Central Intelligence

DIA   Defense Intelligence Agency

DOD   Department of Defense

ECM	Electronic Warfare
EEC	European Economic Community
FEBA	Forward Edge of Battle Area
FOBS	Fractional Orbit Bombardment System
GAO	General Accounting Office
HEST	High Explosive Simulation Test
ICBM	Inter-Continental Ballistic Missile
IDA	Institute for Defense Analysis
INT	Intelligence and Reports (Department of State)
LLLTV	Low Light Level TV
MAD	Magnetic Anomaly Detector
MCPL	Members of Congress for Peace Through Law
MIRV	Multiple Independently-targeted Re-entry Vehicle
MOL	Manned Orbiting Laboratory
MRV	Multiple Re-entry Vehicle
MSR	Missile Site Radar
NIE	National Intelligence Estimate
NSA	National Security Agency
NSC	National Security Council
OSD	Office of the Secretary of Defense
OTH	Over the Horizon Radar
PAR	Perimeter Acquisition Radar

PBCS	Post Boost Control System
PP	Project Prime
PPE	Purchasing Power Equivalent
R&D	Research and Development
RDT&E	Research, Development, Test & Engineering
RETORC	Research Torpedo Configuration
RFP	Request for Proposal
RV	Re-entry Vehicle
SABRE	Self-Aligning Boost and Re-entry
SALT	Strategic Arms Limitation Talks
SAM	Surface-to-Air Missile
SAR	Selected Acquisition Report
SCAD	Subsonic Cruise Armed Decoy
SLBM	Submarine-Launched Ballistic Missile
SNIE	Special National Intelligence Estimate
SRAM	Short-Range Attack Missile
SRGS	Survivable Radio Guidance System
SUBROC	Submarine-Launched Rocket
ULMS	Undersea Long-Range Missile System
USIB	United States Intelligence Board

The Economics of Defense

INTRODUCTION
by Senator Mark O. Hatfield

This book is the product of a new concept at work in the U.S. Congress.

Over the years, Congress has witnessed many new personalities. Party control has shifted back and forth, and with that have come various ideological preferences. Seldom, however, have new organizational concepts caught hold in this tradition-bound body.

The new concept at work today is on the one hand idealistic and on the other revolutionary--idealistic because it calls for the best from men, revolutionary because it offers an alternative to the traditional play of power, politics, and party loyalty.

This concept has both spirit and form. The organization is called Members of Congress for Peace Through Law (MCPL). The spirit is less definable but is shown in the enthusiasm of the 105 Members of Congress of both Houses who have voluntarily joined our ranks.

The organization had its origin at a breakfast meeting called by former Senator Joseph S. Clark in 1959. Sparked by parliamentary groups in Great Britain and Europe, he hoped to rally U.S. support for the concept of enforceable world law. With the bipartisan support of Senator Jacob K. Javits and Congressman James G. Fulton and the fifteen other Members present, an informal bicameral organization was formed, called Members of Congress for World Peace Through the Rule of Law. For seven years, until 1966, this group held luncheons with prominent world figures such as President Habib Bourguiba of Tunisia and former Secretary of State Christian Herter.

In 1966, the momentum of the group swung in a new direction. A full-time permanent staff was authorized, headed by Executive Director Joan L. McKinney. Senator Clark became the group's Chairman. Within a few months, the Members agreed upon priority issues and a method of operating. The Members decided to carry out investigation of issues in small subcommittees, reporting back to the parent body with recommendations or legislation. The first committees dealt with Viet-Nam, the United Nations, and U.S. Military Spending.

This committee approach to problems was enthusiastically
encouraged by Congressman F. Bradford Morse, the newly
elected Chairman in 1968. In recognition of his service and
dedication, Senator Clark was made the permanent Honorary
Chairman.

As the organization continued to pick up new Members, it
branched into several new subcommittees. Chairmen were
elected to head committees investigating East-West Trade,
International Law, U.S.-China Relations, the Middle East,
and Economic Development. In some cases, such as U.S.-
China Relations, the work of these committees is unprecedented
in the Congress.

It is worthwhile to inquire what has triggered the growth
of this organization from 15 to 105 Members of Congress.
Congressman Charles W. Whalen, Jr., has put it well: "MCPL
meetings are an oasis on Capitol Hill where party affiliations
and the formalities of Congress are left outside the door. Here
we can examine the problems which agonize the world as individuals in an atmosphere of mutual concern and a shared determination to find solutions."[1] Senator George S. McGovern
has emphasized the urgency behind MCPL's activities: "Through
MCPL, Members of Congress are searching actively and with
growing effect for alternatives to the rule of fear and force.
No task is more urgent. In a nuclear age, each decision may
effect the survival of our society and of all mankind."[2]

The uniqueness of MCPL is readily observable. Where
else would a senior Democratic Senator serve under the chairmanship of a House Republican? What freshman Senator or
Congressman was ever elected to a committee chairmanship?
How many times have two men running for the same office
worked together on a project, even during their campaign?
Yet all of these things have happened in MCPL. The flexibility
and freedom within MCPL is one of its most attractive aspects.

MCPL has made an impact in many areas, but it is perhaps
known most for its in-depth analysis of U.S. military programs.
In 1969, I had the honor of being asked to serve as Chairman
of the Military Spending Committee. The Committee had a
good base to build upon. Several MCPL Members began expression of the fight against the Anti-Ballistic Missile System
(ABM) as early as October of 1967.

---

1. Charles W. Whalen in "What's MCPL?," (Washington,
D.C.: Members of Congress for Peace Through Law, November, 1969). (Brochure.)

2. George S. McGovern, ibid.

We were faced with immediate challenges. The problems facing any thorough examination of U.S. military policies and weapons are staggering. The new weapons are extremely complex and technical. Defense strategies and contingency plans rarely are available even to Members of Congress. Furthermore, the military budget defies easy analysis. All of this suggested that any honest examination of U.S. programs had to be rigorous but limited. No one Member could hope to master all the intricacies of modern weaponry. Nor could we hope to duplicate the analysis that comes from thousands of Pentagon employees. We chose, therefore, to be selective and thorough, concentrating our resources on manageable projects.

In 1969, each Committee member picked one weapon system or policy to analyze personally. Each office then engaged in extensive background research, isolating the critical arguments about its system and committing these to paper in a uniform format. The Committee met several times during this process to exchange progress reports and coordinate timing. The end product was a forty-page document called the 1969 Report on Military Spending. Fifteen Committee members were involved in the preparation of this Report which analyzed nine different areas of military spending, and a total of over fifty more Members of Congress co-sponsored the project. Released in July of 1969, the Report called for legislative action to reduce military spending by $3 billion, including cutbacks in the ABM, aircraft, aircraft carriers, chemical warfare, and the Main Battle Tank.

Competent research, of course, is by itself without impact. It must be committed to legislation. To this end, Committee members sponsored a number of amendments to the House and Senate Military Authorization Bill. By and large, these specific amendments did not pass. Their effect, however, was not lost on Congress.

At the time of the 1969 Report, several major Pentagon programs were either cut back or disbanded. The Manned Orbiting Laboratory (MOL) is a case in point. The entire program was dropped from the Department of Defense (DOD) budget. Although it is not possible to document that our research on the MOL was a causal factor in its elimination, we certainly feel that Congressional skepticism contributed to the scuttling decision. In a similar fashion, some recommendations were not immediately acted upon by DOD, but later decisions had the effect of implementing certain of our suggestions. The chemical-biological warfare research conducted

by Congressman Richard D. McCarthy provided an example
of this delayed reaction. In addition, there is no way of measuring how our recommendations affected subsequent Administration requests or Congressional committee actions, but it
is likely that some influence occurred.

Our research also had other indirect consequences. The
visibility given these systems and the attendant controversies
intensified the scrutiny of the Congressional Standing Committees. This has resulted in the Appropriations Committees of
both Houses making cuts in the military budget in the last two
years.

Early in 1970, the Military Spending Committee met to
map out its strategy for the first session of the Ninety-first
Congress. The Committee decided to expand its research
into policy areas such as economics, intelligence, and manpower levels, and to invite all Members of Congress to join
in an ambitious military research project. As with the previous year, each Senator or Congressman chose one system
or policy to investigate. The MCPL staff coordinated this
operation, compiling and editing the research papers for this
book.

One cannot grasp the full significance of this study without a short look back to the years when the military budget
passed through Congress almost automatically or in some
cases was increased beyond original requests. Through the
1960's, the United States was concluding a rather massive
buildup in strategic weapons. Sputnik, the "missile gap," and
the Cuban crisis of 1962 reinforced this arms acquisition process. In a period of dynamic arms procurement, the tendency
in Congress is to facilitate, not hinder, military appropriations.
Congress obliged by generally allowing carte blanche for military requests. In retrospect, it is interesting to note former
Secretary of Defense Robert McNamara's comments that this
buildup was not justified in terms of Soviet programs. It was
a costly overreaction to a nonexistent threat.

By the late 1960's, however, the disposition of Congress
began to shift, almost imperceptibly. National economic
strains appeared, generated by the inflationary financing of
the Viet-Nam war. The Soviet Union was recognized as approaching parity with the United States in numbers of strategic
weapons. The myth of the world communist monolith had been
convincingly dispelled. Slowly these facts exerted their weight
on Congress and some calls for rethinking were heard.

The military budget came under closer scrutiny both by
the relevant committees and also by certain Members of

Congress who felt a responsibility to speak out. For the most
part, these efforts were individual in character. They took
two forms, amendments on individual weapon systems and
amendments limiting overall spending. In 1962, different
amendments were offered by Senators Clark, Hart, and Williams of Delaware in an attempt to place a ceiling on defense
bills. With the exception of Senator Williams' 3 per cent cutback, these amendments found little sympathy in the Senate.

Contrast this attitude, then, with the spirit of Congress
in 1969 and 1970. The military budget for FY 1970 was cut
about $5.6 billion and the FY 1971 budget reduced $2.2 billion.
The Armed Services and Appropriations Committees of both
Houses deserve special commendation for their leadership in
this area. An attempt to limit the size of FY 1971 military
expenditures (Proxmire-Mathias Amendment) was narrowly
defeated, 42-31, a surprising tally that reinforced the subsequent work of the Appropriations Committees.

Other forces also have been at work. The General Accounting Office (GAO) diligently examined weapon systems for
cost overruns and made this information available to Congress.
It became all too evident that many U.S. weapon programs
have experienced rather dramatic cost growths.

Also concerned, the Defense Department undertook a review of weapons development and procurement procedures.
Deputy Secretary of Defense David Packard characterized his
findings in a blunt, straightforward statement: "Let's face it--
the fact is that there has been bad management of many Defense
programs in the past. We spend billions of the taxpayers' dollars: sometimes we spend it badly. . . . However, most of
it has been due to bad management, both in the Department of
Defense and in the Defense Industry."[3] "When we are not in
a hurry to get things done right, we over-organize, over-man,
over-spend, and under accomplish."[4] The President's Blue
Ribbon Defense Panel (Fitzhugh Report) likewise cited deficient
DOD practices.

Recognizing that it is very helpful that these reviews of
DOD have been undertaken, the primary responsibility for
military problems nevertheless remains with Congress. The
present situation is too serious for retrospective blame-placing.
Each branch of government must exercise good judgment and

---

3. David Packard, Speech before the Armed Forces Management Association, Los Angeles, August 20, 1970 (Department of Defense Release No. 681-70).

4. Ibid.

pay persistent attention to the development of new weapons and
policies. In this, Congress has a unique Constitutional responsibility, one clearly envisioned by the Founding Fathers.

In the nuclear age, foreign policy and military policy are
almost inextricable. Weapons determine military strategies,
which in turn are based upon political and historical judgments
about national security. This interrelationship makes it even
more important that Congress carefully screen the military
budget.

The Members of the Military Spending Committee feel a
definite responsibility to provide more than piecemeal criticism. First, we uncovered the facts. Then, armed with
sound data, we offered alternative approaches to present policies. The underlying principle of all this research is the con-
viction that reductions can be made in military spending <u>with-
out any corresponding weakening of national security</u>. In the
long run, the increase in efficiency and management we recommend undoubtedly would strengthen our military posture.

Several other themes thread through this volume. First,
we recognize that research and development (R&D) lays the
base for our future military security. It is also well known
that weapon systems have built-in pressures for deployment.
Therefore, at the critical decision point of procurement, we
recommend a searching evaluation of the utility and need for
these weapons. In much of our research, we have found that
the R&D effort has not warranted the deployment of the weapon.
In these cases, we urge further research and development and
categorically reject the tendency toward concurrent development and production.

In some cases we have favored the continued funding of
major programs, particularly with regard to sea-based deterrents. This is not an expression of doctrine on our part but
simply an awareness that the invulnerability of our deterrent
is a critical component in strategic planning. Similarly, we
are increasingly concerned that fixed-based missiles are becoming more vulnerable to accurate re-entry vehicles. Turning this problem around, we also express the fear that the
Minuteman III Multiple Independently-targeted Re-entry Vehicle
(MIRV) will appear to be a first-strike weapon to Soviet planners. In this case, weapon accuracy is the key variable.

The material in the following chapters was put to good
use by the Senate and the House. It is quite self-explanatory
and needs no further interpretation here. Let me stress in
closing, however, that the questions we grapple with today
will determine our posture many years from now, not only
militarily but domestically.

I feel that the forces of reason and patience are with us, in Congress, at the arms limitations negotiations, and across our nation. A small offering this is in a world so clouded with doubt. But even small offerings measure faith.

PART

I

MILITARY
SPENDING AND
CONGRESS

1

THE
DEFENSE
DOLLAR

In real terms, U. S. economic growth has nearly halted over the past five years. Although all actual production measures have shown upward movement since 1965, inflation has simultaneously wiped out real gains--and attempts to check it have only worsened the situation.

The 1965-70 period suggests that conventional tools for economic balance are rendered impotent when there is a tendency to mobilize for massive defense spending.

Inflation, gauged by changes in the consumer price index (CPI) and the GNP Implicit Price Deflators, began at a steady 2 per cent rate in 1965, sped up to over a 3 per cent annual rate through 1966 and 1967, moved up to over 4 per cent in 1968, was above 5 per cent in 1969, and continued at around 6 per cent for early 1970.

Each proposed remedy for this problem--whether of the fiscal or monetary variety--either made no dent or caused some unwanted side effect, such as the collapse of the housing sector after the government pushed up interest rates in an effort to stem consumer spending. The only course not attempted was large reduction in defense spending.

Yet the failure of all other economic tools indicates that we may isolate the cause for current problems as the failure to cut defense.

Federal spending in total rose only 2 per cent in 1965. It jumped 15 per cent in 1966, and another 16 per cent in 1967. Restraints were applied in 1968, but spending still rose 9 per cent and moved upward an additional 6 per cent in fiscal 1969. Attempts were made to limit total government spending, but as long as war held precedence the squeeze was not applied to the largest of all sectors.

This limitation on budget constraint was so telling that in the end it meant that no tool could be effective, no matter what policy mix was tried. The imbalance caused by massive defense spending threw out of whack the delicate devices used for peacetime stabilization.

Quantitative effects of huge defense budgets are just one factor behind recent inflation; just as important are many qualitative effects.

For one example, social benefits are less from each marginal dollar invested in the defense sector than they would be from investment in education. Although there is some technological spillover from the military to the civilian economy, the end-use of most defense investment does little to promote real economic growth and development.

On another level, the expanding defense budget shifted resources from other sectors and excess demand developed in non-defense areas. The effect came on two sides. Resource shifting meant that resource costs would rise, thus increasing production costs. At the same time, consumers, seeing less goods available, tended to up their price bids. The result was to create a series of inflationary pressures emanating from both suppliers and purchasers.

In theory, economic policy was aimed to forestall such pressures. The intent of the surtax was to cut back on potential demand; interest rate curbs were to tighten credit; and the market was to settle back to some new equilibrium.

But there was a catch. Although it was intended to reduce inflation, the surtax also was the prime means of financing the war and other defense spending increases. The net result, taking into account various multiplier effects, was an increase in the imbalance of resources flowing into the defense sectors. And these resulting distortions and inefficiencies eventually caused unemployment and promoted inflation.

WHY CUT DEFENSE?

Often in inflationary periods, conventional wisdom suggests imposition of mandatory wage-price controls. The simple theory holds that high wage rates--large contract settlements--are the most visible factor. Pressure applied on them is held to have positive effects throughout the entire system.

Although fine in theory, the wage-price freeze has yet to prove effective in long-term use. Controls worked to some extent during World War II, but when they were lifted after the war, the consumer price index rose nearly 33 per cent over two years. Guidelines--non-mandatory controls--were also partially effective from 1962 to 1965, but when they were first broken and then ignored past mid-1965, the current inflation took hold.

Traditional wisdom fails here because it aims for the wrong target--at least on a long-term basis. On a purely short-range level, controls undoubtedly do work, but the evidence indicates that their effectiveness diminishes the longer they are in existence. Over the long run, the controls will never be an optimal solution. Inflation must be treated as if it were a fever, an indication of sickness rather than the malady itself. Fevers are not cured by freezing the thermometer, and inflation is not halted by constraining wage and price levels.

Inflation results from a distorted economy, and the chief distortion in the current economy is huge investment in the ultimately unproductive area of defense. Yet in times of budget-cutting pressure, the tendency has been to slash social welfare rather than military programs. The proportion of resources devoted to social welfare (mainly education and health-care services) has decreased whenever defense allocations have risen.

The problem is that the demand for social welfare services continues to grow. In the seven years between 1958 and 1965, the social services component of the CPI rose a total of only 16 per cent, or a bit over 2 per cent annually. Then, from 1965 through April, 1970, the index jumped 30 per cent. It rose at a low 2 per cent rate during 1965, advanced 1 per cent per year through 1966, 1967, and 1968, increased around 7 per cent in 1969, and 8 per cent between April, 1969, and April, 1970.

So we have the prospect of heavy inflationary tendencies in the social welfare sector over coming years as demand for such services continues to rise, and while overall government policies favor constrained spending. It is clear that the only escape from this inflationary pressure is to cut spending not in services but in defense.

REAL COST OF NATIONAL SECURITY

Any discussion of defense spending should begin with a recognition of ignorance--we do not know what the real costs are.

We do not know the total monetary cost because the Pentagon typically understates and underreports or conducts essentially military and paramilitary spending under various non-defense appropriations. Many governmental activities, ostensibly civilian, should have some portion of their costs allocated to defense. Programs in transportation and communications, for example, cost more than they would if only non-defense functions were accounted. The expenditures of the Central Intelligence Agency (CIA) are not explicitly reported at all. Moreover, government cost estimates are arbitrary and do not normally reflect real costs, which tend to increase enormously between contracting and delivery of weapons or services.

As a rough approximation, 70 per cent of total world military expenditures are borne by the United States and the Soviet Union, with the United States leading all other countries in the real cost of defense per capita. True, the argument is usually made in terms of percentage of gross national product, whereby the U. S. effort seems relatively smaller. But real cost in purchasing power equivalent (PPE) gives a better idea of the sacrifice entailed. The following figures represent 1966 costs:

	Real Cost in Purchasing Power Equivalent	Real Cost Per Capita in PPE	Armed Forces Per 1,000 Population
United States	$63,283 million	$322	15.7
Soviet Union	$44,500 million	$191	13.6

The magnitude of this effort is dramatized in comparison-- the United States spends $322 per capita by this measure; the United Kingdom, $105; France, $94; United Arab Republic, $17; North Viet-Nam, $18; North Korea, $37; and Mainland China, $9.

Another way of coming at the "true cost" of defense is to consider alternatives foregone. This concept of "opportunity cost" is relevant here both in narrow money terms and, more broadly, in terms of "costs" to the society. Arguments on national priorities between defense and civilian programs illustrate the opportunity-cost idea--what "might have been."

The intangible cost, moreover, of focusing so much of our material resources, political energies, and executive attentions on an elusive military goal may be higher than is usually recognized. In foreign policy, we should consider the cost of initiatives not taken and attention not given to our affairs in Europe, Africa, and South America as well as in other Asian countries, such as Japan. In domestic affairs, we should take account not only of foregone social programs, but also of widespread civil strife and demoralization.

The sum of all these (and other) costs, tangible and intangible, direct and indirect, should make up any real tally of the price of national security as we now pursue it.

GROWTH AND DEFENSE EXPENDITURES

It is generally agreed that the characteristics of a healthy U. S. economy include (1) maintenance of effective demand to sustain reasonably full employment and relatively stable prices; (2) a level of savings, investment, and innovation sufficient to keep the economy growing at least as fast as the annual average (4 per cent); (3) a large measure of consumer sovereignty; (4) equitable income distribution; and (5) some reasonable balance between the public and private sectors in economic decision-making.

Apologists for the military--as well as leftist critics of the "warfare state"--seem to agree that massive defense spending is a boon to the U. S. economy. This is false. Although the direct beneficiaries of military spending form a powerful constituency in favor of it, the U. S. economy as a whole would be far healthier with a much smaller defense budget.

Comparative economic analysis demonstrates that the substitution of other types of expenditures, whether public or private, would over a relatively short period create more income and employment than would be lost through cutbacks in military spending.

There would, of course, be some transfer costs associated with any substantial shift away from defense. Included would be the cost of specific sectoral and locational shifts, affecting, for example, the aircraft industry and California. There would be rapid depreciation of specialized skills and equipment. And there might be some temporary falling off of total demand and economic momentum.

But these magnitudes tend to be overstated. We are now smart enough and have sufficient fiscal tools available to handle the transfer smoothly and without undue turmoil. For in aggregate terms, the impact of disarmament itself would be barely noticeable.

If, as seems likely, one dollar of defense spending on the average is less stimulating to the economy overall than a dollar of private spending, then the continued diversion of scarce skills, materials, and other resources to the defense sector may actually impede economic growth. Lower defense expenditures could mean lower taxes, hence greater disposable income, and a resultant expansion in private purchasing power (accompanied by less inflation) to offset the original reduction of defense spending.

Because the Pentagon shopping list is very different from the average citizen's, a cutback in defense spending would produce demand increases in some industries and markets while others slacked off. Over a relatively short period of time, sales and induced investment would be rechanneled as the composition of total demand changed.

A quantitative basis for analyzing the problem was provided nine years ago in a famous article appearing in Scientific American by Wassily W. Leontief and Marvin Hoffenberg. [1] Through the use of input-output tables, the authors traced the aggregate and sector-by-sector results of an assumed 20 per cent defense cut accompanied by an equal increase in non-military expenditures. Since their article was published, the military budget has nearly doubled. Updating their figures, one would assume a $16 billion cut in a close to $80 billion budget.

Not surprisingly, the authors found that the industry group most affected by such a cut would be "Transportation Equipment and Ordinance," aircraft, motor vehicles, shipbuilding, railway equipment, and munitions proper. The next most affected groups were "Instruments and Related Products" and "Electrical Machinery." They also found that the industry groups--"Transportation," "Trade," and "Service and Finance"--are less dependent on military demand, and would benefit from any increased demand in the civilian sectors.

Under their assumptions of an $8 billion cut in a $40 billion military budget, the authors found the result was a net increase of 288,888 jobs in "Business Employment," but a net deficit in "Total Employment" of 121,000 jobs for the short term (over 200,000 in present terms). After the initial dislocations are overcome, however, past experience as well as comparative labor intensity and multiplier statistics suggest that employment growth would grow more rapidly with a greater proportion of civilian spending. After World War II

and the Korean War, the U. S. economy responded with ac-
celerated growth and employment expansion to relatively unplanned and precipitate challenges of adjustment.

A related issue is the probable impact of defense cutbacks
on research and development and hence on U. S. technological
leadership. The Department of Defense supports better than
half the R&D work done in three industries--airframe and
aircraft, electrical equipment, and communications--yet provides less than 10 per cent of the funds for many others--food,
chemicals, petroleum, and primary metals industries. Of the
total R&D effort, most is conducted in government facilities,
next most in industry facilities, and least in colleges and other
non-profit institutions.

A few years ago, it was calculated that a 50 per cent de-
cline in defense spending would lead to a 23 per cent cutback
in the employment of scientists and engineers. The salaries
of scientists and engineers comprise only one fourth of R&D
costs in American industry.

Again, there would be some short-run adjustment problems, but the rate of growth in employment of scientists and
engineers is greater than any other occupational group. And
their mobility is among the highest. At the same time, several forces are at work to assist their adjustment: (1) increased
demand for programs designed to combat the deterioration of
the environment; (2) concern for the rebuilding of cities and
the solving of urban problems; and (3) increasing attention on
the part of defense-related firms to apply high technology and
systems analysis capabilities to civil activity.

The conventional wisdom holds that military R&D yields
a bountiful crop of favorable spinoffs to the civilian sector--
in the economist's jargon, "externalities." The assumption
is, further, that the market would allocate a lesser amount
to R&D in the absence of public policy decisions to do so. Yet
if the photoelectric cell that allows us to leave the supermarket
without touching the door is a product of submarine R&D of an
earlier date, perhaps World War II was an excessive price to
pay for this convenience. In any case, there is no reason our
society could not decide--like Japan--to devote more resources
to civilian R&D after defense spending is reduced.

Military R&D, moreover, is turning increasingly to areas
of little relevance to the civilian economy. In fact, a strong
case can be made that continued growth in military R&D, space,
and Atomic Energy Commission activities has retarded civilian
R&D by bidding up salaries and bidding away the cream (and
bulk) of scientists and engineers from civilian laboratories.

The freeing of military-related R&D resources could well
result in higher yields elsewhere in society. Again, the
examples of Japan and Germany, with relatively low defense
spending and high rates of innovation and growth, suggest
that R&D is more catalytic economically in the civilian sector.

There are other unfavorable effects of massive and sustained military spending worth noting. If direct controls are
instituted, this comes at real cost to a free economy. High
tax burdens may reduce work incentives. The side effects of
having government "do our shopping" through defense procurement impairs consumer sovereignty and market structure.

For one example, military spending contributes to the
concentration of industry and may encourage collusive and
monopolistic practices elsewhere opposed (or forbidden) in
U.S. policy. Recall that three fourths of military contracts,
by value, typically go to 100 of the largest companies and less
than 15 per cent go to small businesses. Seven industry groups
comprising about sixty-five companies get 90 per cent of the
total (principally aircraft, vehicle, missile, electronic firms).
It is also worth noting that large businesses on the average
employ far fewer marginal workers per dollar of investment
than small businesses. Thus the concentration of defense
spending in large businesses may divert resources from areas
of the economy that might give jobs to the unemployed.

Despite occasional benefits, military spending also serves
poorly as a fiscal device. It has none of the advantages of the
automatic stabilizers, and its discretionary criteria are ir-
relevant to the stage of the economy in the business cycle.
Finally, the production of non-defense capital goods is better
for the overall economy and for living standards than the production of defense goods and services in both the long and the
short run. Yet for some time now, military outlays have
exceeded by several billion dollars the combined net annual
investment in manufacturing, services, transportation, and
agriculture. And this calculation does not consider spending
on education and human resources, which has been estimated
to be the single most important long-term factor in economic
growth.

INFLATION AND DEFENSE EXPENDITURES

The economy now suffers from inflation of both the
"demand-pull" and "cost-push" variety. On one hand, certain

sectors dominated by defense show an inflationary gap between
spending and existing capacity; and, on the other hand, wage-
price bargains in imperfectly competitive markets are causing
price levels to rise even though total spending is less than a
full-capacity economy would require.

Present defense-related inflation (1) impairs efficiency
in the economy by changing the measuring rod of costs; (2)
impairs work incentives and alters the savings/consumption
patterns; (3) creates a demand for direct controls; (4) lessens
confidence of the citizenry in government and the economic
system; and (5) distorts crucial sectors and creates imbalances.
Also of major significance is the fact that military spending is
not only the major cause of inflation but is itself a major victim
in terms of increasing the cost of its own operations. This is
one of the cycles that must be broken.

In analyzing the present economic situation, a key consideration is the specific impact of Viet-Nam war financing.
Government outlays for military goods rose from $50 billion
in 1964 to an estimated $79 billion in 1968, a 12 per cent
annual rate increase. Total real output grew at a 5 per cent
rate during this period, so that a steadily greater proportion
of the nation's production was used in the defense effort. The
real cost of the Viet-Nam war is probably incalculable because
of the intangible cost to our economy in lost opportunities and
the further shift to defense production away from consumer
production. But perhaps as important as the actual increase
is how it was financed.

In fiscal year 1967, there was an anticipated deficit in the
administrative budget of $1,847 million. The actual deficit for
fiscal year 1967 was $9,869 million. But this $8 billion mis-
understanding was dwarfed in fiscal year 1968, when the
anticipated budget deficit was $8,096 million and the actual
deficit was $28,286 million. The Administration's unwilling-
ness to acknowledge at the time that it was fighting a war
probably explains the reluctance to finance it.

In any case, this series of deficits caused by the Viet-Nam
war and the unwillingness to plan for its cost are what started
the present inflation and high interest rates. In the government's desperate attempt to finance these totally unplanned
costs, it seriously distorted the money market. This distortion continues today.

No previous war has been financed by a tight money policy.
Every war has been financed by an easy money policy. In
previous wars, the future national debt burden thus was not
financially crippling for coming generations. The reverse

policy is being pursued for the financing of the Viet-Nam war.
Deliberately established high interest rates are creating a
heavy future debt service.

Because of the unwillingness to face the realities of financing a war, billions and billions of dollars are being added
to the national debt. In such a situation, inflationary expecta-
tions are correct. Further inflationary pressures are caused
by the fact that defense spending tends to pump money into the
private economy while generating relatively few marketable
goods to soak it up.

Cost-benefit analysis has become a common notion in considering defense matters. The concept is useful in treating
rather specific connections such as the relationship between
changes in the reliability of a rifle and changes in its cost.
And it is helpful in considering on a grander level the relationship between changes in military expenditures and changes in
national security.

Importantly involved is the economist's principle of
diminishing (marginal) utility. The cost-benefit curve is determined as different levels of costs plotted on one axis and
measured against yields associated with those cost levels.
The typical cost-benefit curve looks like the following:

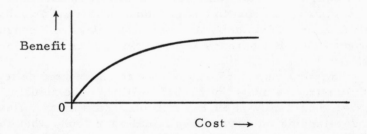

What is here argued is that present levels of defense
spending already find us way out on "the flat of the curve"
and that increases in defense expenditures (with all the other
non-monetary costs cited earlier) bring slight or no increase
in our national security (benefits). Indeed, we are probably
in the position where the curve turns downward as the weight
and impact of defense activities impair what is perhaps our
greatest material asset, the underlying strength of the U.S.
economy.

THE PEACE DIVIDEND

In mid-1968, the phrase "peace dividend" emerged as a
useful concept in planning for economic conversion and for
new domestic programs as the Viet-Nam war wound down. The
peace dividend measures the new funds made available for civilian needs as a result of cutbacks in Viet-Nam spending.

Congress and the Peace Dividend

Under the Constitution, Congress is given power over the
federal purse. In the process of appropriations, Congress
must make judgments on priorities between military and
civilian spending.

As the Viet-Nam war continues, with spillovers in Laos,
Thailand, and Cambodia, Congress is faced with the stark
questions of when the peace dividend will be available, how
much for how long, and where the funds released from war
spending should go.

Answers to these questions necessarily start with assessments of the actual dollar costs of U. S. involvement in Southeast Asian countries.

In 1968, Melvin Laird, then Member of the House of
Representatives, testified:

> For the last 2 or 3 years, the problem we have had
> in this committee has been the underestimation of
> defense costs. We have had to come forward here
> with a $10 billion or $11 billion supplemental in 1966,
> a $13 billion supplemental in 1967, and now this re-
> programming plus new obligational authority request
> of over $6 billion which we are considerning now. [2]

This repeated underestimation of the dollar cost of the
Viet-Nam war, together with conflicting testimony from different Administration witnesses, has led Members of Congress
to criticize Viet-Nam cost-analysis as a "numbers game" and
to demand that the real cost of the war be disclosed to Congress
and the American people. In response to this demand, Congress
has been presented with what might be called war-costs options.

In 1968, Secretary of Defense Robert McNamara testified
before Congress that "incremental cost" constituted the most
meaningful figure on Viet-Nam spending. Incremental cost

is the amount of Southeast Asia conflict costs over and above
normal costs of the defense establishment.   On the basis of
incremental costs, McNamara judged Viet-Nam spending to
be in the order of $17 to $20 billion (FY 1969). [3]

At the same time, Assistant Secretary of Defense Robert
Anthony told Congress that within the incremental cost concept
there was much room for dispute over details, and he submitted
that the cost of the war was in the order of $25 to $26 billion
(FY 1969). [4]

In the same year, Secretary of Defense Clark Clifford
presented Congress with his assessment and projected that
Viet-Nam would cost us perhaps $27 billion (FY 1969). [5]

What about the "full cost" concept of computing Viet-Nam
dollar cost?   In response to Congressional inquiry, the Administration gave Congress a choice between $30. 7 billion
and $32. 2 billion (FY 1969).

In 1970, due to the secrecy over the rate and timing of
troop withdrawals, the Administration decided to withhold from
Congress and the public the current cost of the war in Viet-Nam.
For some inkling of the cost, we are asked to rely on the estimate given by Defense Secretary Laird in October, 1969, that
Viet-Nam spending should be at an annual incremental cost
rate of about $17 billion by mid-1970.   Beyond that, we can
speculate on budgetary costs by inference from the President's
announced intention to continue troop withdrawals and from
known military policy decisions, such as the President's
decision to move into Cambodia.

The Peace Dividend in the
Fiscal Year 1971 Budget

A look at the original FY 1971 budget shows a request of
$71. 8 billion, including military assistance, for the Defense
Department.   This contrasts with outlays of about $77 billion
for FY 1970 and reflects a saving of $5. 2 billion.

This $5. 2 billion saving, according to Charles Schultze's
analysis published recently by the Brookings Institution,
"results from disengagement in Vietnam. "[6]

Speculating on Viet-Nam costs necessarily depends on the
level of U. S. forces in Viet-Nam and the rate of withdrawal.
By April, 1969, troop withdrawal was scheduled to reach
115, 500.

According to the Schultze analysis, a tabulation of possible
schedule of withdrawal and associated expenditure levels reveals the outlook indicated in Table 1.

TABLE 1

Expenditure Levels for Illustrative
Viet-Nam Disengagement Program,
Fiscal Years 1969-75*

| | Expenditure Level | |
Year	Military personnel (thousands of men)	Incremental outlays (billions of dollars)
1969	538	23
1970	380	17
1971	200	11
1972	50	3
1973	0	1.5
1974	0	1
1975	0	1

*These are purely illustrative estimates. However, through fiscal 1971, they are roughly consistent with the budget document projection of total armed forces personnel strength. All figures are as of the end of the fiscal year to which they relate.

Source: Charles L. Schultze, Setting National Priorities, The 1971 Budget (Washington, D.C.: The Brookings Institution, 1970), p. 27.

The $17 billion figure for FY 1970 coincides with Secretary Laird's projection on Viet-Nam spending at the annual rate of about $17 billion by mid-1970. The cost of Viet-Nam for FY 1971, based on the table above, is estimated at $11 billion, assuming a troop level of 200,000. The President announced on April 20, 1970, that he intends to withdraw 150,000 more troops from Viet-Nam over the next year, indicating a level of not more than 284,000 American troops by the spring of 1971.

If the incremental cost of Viet-Nam is estimated at $17 billion (FY 1970) and the projected cost is $11 to $12 billion (FY 1971), the peace dividend amounts to $5 to $6 billion.

Taking the $5 billion as the more realistic peace dividend figure, we discover, based again on the Schultze analysis, that $1.4 billion may be subtracted from "deferred baseline

requirements"--backlogs and deferrals, such as slowdowns
in training for U. S. forces elsewhere and deferral of modernization and maintenance.

If we subtract for deferred baseline requirements, we
discover a possible FY 1971 peace dividend of approximately
$3. 6 billion.

A close examination of the original FY 1971 budget from
the standpoint of "controllable" dollars reveals a similar peace
dividend. Combing the budget, we find $70 billion controllable
dollars out of the total $200 billion requested for federal ex-
penditures. Of the $70 billion, $47. 7 billion is for defense,
reflecting a $3. 4 billion reduction over controllable dollars
for 1970 defense.

A $3 billion peace dividend for FY 1971 contrasts markedly
with the savings anticipated in defense spending. Moreover,
even this meager sum of savings is in grave danger of being
devoured by future military spending. Consider these possibilities. What if the Administration comes to Congress for
supplemental budget requests for war spending as was the case
in 1966, 1967, and 1968? What if the Administration bunches
up troop withdrawals at the end of FY 1971--as contrasted to
withdrawing troops at the current average monthly rate of
12,500? The peace dividend indeed then may become more
illusive than real.

RECOMMENDATIONS

Congress will be better equipped to discipline defense
spending when the following steps are taken:

1. A Presidential Report on Military Expenditures and
the Economy delivered annually on July 1, the beginning of
the new fiscal year, to a Joint Session of Congress and the
American people. Such a message would include past and
updated war costs, based on one method of cost accounting.
It should provide a uniform basis for cost citation; clarifica-
tion of differing war-cost figures over the years; description
of the impact of military spending on the economy with relevant indicators; and prescriptions.

Such a Report would lead to a common understanding of
war costs and eliminate the confusion that has resulted from
the past war-cost options approach. The latter has created
an expectation-achievement gap regarding the peace dividend.

The Report would also help steer a realistic course

between the extremes of pessimism and optimism regarding
the peace dividend. Already within the Administration we
have heard conflicting outlooks. For Daniel Moynihan, "the
peace dividend turned out to be evanescent, like the morning
clouds around San Clemente. "[7] According to Arthur Burns,
formerly the President's economic advisor, if the war ended
immediately, as much as $8 billion would be available for
"civilian" programs. [8]

Congress as a whole simply must be presented with a
uniform basis of war-cost assessment and with basic data on
the impact of military spending on the economy if it is to have
a meaningful decision-making role in economic policy, including economic conversion from a wartime to a peacetime
economy, and if it is to change spending priorities.

2. A "Pentagon Dividend" can be gained by cutting out
wasteful weapons spending. The Defense Department itself
has a responsibility to weed out excess and waste in military
spending. When the Pentagon fails to weed out unnecessary
programs, Congress must take on this responsibility itself
or saving from reduced war spending will be devoured by
wasteful weapons spending. Preventing the peace dollar drain
to defense is the best way to release funds for new priorities.

NOTES

1. Wassily Leontief and Marvin Hoffenberg, "Economic
Effect of Disarmament," Scientific American (April, 1961),
p. 47.

2. Hon. Melvin R. Laird, Member of Congress, Hearings
on Second Supplemental Appropriations Bill, 1968, before
Subcommittee of Committee on Appropriations, House of
Representatives, 90th Cong., 2d Sess. (May 28, 1968), p. 732.

3. Testimony of Secretary of Defense Robert McNamara,
Hearings before Subcommittee of Committee on Appropriations,
House of Representatives, 90th Cong., 2d Sess. (1968), Part
I, pp. 92-93.

4. Testimony of Assistant Secretary of Defense Robert
Anthony (comptroller), ibid., p. 460.

5. Testimony of Secretary of Defense Clark Clifford, Hearings on Second Supplemental Appropriations Bill, op. cit., p. 735.

6. Charles L. Schultze, Setting National Priorities, The 1971 Budget (Washington, D. C. : The Brookings Institution, 1970), p. 21.

7. Daniel P. Moynihan, Press Conference, August 25, 1969.

8. Arthur Burns, Speech, National Governors' Conference, September 1, 1969.

2

INTELLIGENCE
AND
POLICY

The way in which developments abroad are perceived, evaluated, and presented is directly linked to the kinds of policy alternatives drawn from them. Ultimately it is the President who determines the degree and form of the response. But prior to his decision there occurs a highly complex and extensive information gathering and analyzing process to obtain the factual data necessary to make such a decision.

When developments abroad are perceived to pose a possible threat to our national security, the President calls upon the CIA, the National Security Council, State and Defense Department officers, and his advisors to evaluate the potential of such a threat. For the most part, the press, public opinion, and Congress are neither consulted nor considered in situations that require an immediate response.

Although Congress has played only a minor role in the formulation of military strategy, its influence may be substantial in developing and revising defense postures. When a Congressional committee receives a classified briefing during an authorization or appropriation bill, that briefing represents thousands of hours of intelligence analysis. Inasmuch as major U.S. weapon programs are initiated from these briefings, it is as critical to understand the intelligence process as it is to identify its products.

THE SOURCE AND FLOW OF INTELLIGENCE

Intelligence information is collected world-wide, falling in four major categories: (1) open sources such as newspapers, periodicals, translated foreign literature, and radio broadcasts from the Foreign Broadcast and Information Service; (2) satellite-derived intelligence used for mapping, targeting, and observation of military construction, industrial capacity, communications, and military deployments; (3) technical collection techniques--intercept of signals, electronic emissions, communications, plus radar data on missile and space events; and (4) human resources such as defectors, agents in place, and interviews with selected travelers and immigrants.

The bulk of intelligence data still comes from open sources, but satellite and technical collection products are increasing in quality and value, particularly with regard to military intelligence. Human resources overall have declined in importance.

Intelligence data is collected initially at many sites, satellites, ground stations, aircraft, ships, and then transmitted by secure means to intelligence processing centers in the United States. Theoretically, the CIA is the central repository for all intelligence inflow. In practice, however, duplicate copies of most incoming cables also flow to the National Security Agency (NSA), Defense Intelligence Agency (DIA), Department of State's Intelligence and Reports (INT), and the intelligence components of the Army, Navy, and Air Force. This information is analyzed by departmental and regional specialists and compared with collateral sources for reliability.

For security reasons, each intelligence agency is compartmented into numerous divisions, each restricted to certain types of information. Under the principle of "need to know," only information relevant to a specific responsibility is released to any one person. Access to information in other channels of flow is strictly regulated. Every intelligence document bears a classification and control, the classification being the highest level of information involved, the control being a restriction regarding who has access to the information.

INTELLIGENCE PRODUCTS

Intelligence products are distinguished by time period, subject, and consumer.

Each day, the President receives a personalized brief of world events gathered from all sources, open and clandestine. The Secretary of Defense, Secretary of State, and a small number of other officials receive a similar, slightly expanded document. A rather large group of lower officials receive a document at a lower classification. Longer articles than these paragraph "briefs" often are included in weekly wrap-ups.

In-depth analysis of particular subjects such as Viet-Nam or missile and space data often are distributed independently of the daily brief. Each major component of intelligence agencies generally tries to produce its own specialized intelligence product at the highest classification permitted, a symptom of inter- and intra-agency rivalry. Some of these intelligence products are obviously competitive.

National Intelligence Estimates (NIE) are produced by a fourteen-odd man Board of National Estimates of the CIA. Board members generally are veteran intelligence officers with areas of specialization. Estimates from the Board are presented to the United States Intelligence Board (USIB), comprised of representatives from CIA, DIA, NSA, I&R, intelligence components of the Atomic Energy Commission, the FBI, the Army, Navy, and Air Force, the latter three non-voting. It is chaired by the Director of Central Intelligence (DCI), who, in theory, directs the intelligence establishment while under a second hat is director of the CIA. In practice, the fiefdoms of DIA and NSA afford considerable latitude for independence.

Some NIEs are periodic--for example, yearly estimates of the capabilities and intentions of Soviet strategic weapons programs. Others assess political conditions in strategic regions or countries. Most nations are covered, though not all every year. On occasion, at the request of the President or USIB, special quick NIEs (SNIEs) are drawn up to meet pressing conditions.

The NIE is a succinct document with conclusions always presented first. In order for the NIE to be accepted by the USIB, there must be unanimous consent as to the presentation and conclusions. When views differ and cannot be reconciled, a USIB representative can take a footnote, stating his reservations. Footnoting is discouraged but occurs fairly frequently in military and political estimates. Footnoting, it is suspected, has been used by the Army, Navy, and Air Force to retain specific threat evaluations that justify current or proposed funding programs.

OTHER INTELLIGENCE FUNCTIONS

In addition to regular intelligence gathering, intelligence agencies engage in certain covert activities. This refers to all programs that are not to be identified with the U.S. Government. Covert action programs are not self-initiated. A small committee including the President, Secretary of State, Secretary of Defense, Director of Central Intelligence, and at times a Presidential foreign policy or national security advisor directs covert action programs. Although little is known about the operation of this committee, covert action programs appear to be sanctioned when attribution to the U.S. Government is not acceptable yet the action is deemed necessary. There is a tendency for some of these programs to be expensive in terms of resources and image. The Bay of Pigs clearly demonstrated that the intelligence community had stepped in over its head by trying to coordinate a large-scale covert action program.

Two other intelligence functions deserve mention. (1) Counter-intelligence operations are employed domestically and abroad to defend against penetration by other intelligence units. Foreign counter-intelligence operations generally are run by the CIA and military components; domestic operations are the prerogative of the FBI. Cooperation between the FBI and CIA is quite close, however, and some overlap of jurisdiction occurs. (2) U.S. intelligence agencies exchange liaison personnel with other friendly intelligence agencies, notably the Commonwealth nations.

INTELLIGENCE ASSESSMENT AND
DECISION-MAKING

Paramount in the evaluation of intelligence is the role of the CIA. The concern here is how, and to what extent, does the CIA depart from its presumably objective data analyzing function and enter into the realm of objective policy? Of particular concern is the following question: To what extent is the evaluation process governed by selective perception or by bureaucratic inflexibility? Although the answer is impossible to determine with precision, it would be foolish to discount these factors as insignificant.

Another, equally crucial question pertains to the presentation of intelligence data to the President. How are these

facts placed in their proper perspective, thereby providing
for high-level policy decisions affecting our national security?
The problem here is that new intelligence data presented to
the President may often be inconsistent with previously submitted data, upon which a major policy had been established.
In such cases, when conflicting data might undermine the
position of the intelligence officer, there may be a tendency
to withhold or downplay new information. By determining what
information the President will see, the intelligence officer
plays an integral role in policy-making.

The contention here is that the President does not always
receive an unbiased interpretation of the facts germane to a
decision on national security. This problem stems in part from
the CIA functioning as a body protecting its own credibility. In
addition, given the nature of the decision-making process, one
could assume that a friendly competition exists among the
President's advisors (civilian and military, professional and
independent) on national security, with the goal being maximum
consideration of a party's views. This calls to attention the
problem of whether the President actually makes the decisions
or merely selects from those already made by his advisors.

In a situation such as this, whereby the President relies
upon advice that may be significantly subjective, there is a
clearly defined need for Congress to become involved in matters pertaining to national security. Inasmuch as the assessment of a military threat is often concluded with a personal
perception of the situation, there is valid cause to broaden the
group responsible for determining who or what constitutes a
threat. The more responsible people (from diverse back-
grounds) that can be drawn into this process, the less chance
there is that the final evaluation will be based on value judgments, political or ideological bias, or self-fulfilling prophe-
cies (as national intelligence estimates may at times be).

Congress as a whole is ill suited to deal with matters affecting national security. The problems of maintaining security within so large a body are enormous. Another problem
is the possibility that regional interests and political allegiances
will inhibit members' ability to objectively assess these matters. Nonetheless, the responsibility to evaluate national intelligence estimates should be extended to Senators and Congress-
men other than members of their respective Armed Services
Committees, which have access to some of these data.

Criticism has been raised that these committee members
have neither been responsive to nor representative of the Congress as a whole, thus precluding the broad spectrum of opinion deemed necessary. Moreover, although national security

matters usually involve the military, there is often a spillover
into the realm of foreign policy. In considering problems in
which a sound knowledge of international affairs is important,
it would be wise to draw upon the expertise of members of the
Foreign Relations Committees.

CONGRESS AND INTELLIGENCE ASSESSMENT

As evidenced by the ever-growing debate (both within and
outside the Federal Government) over the need for strategic
weapons and defense systems, there is an apparent need for
Congress to become directly involved in the processes in which
strategy is formulated.

With these considerations in mind, a strong case can be
made for establishing a Joint Congressional Committee on
Intelligence. Participants would include selected members of
the Armed Services and Foreign Relations Committees, as well
as a few members chosen from Congress at large. Ideally,
such a committee would be co-chaired by representatives from
each of the two committee types.

The committee's functions could range from reviewing intelligence data to serving as an official liaison for Congress
with the National Security Council (NSC). It might also be
used to reconcile U.S. strategic plans with foreign policies.
Considering the mounting criticism of CIA activities in the last
decade, a Congressional watchdog committee could add insurance that intelligence operations do not interfere with, or under
mine, non-strategic interest activities such as foreign aid and
educational programs abroad. This could reduce the ways in
which covert intervention in the affairs of other countries might
pose ethical or political problems. And by matching intelligenc
information with press reports, independent observations, and
classified military briefings, Congress would be gathering data
from diverse sources. As a result, Congress would be aware
of possible conflicting intelligence reports, and would also bene
fit by receiving data from various perspectives.

If these committee functions were to be properly carried
out, the danger of an intelligence officer becoming a policy-
maker could be minimized. It should be made clear, however,
that the purpose of an Intelligence Committee is not to manage
the affairs of the CIA or any of the other intelligence agencies.
Lack of experience in this area and the complexity of the organization render such a task impossible. In any case, the

administrative functions of the intelligence agency are not in question here. The CIA in some areas has performed its tasks with an extraordinary amount of expertise. What is being questioned is the objectivity of information presented to the President. And the underlying assumption here is that that which is not objective is not necessarily the result of deliberate or conscious efforts.

The creation of a Joint Committee on Intelligence would not undermine the jurisdiction of the Armed Services Committees. On the contrary, it could complement the work of the committees by providing them with information on the need for strategic military weapons and for the maintenance of forces in certain sensitive areas.

History has demonstrated that a misperception of a potential threat has provoked a misuse of force. In such cases, the effect has been to undermine the government's position in international affairs and to precipitate dissension at home. Broadening the assessment would not only strengthen our foreign policy, but would also enable us to formulate a more realistic appraisal of our defense postures and strategic concerns.

RECOMMENDATIONS

1. There should be a drastic curtailment of covert action programs. Where appropriate, these programs should be continued overtly by the Department of State, Department of Commerce, or AID.

2. The intelligence community should end the use of legitimate U.S. business and government agencies for operational cover overseas and domestically.

3. Clearer lines of responsibility must be drawn between the CIA, DIA, and NSA.

4. Information obtained by intelligence satellites in the earth resources, fishery, forestry, and crop management fields should be declassified and shared with competent scientists world-wide.

5. Whereas inter-service parochialisms distort the estimative process and lead to unnecessary weapon procurement, all military services should be required to cite only the majority position on NIEs before Congress, rather than their service footnote.

6. The Board of National Estimates should include representatives from a non-intelligence, non-government source.

7.   The number of personnel working in covert action and human resource programs should be cut back drastically.

8.   There should be an official Congressional inquiry into the use of selected intelligence data to justify U.S. weapons development programs.

The Secretary of Defense in his FY 1971 Posture Statement said that the primary objective of our strategic forces is deterrence:

> We must continue to rely on the retaliatory power of our strategic offensive forces to deter the Soviet leaders from launching a nuclear attack on our cities. . . . Our strategic forces are primarily designed to deter such an attack. Thus, regardless of how we interpret Soviet intentions, we still must deal with Soviet capabilities in assessing the sufficiency of our strategic forces for deterrent--now and in the future. [1]

To carry out this policy of deterrence is expensive. Strategic forces account for approximately $18 billion or 22.5 per cent of the FY 1971 defense budget, including $8 billion in explicit expenditures for weapons system procurement and operation, and an estimated $4 billion in training, intelligence, communication, and research and development. In addition to the funds needed to maintain the existing force, the Defense Department asked for money to purchase a series of extensions and enlargements of the force and to develop what it considers the next "generation" of new strategic weapons. Some of the costs for research, development, and procurement of these new weapons include:

Conversion of Polaris submarines to accommodate the MIRV-carrying Poseidon

missile, and purchase of the associated
missiles...........................$1,100 million
Incorporation of multiple warheads (MIRV)
on the Air Force's Minuteman missile,
and other "upgrading" of that system... $656 million
Continuation and expansion of Safeguard
ABM system...................... $1,490 million
Development and procurement of a new
air-launched missile (SRAM) and an
armed decoy (SCAD) to be carried by the
B-52 bomber or the proposed B-1...... $297 million
Advanced Manned Strategic Aircraft
(B-1)................................ $100 million
Total............................. $3,673 million

Funds were also requested for developing the weapons that
will succeed all of those now deployed or currently being deployed:

New re-entry vehicles beyond MIRV,
providing increased accuracy and self-
guided, maneuverable warheads....... $110 million
New types of bases for the Minuteman
missile, including the possibility of
constructing silos in hard rock and the
development of mobile missiles, carried
on truck, rail, or barges.............. $77 million
New ABM concepts................... $158 million
ULMS--a long-range, submarine-based
system, to replace the Polaris/
Poseidon........................... $44 million
New bomber warning and air defense
control system...................... $87 million

Before any of the expenditures for these current or proposed strategic forces are approved, or rejected, the Congress
should, for the first time, debate the strategy of nuclear deterrence.

DETERRENCE STRATEGY

American strategic forces must meet two essential requirements and are subject to one major limitation. They

must be of sufficient size and survivability to guarantee our deterrent assured destruction capability. At the same time, they must not become so large that they threaten Russia with a disarming or pre-emptive first strike. The limitation on strategic weapons is that they are chiefly useful in deterring strategic attack but constitute no panacea against conventional threats.

Our deterrent lies in an ability to inflict, if need be, an unacceptable level of damage on Soviet society. This is generally taken to be some 25 per cent of the population (chiefly urban) and 75 per cent of industry. Such results can be obtained, in extremely conservative estimates, by the delivery of 400 one-megaton warheads. For a secure deterrent, some allowance must be made beyond this figure to account for malfunction and for missiles destroyed in a Soviet attack.

But even with such an allowance, our forces are probably excessive. The United States can now deliver over 4, 200 strategic nuclear warheads against the Soviet Union. By MIRVing both our Minuteman and Polaris forces, an operation now in progress, we could double the number of warheads from 4, 200 to 9, 600--still to assure the same objective of the secure delivery of only 400.

When research and support units are included in the total, the Brookings Institution calculated we spend some $18 billion annually on the strategic deterrent. This sum should be reduced as far as consonant with national security. More important, such reduction is dictated by sound strategy as well as economics.

If we allow our deterrent force to grow too large, it will become capable of launching a first strike against the Soviet Union. The conservative Russian planner cannot know our intentions, nor indeed by his eyes does he have any particular reason for trusting them. Like us, he will assume the worst and judge the matter by our capabilities.

To preserve his deterrent in such circumstances, the Soviet planner will have to adopt some doctrine detrimental to our best interests. He can expand his forces to match ours, producing another spiral in the arms race. He could adopt a doctrine of "launch-on-warning"--with all its dangers of accident, ambiguity, excessive speed, and lack of time for communication and negotiation. Or he can adopt or expand such technical devices as the ABM and MIRV with their destabilizing effects.

Any of these alternatives would place us in a more dangerous world than we inhabit now. It must always be borne in

mind that armaments are only the means to a desired political
end. Weapons must be judged by the impact they will ultimately
have on international relations. If we possess too few, we will
be insecure. If we possess too many, the Soviets will be equally insecure, edgy, and prone to dangerous haste in order to
escape the risk of being destroyed on the ground. Our foreign
relations will be ill served by such superiority. The well-con-
ceived deterrent force should be one that fosters restraint and
prudence on both sides.

FORCE LEVELS

The degree of damage that can be inflicted on Soviet
targets was disclosed by Defense Secretary Robert McNamara
in a damage table published in January, 1968, here reproduced
in Table 2.

U.S. strike force levels designed to implement the policy
of nuclear deterrence have been variously designated in Defense
Department posture statements as shown in Table 3.

It is now known that the Polaris A-3 throws a cluster of
three warheads (Multiple Re-entry Vehicles, or MRVs). Twenty
eight of the total force of forty-one Polaris submarines are
equipped with A-3 warheads at sixteen missiles per boat, afford
ing an additional force loading of 896 on these twenty-eight boats
It is thus probable that the 4,200 figure understates the actual
number of force loadings, which is probably closer to 6,000
warheads. A Minuteman II configured to throw three MRVs
would lead to an even larger figure for total throwable warheads

If we accept the 4,200 warhead total, this number is 21
times larger than a figure of 200 on-target warheads required
to kill 52,000,000 Soviets in a retaliatory raid. The fewer than
70 Galosh ABMs deployed around Moscow would not materially
alter this factor of overkill. Bomber defenses would be more
significant, possibly knocking out 50 per cent of the heavy bombers, but this would still leave more than 3,000 warheads to be
targeted. Heavy bomber losses could be compensated for many
times over by using the 4,000 fighter-bombers and carrier-
based planes to deliver additional weapons.

Given this assessment of the strategic retaliatory inventory, it becomes evident that the survivability of U.S. strike
forces must be the rationale for such a degree of overcapacity.
The Secretary of Defense maintains that the vulnerability of
1,000 land-based Minuteman inter-continental ballistic missiles

TABLE 2

Soviet Population and Industry Destroyed
(assumed 1972 total population of 247 million;
urban population of 116 million)

1 MT Equiv. Delivered Warheads	Total Population Fatalities		Industrial Capacity Destroyed (Per Cent)
	Millions	Per Cent	
100	37	15	59
200	52	21	72
400	74	30	76
800	96	39	77
1,200	109	44	77
1,600	116	47	77

Source: Robert McNamara, Defense Budget FY 1969
(Washington, D.C., January, 1968), p. 57.

TABLE 3

U.S. Strategic Force Levels, 1966-72

Item	10/1/66	10/1/67	9/1/68	9/1/72
ICBM Launchers	934	1,054	1,054	1,054
SLBM Launchers	512	656	656	656
Total	1,446	1,710	1,710	1,710
Intercontinental Bombers	680	697	646	581
Approximate No. of Warheads	--	4,500	4,200	4,200

Sources: Clark M. Clifford, Statement in The 1970 Defense Budget and Defense Program for FY 1970/74, p. 42; Defense Posture Statements for 1967, 1968, 1969.

(ICBMs) is so endangered by the continued deployment of
Soviet SS-9 ICBMs that it is essential to have Phase I of Safeguard to provide ABM protection of the missile silos. [2]

The Congressional debate on Safeguard examined the ade-
quacy of the U.S. nuclear deterrent. It demonstrated that the
Defense Department's case for the vulnerability of U.S. nuclear
strike forces to a Soviet first strike focused on one component
of the total strategic forces, the land-based ICBMs. If one
accepts the contention that 950 Minuteman missiles might be
knocked out in a first strike, one may still rely on the varied
and widely dispersed aircraft and missiles making up the rest
of the U.S. strike forces.

If each of the 1,000 Minuteman missiles is credited with
a single warhead, they make up only 24 per cent of the 4,200
warheads specified by the Posture Statement. To strike at
the remaining 76 per cent, the enemy would face an impossible
strategic assignment. Given the geographic distribution of the
aim points represented by these 3,200 warheads, it would be
impossible to time-phase a first strike for nuclear blows
simultaneously on all targets, even if the enemy could manage
somehow to know where the U.S. Polaris submarines were
located--or even, more implausibly, where these aim points
would be at the exact time of warhead impact. Soviet missile
warheads could not simultaneously strike NATO aircraft bases,
carriers at sea, B-52 bases, Polaris subs at sea, and U.S.-
based ICBMs. This is a physical impossibility. The planning
for such a coordinated attack must also remain undetected by
our various intelligence networks.

The fact is that Soviet planners could never be sure that
a first strike, even if technically possible, would be effective
in knocking out the Minuteman fields because of the prime uncertainty about the U.S. decision to keep the Minuteman missile in its silo when early warning systems signal the identification of a massive attack. This is not a matter of U.S. policy
specifying launch-on-warning. It is simply that Soviet planners
could not be sure that the multidepth U.S. system of early warning would not trigger such a decision. We note, for example,
that the 1971 budget contains provision for $219 million for
"Development and Deployment of new satellite strategic surveillance system." This is in addition to the following existing
systems:

Ballistic Missile Early Warning Systems (BMEWS)
Over the Horizon Radar Systems (OTH)
Perimeter Acquisition Radar (PAR)
Warning systems for submarine-launched ballistic missiles.

It can be rightly argued that in a matter of such critical importance as maintaining the nuclear balance of terror, the Department of Defense is justified in erring on the side of caution. After all, the nation's security is at stake. But too heavy a hand on the nuclear scales can have an adverse effect. It can motivate the enemy to respond with an ever-mounting deployment of more weapons that add greater weights of armaments to both sides of the balance. No greater measure of security is achieved, and each nation is the poorer in having diverted urgently needed funds and resources from satisfaction of domestic needs. A new feature of the nuclear arms race is that more weapons do not necessarily mean more security.

The problem of determining relative strategic strength on each side has been complicated by two technical developments: the Anti-Ballistic Missile System (ABM) and Multiple Independently-targeted Re-entry Vehicles (MIRV). Of these, the ABM issue is at present of less significance in terms of balance of nuclear power than MIRV. For example, the impact of the Soviet ABM on the balance of nuclear power--some sixty launchers--must be reckoned as meaning the interception of perhaps thirty strategic warheads. In anticipation of the expansion of this ABM-1 system to other target complexes, the United States has decided to deploy its Poseidon MIRV force on thirty-one submarines. This represents an increase of some 3,000 warheads in the U.S. offensive force--one hundred times that interceptable by the existing Moscow defense system.

MIRV's impact on the arms race is extremely destabilizing because it introduces a complex mathematics into arms control and into the exercise of judging nuclear sufficiency in the absence of adequate arms control. An arms accounting or balance becomes exceedingly difficult when one missile can no longer be counted as one unit of offensive fire-power. For example, the heavy throw weight Soviet SS-9 ICBM can hurl a single warhead of 25 megatons in power, i.e., 25 million tons of TNT or more than a thousand times the power of the Nagasaki A-bomb of 1945. If the single warhead is split into three individual warheads each falling in a triangular pattern on closely spaced aim points such as Minuteman silos, then the separate warheads can each be as much as 5 megatons in weapon yield. Split-up of the single warhead package into six MIRVs would decrease the individual weapon yield to 1.5 megatons. Such a sixfold MIRV (sextet) weapon would have to achieve a modest 0.2-mile accuracy to knock out a missile silo of the Minuteman type.

On the other hand, the Minuteman III will have far less MIRV potency because of its lower throw weight. Minuteman

III has a triplet MIRV each of which has approximately 0.2 megatons of yield. Thus in any arms limitation of strategic weapons, the United States and the Soviet Union are trying to balance asymmetric missile systems.

Asymmetry in weapons would not preclude arms control agreements provided that each side could be confident that the other lived up to the letter of the terms. However, verification through some form of inspection is a necessity for any strategic arms limitation treaty. Here the MIRV development profoundly complicates the situation in that orbital cameras cannot look inside a silo and determine how many MIRVs are on board each SS-9 or Minuteman III. Almost continuous on-site inspection may be required to verify the MIRV quality of each missile.

The United States has halted the deployment of strategic systems at the 1,054 level for land-based launchers and at the 656 level for sea-based launchers. However, the MIRV test program, designed to alter the quantity of the strike force of these launchers, has proceeded to a point where the Air Force deployed some Minuteman IIs (MIRVs) in June, 1970. The Soviet lag behind the United States in MIRV technology. It is hardly likely that they would agree to a MIRV test ban and accept a position of inferiority. On the other hand, in the absence of a test ban, the Soviets would have to assume that the United States will proceed to convert Minuteman Is and IIs into Minuteman IIIs. By 1974, the United States plans to have 500 Minuteman IIIs deployed, but the Soviets might make the worst assumption that every one of the 100 Minuteman silos contains a Minuteman III. The U.S. Navy has eight of its Polaris submarines under conversion to a Poseidon configuration; the first of these will undergo sea trials and be Poseidon equipped as of January, 1971.

Table 4 presents the 1974-75 force loadings resulting from the MIRVing of Minuteman III and Poseidon.

In other words, the Defense Department is programming an increase of 5,400 warheads, or 129 per cent, for strategic offensive weapons systems. This is the probable program, but it is by no means the maximum force loading that could be achieved. For example, this ignores the force loading that could be delivered by 4,000 tactical aircraft.

The Defense Secretary stated in his Posture Statement that the FY 1971 budget was transitional and that restraints were imposed on that budget. Yet he requested $4 billion in FY 1971 for development and deployment of major strategic programs; that was little evidence of restraint. Indeed, the Posture Statement contained requests for funding of major new

TABLE 4

U.S. Strategic Force Loadings, 1974-75

Missiles and Aircraft	Quantity	Warheads
Minuteman III	500	1,500
Minuteman II	500	500
Polaris A-3	160	480
Poseidon	496	4,960
ICBMs + SLBMs Subtotal		7,440
B-52 C-F 3 Sqdr.	45	--
B-52 C-H 17	225	2,160
FB-111 4 Sqdr.	60	--
Total force loadings		9,600

Source: Compiled by Military Spending Committee, based on announced DOD force levels and projections.

weapons development like the strategic bomber (B-1), the Subsonic Cruise Armed Decoy (SCAD), the Undersea Long-Range Missile System (ULMS), and programs to rebase Minuteman in a mobile or superhardened silo form. It was implied that if the Strategic Arms Limitation Talks (SALT) do not succeed in limiting strategic weapons, then the United States will undertake a new round of armaments.

The comparative record of U.S. and Soviet missile deployments shows that the United States has always enjoyed both a quantitative and qualitative superiority in ICBMs and Submarine-Launched Ballistic Missiles (SLBMs). The U.S. initiative in fielding large numbers of Minuteman missiles may have stimulated a response by the Soviets which they might not otherwise have made. In describing the decision to undertake a massive missile buildup, Defense Secretary Robert S. McNamara later explained: "Since we could not be sure of Soviet intentions--since we would not be sure that they would not undertake a massive build-up--we had to insure against such an eventuality by undertaking ourselves a major build-up of the Minuteman and Polaris forces."[3]

Here we see evidence of the fact that decision-making in the Defense Department is keyed to making the worst assumptions about enemy intent and capability--patterning our future forces on estimates of what the enemy might do, not what he is actually doing. This is not a cycle of action-reaction, but rather a one-way street for defense planners. It is a result of the closed system in which those charged with defense planning also have responsibility for interpreting and evaluating potential threats to our national security. Their basic assumption--that the Soviets are seriously determined to exceed all U.S. strategic deployments--seems unrealistic; the Soviet economy, only half the size of the United States', is already under severe strain. Congress should explore the Soviet threat for the 1970's in light of such economic and political constraints.

The decisions on the Minuteman force illustrate the failure of the Congress to inquire incisively into the quantity and quality of the missiles. For example, the decision to deploy missiles on U.S. soil failed to take into consideration the fact that an enemy strike at such missile sites would constitute a massive attack on U.S. population centers. Any serious attempt to first-strike the Minuteman silos would involve many thousands of megatons of warheads, the fallout from which would envelop the densely populated regions of the United States. Furthermore, fixed ICBM bases would in time become targets attracting enemy fire once missile accuracy became adequate for this purpose.

The relative military worth of fixed land bases vis-à-vis sea bases for missiles has not been properly studied by the U.S. Congress. The result is that some $17 billion has been committed to Minuteman missile forces (research, development, test, and engineering plus silo construction and deployment of Minuteman I, II, and III). If nuclear warhead costs and operations are included, this adds up to a more than $20 billion national investment.

In early 1970, the Secretary of Defense claimed it was essential to protect the Minuteman bases against a first-strike threat by deployment of Phase I and then Phase II of Safeguard.[4] If we consider amortization of ABM research and development and Safeguard costs, this adds at least $8 billion more to the Minuteman system costs. Thus, a system of diminishing utility has to be protected by a system of doubtful effectiveness.

Congressional debate over the Safeguard program last year served to involve many Members in the study of nuclear deterrence--a subject previously more or less left to the members of the special committees dealing with defense issues. As a result, the Congress is in a better position to assess the defense choices of the 1970's. This volume, in effect, symbolizes a determination on the part of some Members of Congress to take an active role in making sure that these defense choices are soundly based.

We should not expect instant agreement at the SALT discussions nor should we be discouraged if the negotiations drag out. The important fact is that the two great nuclear powers are sitting down at the same table to talk over the most serious issue on the world agenda--the arresting of the nuclear arms race. The Soviets, for their part, could ease the nuclear tensions gripping the world if they would curtail deployment of their land-based missiles. For our part, we can exercise moderation in adding to our strategic weaponry. Both sides should be motivated to prevent spiraling upward the arms race in another costly circle of weapons which will in the end assure neither of any improvement in security.

The negotiators at the SALT table must do more than strive to reach a militarily and technically sound agreement on limiting arms; they must formulate one that will be acceptable to the American people. It is not sufficient for Congress alone to understand the issues involved. This comprehension must be broadly based and extend to the grass roots of America. In 1920, H. G. Wells wrote, "Human history becomes more and more a race between education and catastrophe." Fifty years later, we find that the forces of destruction have multiplied, seemingly out of control, while men inch along on a plateau of limited understanding.

If our strategic armaments are to be brought under control, it becomes necessary for the great issues involved to be fully examined in the public forum--that crucial intersection of national interest and public policy.

RECOMMENDATIONS

1. Initiate a serious Congressional dialogue concerning: (a) the concept of deterrence and what is sufficient deterrence; and (b) the rationale for maintaining three separate deterrent forces--land-based missiles, sea-based missiles, and bombers--each capable in itself of inflicting the requisite level of assured destruction.

2. We are currently spending on the order of $18 billion

annually on strategic forces. The adoption of a restrained
yet awesomely powerful posture would produce significant
budgetary savings each year. Such a posture would accept assured destruction capability as the essential requirement of
our forces. But the more restrained posture, unlike current
policy, would not need to go beyond assured destruction capability and would estimate the forces needed for such capability
in somewhat more reasonable terms. In particular, this posture would alter the FY 1971 budget as follows:

    a.   Modify the Safeguard ABM program with cuts ranging
         from $404 to $1,085 million;

    b.   Continue but not speed up the Poseidon MIRV program;

    c.   Cancel deployment of Minuteman III MIRVs, cutting
         $575.7 million;

    d.   Postpone indefinitely the procurement of the Advanced
         Manned Strategic Aircraft, B-1, cutting $100 million;

    e.   Continue spending on ULMS (Underwater Long-Range
         Missile System) research and development.

The United States would still be left with awesome nuclear
deterrence. More than 7,000 deliverable warheads, carried
on three distinct delivery systems--1,054 possibly vulnerable
land-based missiles, 656 partially MIRVed and invulnerable
submarine systems; and 450 B-52 bombers which could deliver
1,800 warheads on target.

NOTES

1. Melvin R. Laird, Defense Program and Budget FY 1971
(Washington, D.C.: U.S. Government Printing Office, 1970),
p. 39.

2. Ibid., pp. 46-48.

3. Robert McNamara, "Remarks before the United Press
Editors and Publishers in San Francisco, September 18, 1967,"
Bulletin of the Atomic Scientists (December, 1967), pp. 26-31.

4. Washington Post (January 4, 8, 12, 1970); New York
Times (February 25, 1970).

4

The Safeguard program has been presented as having three missions:

1. <u>Accidental or Unauthorized Soviet Launch.</u> This provides for a reduction or elimination of American casualties should a small number of Soviet missiles be launched by accident or without authorization. Elimination of casualties would lessen the pressure on the President to retaliate and thereby escalate into total war.

2. <u>Chinese Attack.</u> A Chinese attack presents a problem similar to that of the accidental Soviet launch. A small number of missiles would be directed at U.S. population centers.

3. <u>Hard-Point Defense.</u> The purpose of hard-point defense is to preserve the land-based ICBMs as an independent second-strike deterrent. To be effective in this role, not all silos need to be protected, but enough Minutemen must survive to destroy significant portions of the Soviet Union even if there were some catastrophic failure in U.S. submarines and manned bombers.

In addition to its three military functions, Safeguard is considered as a bargaining counter in arms talks with the Soviet Union.

AREA DEFENSE

Components

Each area defense complex can protect an egg-shaped area approximately 900 x 600 miles. [1] An area defense complex

consists of a Perimeter Acquisition Radar (PAR), a Missile
Site Radar (MSR), and a number of Spartan missiles plus
enough Sprints to intercept warheads not destroyed by Spartan
and to protect the complex itself. The twelve complexes proposed for Safeguard Phase II cover the continental United
States with no significant blank spaces. Area defense is also
called "thin" defense because it is relatively easy to penetrate.

PAR

The Perimeter Acquisition Radar is a long-range radar
(about 1,500 miles)[2] that can pick up and track incoming warheads. PAR cost about $150 million each. Safeguard Phase
I calls for two PARs; Phase II calls for seven PARs in a ring
around the continental United States. Whiteman Air Force
Base (the third site requested in 1970) will not have a PAR,
since it is inland. PARs at various sites can overlap and
interlock to form a network.

MSR

The Missile Site Radar is a short-range radar (about
500 miles) which picks up from PAR the role of predicting
the re-entry path of enemy missiles and tracks the re-entry
vehicle (RV) with high accuracy while at the same time tracking the ABM anti-missile missile and guiding it to interception. Each ABM complex will have one MSR. The cost is
about $200 million each. Due to their short range, there is
no overlap between MSRs.

Spartan

The Spartan is a long-range missile (600 miles)[3] that
costs about $3 million each, including launcher. (This is a
1969 figure--the current figure is classified.) Its warhead
of about four megatons [4] relies on neutrons and x-rays for
kill. It uses outer-space interception only because it lacks
the acceleration necessary for atmospheric interception.
The kill radius is claimed to be twelve miles. [5]

Improved Spartan

This is basically a Spartan with a smaller warhead and
therefore longer range and better maneuverability. It is designed for lower altitude interceptions of sea-launched missile

warheads at greater horizontal distances from its ABM site than the standard Spartan. It is designed to complement but not replace the standard Spartan.

Critique

Offense can counter an area defense by any one or any combination of the following:
1. Chaff: RVs can disperse large clouds of aluminum foil or fine copper wires, which are opaque to radar. Defense may not know where the RV is in the cloud.
2. Decoys: The RV can deploy a large number of foil-covered balloons of the same size and shape as the RV. The defense may not be able to tell which is real and which is the decoy.
3. Blackout: A nuclear explosion creates a "blackout cloud" which is for practical purposes opaque to radar. RVs behind the cloud cannot be tracked. The parameters of the cloud are complicated, but, in brief, it is feasible to set up an anti-PAR cloud of 200 x 450 miles[16] diameter that will last for several minutes. This might be done by a large precursor warhead detonated at high altitude specifically for this purpose. There also might be self-blackout from the Spartans sent up against the first RVs. Overlapping of PARs would enable the defense to "look around" the blackout cloud to some extent, but a heavy attack would set up a pattern of several clouds which would make this difficult.

All countermeasures against a point defense can also be used against an area defense, although the converse is not true.

POINT DEFENSE

Components

A point-defense complex consists of a single MSR and a number of Sprint missiles scattered at several sites.*

---

*Some of the Safeguard point-defense complexes are combined with area-defense complexes and include Spartans and a PAR, but the contribution of these components to point defense is small and their cost is probably not justified except as part of an area defense system.

Sprint

This is a short-range, very high acceleration ABM interceptor designed for atmospheric intercepts at altitudes of 10,000 to 100,000 feet.[7] A Sprint can protect an area of approximately fifteen miles' radius.[8] The warhead is about two kilotons.[9]

MSR

This is the same as is used in area defense. A longer-range radar, such as PAR, is not necessary for point defense.

A new radar, not yet named, also is under development. A smaller, shorter-range, cheaper MSR, the plan is to put perhaps four or five of these at each Minuteman farm, thus attempting to reduce the Achilles' heel vulnerability of the Safeguard radars.

Critique

Blackout and decoys are of very limited use against a point defense. Instead, penetration of point defense relies on three basic strategies:

1. Saturation: The offense presents the defense with a larger number of RVs than the latter's radar and computers can handle at one time.

2. Exhaustion: Offense presents the defense with more RVs than the latter has Sprints. The Sprints are used up by the first RVs; the remainder get a free ride. The question here becomes whether or not it is cheaper for the offense to increase its RVs or for the defense to increase its Sprint force.

3. Radar destruction: The offense directs its initial warheads against the MSRs or the "new radars" and takes them out, and the remainder of the attacking force gets a free ride. As with exhaustion, the feasibility of this approach becomes a matter of cost comparison.

ABM COSTS AND TRADE-OFFS

All cost figures must be taken skeptically due to the rapid escalation factor. As shown in Table 5, for example,

TABLE 5

ABM Unit Costs

Item	Number of Units in Full Safeguard Phase II	Estimated Unit Cost (in millions)	
		1969	1970
Sprint	a	2	2
Spartan	a	3	a
MSR	12	165	200
New radar	about 16 (unofficial)	b	b
PAR	7	130-60	b
Improved Spartan	a	b	a

aClassified. This data should be made available.
bClassified or not yet established.

Source: Compiled by Military Spending Committee, from House and Senate Armed Services and Appropriations Committee Hearings for 1969 and 1970.

in 1969, the unit cost of an MSR was described by DOD as $165 million. By 1970, the figure was $200 million.

Total Safeguard system projected cost now runs about $12 billion, which is about $1.5 billion above the 1969 estimate.

The following is a popular pro-ABM argument: It is cheaper for us to increase our Sprint forces than for the Russians to increase their SS-9 ICBM force. Figure $2 million each for a Sprint. Estimate 100 Sprints per MSR, prorate the $200 million MSR among them; this adds $2 million for a total of $4 million per Sprint. One SS-9 with three warheads costs about $30 million, or $10 million per warhead. Thus, we have a cost-exchange advantage of 2 1/2 to 1.

By way of rebuttal, further cost comparisons become

clear. For example, the offense can "jackpot" by taking out
the MSR, producing a radically different cost-exchange ratio.

Accept the Pentagon's assumptions that the SS-9 has 80
per cent reliability, 1/4-mile accuracy, and sufficient payload to carry one 25-megaton warhead or three five-megaton
warheads. (If the Soviet force is less effective than this,
Minuteman is not threatened and we do not need a hard-point
ABM.) Assume the Safeguard system has an effectiveness of
70 per cent. Using standard statistical procedures based on
the binomial distribution, it can be calculated that an attack
by twenty warheads of 100 kilotons each would have a better
than 99 per cent probability of destroying an MSR. These
warheads could be carried on MIRVed SS-9s, SS-11s, SS-13s,
or any combination thereof.

As yet, the Soviets do not have operational SS-9, SS-11,
or SS-13 MIRVs, nor do they have small-unit, high-multiplicity,
radar-killer MIRVs for the SS-9. But the cost and lead-times
involved in developing and deploying these warheads are far
less than for Safeguard. This is a perfectly feasible response
on their part if we go ahead with Safeguard. The cost of such
a twenty-warhead attack, carried by two SS-9s or the equivalent, would be about $70 million, based on DOD's estimate
of $30 million per SS-9 and allowing $5 million additional for
the MIRV. This $70 million attack would take out a $200 million radar and incapacitate every Sprint in the complex. One
hundred Sprints at an estimated $2 million each will total
$200 million. Adding in the cost of the radar would give $400
million, resulting in a cost-exchange disadvantage for the
ABM defense of about six to one.

One way of calculating cost-exchange ratios would be to
consider twelve such attacks, one on each MSR, taking out
the entire Safeguard system. In this way, twelve attacks at
$70 million each, totaling $840 million, are balanced against
the cost of the entire Safeguard system, including R&D--cur-
rently about $12 billion and going up. Considering $840 million against $12 billion gives a cost-exchange disadvantage
for the defense of about fourteen to one.

Use of large numbers of small, cheap radars would, of
course, improve the defense's cost-exchange position. But
even if the radars came free, we would have to build 168
(12 x 14) of them in order to bring a fourteen to one ratio down
to one to one. The futility of this approach can be demonstrated by hypothesizing that the new radar will cost $100
million per copy, or half as much as an MSR. In this case,
the cost of 168 radars would be $16.8 billion, or more than

the entire system as currently projected. Even this expenditure would leave us with a $26.8 billion system the Soviets
could neutralize with 180 attacks at $70 million each, totaling
$12.6 billion. So after spending some $40 billion on a vulnerable and obsolescent system, we would still have a cost-exchange disadvantage of more than two to one.

DEFENSIVE POSTURES WITHOUT ABM

What then should the U.S. defensive posture be relative
to the Soviet and Chinese threats? The following statements
reflect how to meet the threat without an ABM.

Situation: Heavy Soviet attack against Minuteman farms.
Posture: It appears that nothing we can do will preserve
the second-strike deterrent value of fixed-base missiles
through the 1980's. Improvements in RV accuracy will permit
first-strike strategies using progressively smaller warheads
and progressively higher MIRV multiplicities. Launched
first-strike missiles will be able to take out a progressively
larger number of silos, making a first strike against fixed
silos progressively more feasible, regardless of Safeguard
protection.

It may be possible to extend the deterrent life of Minuteman by superhardening. This may even be temporarily cost
effective, but it will eventually be neutralized by improved
Soviet RV accuracy.

Announcement of a launch-on-warning doctrine has the
advantage of preserving Minuteman's deterrent value at zero
cost. It has the overwhelming disadvantage of increasing the
chance of accidental war.

The only long-range solution to preserving the strategic
deterrent lies in making it mobile, either on land or under
water. At this time, the second course appears considerably
more feasible than the first.

Situation: Accidental or unauthorized launch.
Posture: Make all appropriate precautions for U.S. weapon systems, and trust that the Soviets do likewise. Because

an accidentally launched Soviet missile may be expected to
have penetration aids, only a point-defense ABM would provide protection with any confidence.

Safeguard provides no point defense for population centers, except possibly in Washington, D.C. In order to defend
against accidental launch, point-defense complexes would have
to be built at each city to be defended. The cost would run
into tens of billions. It would still leave many cities unpro-
tected. It would still have to work perfectly the first time it
was used.

Situation: Chinese attack.

Posture: Rely on deterrence and a reasonable foreign
policy. If the Chinese are really determined to kill several
million Americans, we cannot stop them. If they have twenty-
five or more ICBMs, they can target them all on one city and
have extremely high confidence of penetrating Safeguard's
area defense. Alternatively, there are cheap and reliable
methods of delivery of a thermonuclear bomb to an American
city without using a ballistic missile at all. (See following
discussion, "Unorthodox Nuclear Delivery Systems.")

Therefore, we must rely on deterrence to protect us
against a Chinese attack, just as we rely on it for protection
against a Russian attack. The Chinese have been traditionally
cautious in foreign affairs. There is no reason to expect them
to provoke the obliteration of their country for the satisfaction
of killing a few million Americans. All we have to do is re-
frain from pushing them over the brink.

UNORTHODOX NUCLEAR DELIVERY SYSTEMS

At one point, the Nixon Administration stated that it was
"absolutely essential" to deploy an area defense Safeguard
ABM system to counter nuclear blackmail threats of Red
China and that such a system would be "virtually infallible."
It is worthwhile examining, therefore, several non-ballistic
modes of nuclear delivery systems for which the ABM would
be useless.

One possible threat avenue is transportation of high-yield
thermonuclear weapons via cargo ships or undersea craft.
Here we understand "high-yield" to mean superweapons 100
megatons or more in explosive equivalent.

The principle of the 100+ megaton weapon was tested in 1962 by the Soviet Union when a 58-megaton air-burst was made. Analysis of the bomb debris showed that Soviet experts had jacketed the superbomb with a mantle of ordinary lead. The latter substituted for natural or depleted uranium as the third state of a fission-fusion-fission weapon. Lead does not fission under fast neutron bombardment, as does uranium-238, and it has the virtue that neutron absorption in general leads to stable isotopes of lead so that radioactivity in the bomb residue is minimized. If, however, uranium had been used in place of lead, fast fission would have occurred with energy release that would have made the total yield of the weapon exceed 100 megatons. In theory, there is no upper limit to the yield of such superweapons, but in practice their package weight restricts their delivery. We may assume a specific yield of six megatons per ton of package weight.

A very high-yield (gigaton) bomb with a power of one billion tons of TNT might be constructed as a single unit, or it could be equaled in power by simultaneous detonation of fewer than ten individual 100+ megaton explosives. Total package weight for a gigaton weapon can be estimated at 160 tons. This equivalent of one billion tons of TNT could be fitted into a volume corresponding to a small bedroom.

Given weight and dimensions of this class, it appears practical to transport very high-yield thermonuclear weapons in submarines or, alternatively, they could be stowed as cargo or even concealed in fuel tanks.

The attack mode for such weapons would be in situ detonation at moderate depth or as surface bursts hundreds of miles off the Pacific Coast at locations calculated to produce maximum radioactive fallout on the continental United States.

Deployment of the devices might be made by submerging them as sea mines which could be series-detonated by shock impact from other exploding weapons.

Weapon effects would be limited to (a) tidal waves impinging on the coastal cities and (b) radioactive fallout. The magnitude of the fallout effect would depend on the total megatonnage detonated, the distance off-shore, and the wind conditions.

As a weapon of blackmail, a nuclear explosive might be brought in very close to shore, possibly even into a harbor if the cargo vessel flew an acceptable flag. In such a case, the blast and thermal primary effects from a surface-burst high-yield weapon would be significant.

As a continental attack weapon, the magnitude of the

threat can be assessed as follows. The high-yield weapons
would be assumed to be designed to maximize fission products
so that 70 per cent of the yield would constitute fission fallout.
A 100-megaton (100,000-kiloton) weapon would thus yield
70,000 kilotons of fission products, i.e., fallout associated
with the fission-produced radioactivity of 70,000 kilotons. As
a rule of thumb, Table 6 presents the schedule of radiation
dosage to a person fully exposed on the earth's surface resulting from one kiloton of fission products dispersed uniformly
over one square mile of area.

Because of their proximity, coastal areas would receive
high radiation dosages characterizing the first day of fallout,
whereas more remote inland areas would receive markedly
lower dose schedules. Inland areas would be spared the intense phase of fallout, and, in addition, the dilution of the fallout as the winds disperse the bomb debris would reduce fallout
intensity. However, with multiple explosions, one would expect buildup of intensity due to overlap of the fallout patterns.
Lethal damage due to exposure in the first week would be confined to California, Oregon, and Washington. The most serious radioactive fallout would be to the west of the Continental
Divide, although weapons burst off the Los Angeles-San Diego
zone might overlap Denver with their fallout patterns.

Another unorthodox path to follow in bringing nuclear
damage to the continental United States is that of clandestine
activities involving the smuggling of weapons into U.S. cities.
A form of suitcase warfare is made possible by the development of low-yield weapons of compact size and light weight.
For example, a package the size of a portable color TV set
can conceal a weapon of Hiroshima power. It could be carried
by one person. Introduction of a megaton weapon into a U.S.
city involves a somewhat larger package size and a weight of
half a ton (no larger than a hi-fi console).

A great many risks are attached to smuggling nuclear
weapons into a foreign country, especially if a significant
number is committed. Agent security, communication, timing,
and limited damage of low-yield weapons would all argue
against such a high-risk mode of attack. But if Red China,
for example, is reckoned such a risk that it would resort to
nuclear blackmail by means of a ballistic missile strike at a
few U.S. cities, then presumably it would not be out of line
to take seriously a covert attack with planted nuclear weapons.

TABLE 6

Radiation Dosage Over Time

Time Period	Dosage
2d hour after detonation	5 lethal doses
3d and 4th hours	4 lethal doses
5th hour	1 lethal dose
5-10th	3 lethal doses
10-24th	3 lethal doses
2d day	2 lethal doses
3d day	1 lethal dose
Next 3 days	1 lethal dose

Source: Adapted from statement of Ralph Lapp before the Joint Committee on Atomic Energy, Nuclear War Hearings (Washington, D. C., 1959). See also Ralph Lapp, The Weapons Culture (New York: W. W. Norton, 1960), p. 59.

RECOMMENDATIONS

The following range of alternatives regarding Safeguard are offered in lieu of any one recommendation. All involve modifications of the Administration's FY 1971 request, as amended by the Senate Armed Services Committee.

1. The Safeguard system should be held at the R&D level. No funds should be authorized for Safeguard deployment.

2. Deployment of the Safeguard system should be limited to the two sites approved in 1969. Research and development should continue.

3. Divert R&D funds for Safeguard to R&D on an advanced ABM.

4. Escrow arrangements conditioned on the SALT negotiations. Funds held in escrow could be released at the discretion of the Congress if talks fail. Creation of an escrow arrangement, however, should not be interpreted as indicating a belief that failure of the negotiations would increase the desirability or utility of an ABM system. The weaknesses of Safeguard would be accentuated by a new arms race. New ABM deployments should not be considered as inevitable if the SALT negotiations fail. The escrow proposals follow:

a. Hold in escrow the Safeguard deployment at the
original two sites.

b. Hold the entire Safeguard program (excluding
R&D) in escrow.

There are a number of permutations to each of these options. In all cases, R&D could continue on a non-Safeguard
ABM defense. The potential savings in these options range
from $1,085 million in the first and fourth (b) to $404 million
in the second:

Recommendation	Cost (Millions)	Reduction or Escrow
1	365	1,085
2	1,046	404
3	365	range
4 a	-	781
4 b	365	1,085

NOTES

1. Military Posture and Authorization Appropriation,
1970, House Document 91-53, p. 7059.

2. Ralph Lapp, "From Nike to Safeguard: A Biography
of the ABM," The New York Times Magazine, May 4, 1969.

3. Calculated from House Document 91-53, op. cit.

4. Bulletin of Atomic Scientists, June, 1970, p. 106.

5. Calculated from Space/Aeronautics, November, 1969,
pp. 58 and 64.

6. Space/Aeronautics, November, 1969, p. 58.

7. Military Construction Appropriations for 1971, Part
IV, p. 16.

8. House Document 91-53 gives Sprint short range at
about twenty-five miles. We estimate this to have a ground
projection of about fifteen miles.

9. Space/Aeronautics, November, 1969, p. 62.

5

MULTIPLE
INDEPENDENTLY-TARGETED
RE-ENTRY VEHICLES
(MIRV)

The development of MIRV can be traced to four factors:

1. Dr. John Foster, Director of Defense Research and Engineering, has testified that the original MIRV concept developed from the desire to increase targeting capability. With the increase of satellite observation in the 1960's, a number of new targets appeared, more than the existing Minuteman force could handle. Therefore, MIRV satisfied the new targeting demands without deploying more launchers.

2. Early in the 1960's, construction around Moscow and Leningrad suggested that the Soviets were building a large-scale sophisticated ABM system composed of long-range early-warning radars, a massive central discrimination radar, and various shorter-range missile-intercept radars. In addition, construction appeared at several other sites, known as the Tallinn line, which the Department of Defense determined also had an ABM capability. Other intelligence agencies assessed the Tallinn line as an advanced surface-to-air missile (SAM) system with little or no ABM capability, and this assessment, in later years, proved to be correct. The disputed capability of the Tallinn line, however, plus the significant construction around Moscow, provided another justification for MRV and MIRV--that of ABM saturation and penetration.

3. After a rapid buildup, the United States reached a self-imposed plateau of 1,054 land-based launchers. It was determined that multiple warheads would be more cost effective than additional launchers.

4. Every system has an improvement factor. Modifications are a normal part of system development. Design teams

seek to improve accuracy, fire power, reliability, and cost
effectiveness. When anticipated modifications are extensive,
a follow-on system is developed. All of these are internal
pressures that push weaponry to (and sometimes beyond) its
technological limits. Thus, MIRV, in part, also is the natural
follow-on to the single warhead system, the product of an ener-
getic and skilled engineering community.

U.S. MIRV DEPLOYMENT SCHEDULE

U.S. MIRV development and testing has proceeded nearly
as scheduled. Initial deployment of Minuteman III with its
Mark 12 warhead began in June, 1970, and probably will proceed slowly until about 500 of the Minuteman I and II force are
replaced. Each Mark 12 system includes three warheads of
about 200 kilotons each. Thus, 500 Minuteman IIIs yield 1,500
warheads.

The first Poseidon MIRV system was scheduled for deployment in January of 1971, but production problems forced a
delay until the spring. The full program calls for thirty-one
of the forty-one Polaris submarines to be converted to Poseidon.
Each sub carries sixteen launch tubes, and each launcher will
carry an average of ten MIRVs. This means that 4,960 warheads (31 subs x 16 launchers x 10 MIRV) will be available from
the Poseidon forces. The Poseidon payload will be about twice
as accurate as the Polaris A-3 triplet payload.

Minuteman III and Poseidon forces alone will number 6,460
independently-targetable warheads (1,500 Minuteman III plus
4,960 Poseidon).

SOVIET MIRV DEVELOPMENT

The Soviets began testing a multiple warhead system in
about 1967. Testing has occurred both within the Soviet Union
and to long-range impact areas in the Pacific. As far as can
be determined, the early Soviet warheads were not independently-targeted before late 1970 and even then the technology
was not clear to U.S. analysts. A Soviet MRV could have been
deployed as early as 1970, and a MIRV deployment could come
as early as 1972. Each of the triplet warheads tested in 1969
and 1970 was considerably larger than the Minuteman III pay-
load--5 megatons versus about 200 kilotons.

The Soviets could also outfit some of their SS-11 force
with a MRV capability. SS-11 MRV tests of some kind began
in 1970. And the Soviets will probably develop an increased-
range missile for the Y class submarine, possibly with a MRV
capability.

THE MIRV MISSION

There has been some official confusion as to the mission
of MIRV. First DOD releases claimed that MIRV had the mission of penetrating a heavy Soviet ABM defense, although a
heavy defense had not materialized. Subsequent announcements
suggested that MIRV had some hard-target capability. In April,
1969, Secretary of Defense Melvin Laird spoke of enhancing
the hard-target capability of Poseidon. [1] At other times, and
most recently, reassurances have been given that MIRV is only
one part of our assured destruction capability and not intended
for hard-target use, except in a retaliatory role. Official U.S.
confusion over this point cannot be reassuring to Soviet strategists.

Regardless of the intent of U.S. planners, however, improvements in U.S. MIRV accuracy will have to be judged by
the Soviets as first-strike innovations. U.S. planners would
make the same assumption were the situation reversed.

HOW DOD LOOKS AT MIRV

The Department of Defense is entrusted with the security
of the nation from all foreign threats, real and potential. Due
to the relatively long lead-time now necessary to develop
weapons, assessments must be made about potential enemy
developments without current, firm information. The process
of calculating threats demands that if U.S. protection is to be
assured, every possible threat must be anticipated and met.
This demand for full protection has spawned the "greater-than-
expected" threat. That is, DOD must meet the worst possible
case.

MIRV, it is said, is one measure necessary to meet any
buildup the Soviets are making. Secretary Laird has stated
that 420 SS-9s with MIRVs could be capable of destroying 95
per cent of the 1,000-Minuteman force by 1974 or earlier
if the current Soviet buildup continues. [2]

Not only has the SS-9 and SS-11 force expanded but tests
on the Fractional Orbit Bombardment System (FOBS) and a
new naval missile are continuing. Construction of Y class
Polaris-type nuclear ballistic missile submarines is proceed-
ing at a faster pace at Severodvinsk and other yards. By 1974-
75, the Soviets could have 560 to 800 SLBMs. The Department
of Defense believes that the Soviets are moving forward with
a wide range of effective weapons and that this coordinated
push is a meaningful threat to U.S. retaliatory systems.

The DOD position on U.S. weapon development concurrent
with SALT rests on four points:

1.   The United States has adopted a posture of restraint,
deferring decisions on all new major weapons systems until
after SALT.

2.   Given the rapid buildup of Soviet ICBMs, it is prudent
to move ahead with an ABM system designed to protect part
of our retaliatory force and part of our population from accidental launch or the Chinese threat.   The Soviets are aware
that this is a defensive system--they have one of their own--
and it will not be provocative.

3.   Deployment of MIRV should proceed regardless of
SALT as a hedge against the Soviet buildup and because it
represents only a strengthening of our retaliatory capability.

4.   MIRV and particularly the ABM are excellent bargaining factors which should not be handicapped before bargaining
begins.

THE CASE AGAINST MIRV

The case against MIRV distills down to one central observation: MIRV is more likely to increase the likelihood of war
than assure peace and security.

In the mathematics of deterrence, MIRV introduces figures
that cloud perception of intent and upset the relative balance of
forces. Without MIRV, each launcher with its single warhead
can be accurately counted by national means. With MIRV,
national planners will be forced to assume the worst possible
case--that all launchers are MIRVed. There is no present or
anticipated national means of verifying MIRV deployment,
without on-site inspection.

MIRV greatly expands the number of points that can be
targeted. This alone may not be destabilizing, but combined
with a moderate increase in accuracy, MIRV becomes a

significant counter-force weapon. That is, with sufficient
warheads, accuracy, and reliability, the strategist recognizes
that a first strike could succeed in reducing enemy forces to a
small percentage of their original strength. If, in turn, these
small remaining units are balanced by a defensive ABM system,
the threat of a pre-emptive strike becomes significantly greater.
Both sides will recognize this new state of technology and as a
result may be too quick to react. Regardless of the intent of
either power, the risk of war--accidental, forced, or pre-
emptive--may be heightened.

MIRV is one consequence of unrestrained technology. As
with all other advances in weaponry, MIRV will lead both to
new follow-on offensive forces and new anti-MIRV defensive
forces. At one time, new weapons could be procured at reasonable levels of expenditures. The present technologists, however, are cost intensive. They fuel the arms race with significant jumps in expenditures.

Deployment of MIRV poses serious problems for Soviet
negotiators. Soviet MIRV technology lags behind that of the
United States. Bargaining from a recognized position of inferiority creates psychological pressure, and inasmuch as the
U.S. and Soviet programs are not at comparable levels of development, bargaining likely will involve complex trade-off
formulas or meaningless open-ended ceilings.

With no reliable method of MIRV inspection available to
them, Soviet suspicions certainly will increase. They may
decide to play "catch-up" before bargaining or move ahead with
other major weapon programs. Either reaction would threaten
successful SALT negotiations. Thus deployment of MIRV not
only complicates negotiations, but tends to limit options.

We have seen how the land-based systems actually are
failing as a reliable and invulnerable deterrent and now have
to be bailed out by an even more questionable ABM system.
To MIRV these same increasingly vulnerable land-based systems is far less effective in a second-strike situation than
MIRVing an invulnerable force.

The claim that MIRV and ABM will provide a useful
bargaining position requires serious justification. Will the
acquisition of more weapons make it easier to reach agreement
about arms limitation?

ADVANCED BALLISTIC RE-ENTRY
SYSTEMS (ABRES)

The surprise appearance of MIRV suggests that attention should be given to the research and development phase of major weapon programs. For example, few in Congress have been aware, until recently, of the ABRES program, perhaps the major contributor to MIRV technology.

ABRES is a joint R&D program to improve the maneuverability of ICBM re-entry vehicles and the effectiveness of penetration aids. Part of the program offers the possibility of advancing the MIRV weapons system by adapting individual guidance units to each of the several re-entry vehicles loaded in one ICBM. The MIRV weapon now being tested releases one warhead at a precise point during the missile's trajectory, then shifts course to release the next warhead at another target. MIRV technology developed under ABRES will enable each re-entry vehicle to alter course, maneuver around an anti-ballistic missile system, and guide the warhead to its target.

The ABRES program, in addition, involves continuing R&D on penetration aids such as heat-shields, decoys, chaff, and electronic counter-measures. ABRES also investigates defensive technology such as hardening concepts and characteristics of re-entry vehicles in order to facilitate destruction of incoming enemy warheads.

ABRES has been in operation since 1963. Over $1.3 billion has been spent since FY 1962 on technology and development for ICBM re-entry vehicles and penetration aids. DOD requested an additional $121 million in R&D funds for FY 1970, but was cut by $14 million by the Senate Armed Services Committee. Singer-General Precision, Inc., was awarded a $3.9 million contract in 1970 to develop and build parts for a new guidance system, an indication that the Pentagon intends to go ahead with an advanced MIRV weapon. The total R&D costs for the ABRES program for the next five years are estimated at over $600 million.

RATIONALE AND CRITIQUE
OF THE ABRES PROGRAM

DOD asserts that ABRES is intended to increase the technological data available for new weapons development and does not involve effort on deployed systems. The effort is primarily in the area of improving capability to penetrate Soviet defensive systems, although hard-target capability is improved in some ABRES activities. The central objective of the ABRES program, however, is the maintenance of our deterrent by enhancing the penetration capability of our re-entry vehicles.

Improvement of our hard-target capability, it is claimed, is not directed toward a U.S. first-strike capability but improves our second-strike damage-limiting ability, a secondary U.S. strategic requirement. The portion of the ABRES program relating to an improved MIRV guidance system in fact may decrease our ability to hit hard targets because installation of a guidance system capable of maneuvering around Soviet ABMs requires a trade-off in accuracy and warhead size.

The necessity for maintaining a technological base for future weapons development is generally accepted, even by Pentagon critics, particularly regarding R&D. It is not clear, however, that the ABRES program is confined solely to R&D efforts. The Singer-General contract, for example, is for production of parts for a new guidance system--clearly a step beyond research and development as it is normally defined.

ABRES, like any other new weapons program, develops its own momentum for deployment. Once the technology becomes available for successful introduction of a new system or a system refinement, the pressure for production and deployment often becomes irresistible. Unfortunately, the ABRES program has been so tightly classified that it is impossible to determine what stage of development the components of the program have reached.

With regard to the U.S. secondary strategic mission of limiting damage by destroying hardened enemy missile silos, such a capability clearly is analogous to a first-strike option. A potential enemy, of course, has only the President's word that the option will not be exercised. For an enemy strategic planner to meet contingencies on this basis would surely be too much to ask. Therefore, the damage-limiting mission becomes an excuse for enemy planners to go ahead with weapons systems designed to dig out U.S. missiles, which in turn raises first-strike fears in the United States and sends the strategic arms race into another upward spiral.

RECOMMENDATIONS

1. Every effort should be made during the current SALT talks to put a freeze on MIRV deployment.

2.   The recommendations for retrenchment of MIRV apply
only to the Minuteman III program.   The estimated total system
cost for MIRVing the Minuteman III is about $5.4 billion.   The
request for FY 1971 is $686 million, including $211 million for
R&D and $457.7 million for procurement.   We recommend al-
locating no further funds for MIRVing the Minuteman because
of fixed-base vulnerability and the potential destabilizing effects of MIRV.

3.   We recommend that the ABRES research program continue.   However, there should be a yearly accounting to Congress about strategic systems being developed and improvements in deployed systems.

4.   We recommend that no funding be approved for improving the accuracy of the Minuteman III MIRV.

NOTES

1.   Hearings on Military Posture, House Armed Services
Committee, 91st Cong., March-May, 1969, p. 1748.

2.   New York Times (January 8, 1970).

The B-1, previously designated the Advanced Manned Strategic Aircraft (AMSA), is an intercontinental strategic bomber proposed by the Air Force to succeed the currently deployed B-52 and FB-111. As presently envisioned, the plane will weigh 380,000 pounds, have a payload of approximately 50,000 pounds[1] and have a range variously estimated at from 6,100[2] to 10,000 miles.[3] It will be armed with Short-Range Attack Missiles (SRAM), Subsonic Cruise Armed Decoy (SCAD), and Bomber Defense Missiles (BDM), as well as with nuclear and conventional weapons.[4] Other significant features anticipated for the plane include a small radar cross-section and a low infrared signature (which decreases plane vulnerability to heat-seeking anti-aircraft missiles). The B-1 will cruise supersonically, with a top speed of Mach 2.5.[5] When beginning its bomb run, as much as 1,666 nautical miles from target, the plane will drop to a low altitude (about 200 feet) in order to decrease the effectiveness of enemy radar, surface-to-air missiles, and other defenses, although in so doing it will have to decrease its speed to a high subsonic value, about Mach 0.85.

The number of aircraft tentatively planned by the Defense Department is approximately 250[6] at a cost per plane of $25 to $30 million, when bought in quantities in excess of 200 planes,[7] although higher estimates have been made by other sources. The current research, development, test, and engineering (RDT&E) cost of the entire program is $2.3 billion.[8] To date, about $240 million has been spent on the program, with FY 1971 requested authorization at another $100 million.[9]

71

DESIRABILITY OF THE B-1

In making their case for the B-1, supporters have given the following reasons, among others, for action on this project:

1. The B-52s are aging and must be replaced.
2. The B-1 is a more formidable weapon than the B-52 or FB-111.
3. The B-1 is important in maintaining our bomber superiority over the Soviets.
4. We need a mixed arsenal of both missiles and bombers as a hedge against missile unreliability or improvements in Soviet ABM capability.
5. Bombers have greater flexibility than missiles.
6. Bombers require the enemy to mix his defenses, thus diverting funds from ABM.
7. Bombers, unlike missiles, can be used conventionally.

Each of these arguments are discussed, individually, in detail below.

Replacement of B-52

"The B-52s are aging and must be replaced." This point has been more frankly phrased by General Curtis LeMay, former Chief of Staff of the Air Force, who said in 1964, "I am afraid the B-52 is going to fall apart on us before we can get a replacement for it. There is a serious danger that this may happen."[10] Yet there is substantial evidence that the B-52 G and E models will last well into the lifetime of the B-1 with moderate expenditures on maintenance and improvements in the aircraft.[11] Indeed, a series of modifications in the B-52, beginning in 1962, has increased their lifetime significantly. These modifications include, among others, a new wing box structure, a new bulkhead between the tail and fuselage, and a new aft fuselage skin, all at a fraction of the cost estimated just for B-1 research and development alone.

According to the Defense Department, "there appears to be no reason why the B-52 Gs and Hs cannot be maintained through 1980, if that should prove necessary."[12] Also, the oldest B-52s, constituting series C through F, are gradually being reduced in number, with FB-111s serving as substitutes. The G and H planes, the newest B-52s, will not suffer any deactivation unless the B-1 is deployed.[13] Clearly, the

FB-111s presently being acquired will remain structurally
sound for a long time. In any event, even if structural problems in the B-52 actually did occur and were serious enough
to force the plane's discontinuation, a more inexpensive option
would be to produce a less elaborate bomber, such as the
B-52 H. Thus, modifications in our current bomber fleet appear the more judicious choice.

B-1 Superiority Over B-52

"The B-1 is a more formidable weapon than the B-52 or
the FB-111." Although the B-1 appears to be a remarkable
plane, its advantages over existing aircraft are not as great
as we are led to believe. For example, the B-1 does not have
a supersonic dash capability,[14] whereas the FB-111 is able
to fly Mach 1.2 at sea level.[15] Moreover, a number of the
advanced new weapons slated for the B-1 will also be used on
the B-52 and FB-111. For example, the SRAM will be available on all three aircraft,[16] as well as the SCAD.[17] The
SRAM, bomber penetration aids, and electromagnetic warfare
devices are all being designed, according to the Defense Department, "so that they could be used both on our existing
heavy bombers (B-52s), or on a new AMSA-type bomber, as
well as on the FB-111 where feasible."[18] Their analyses
showed that "the most important factor in manned strategic
weapons systems appears to be the weaponry and penetration
aids carried; the characteristics of the carrier are a secondary
consideration, except as they relate to penetration aid effectiveness."[19] Thus, the problem is not so much a need for a
new aircraft as it is for new penetration aids and weapons,[20]
such as SCAD and SRAM, which are available for existing
aircraft.

Bomber Superiority Over Soviet Union

"The B-1 is important in maintaining a bomber superiority
over the Soviets." Several sources have presented information showing that the long-range heavy bomber fleet of the
Soviets is far inferior to that of the United States both in
numbers and in quality. In the hearings before the House
Armed Services Committee in 1970, Defense Secretary Laird
presented statistics showing that the U.S. intercontinental
bombers outnumbered Russian intercontinental bombers by 581

to 140-45, a ratio of four to one. He went on to state that the
estimate of the Soviet intercontinental manned bomber force
is "essentially the same as noted in previous years. There
is still no evidence that the Soviets intend to deploy a new
heavy bomber."[21] In The Military Balance of 1969-1970,
prepared by the Institute for Strategic Studies, revealing
statistics, here presented in Table 7, were given comparing
U.S. and Soviet bombers.

The B-52 described in Table 7 refers to both the G and H
models, of which the United States has 255.[22] The figures
graphically show the great superiority of U.S. current bombers
over their Russian counterparts in range, speed, and payload.
In addition, Dr. John Foster, Director of Defense Research
and Engineering, told the House Armed Services Committee
in 1969 that there was "no evidence of any follow-on heavy
bomber development" by the Soviets.[23] Since that time, the
Soviets have developed a new medium-range bomber, but there
is no indication that this plane has been put into production.
Clearly, inasmuch as our enemies do not put much stock in
intercontinental bombers, our current bomber force appears
to be adequate in maintaining our superiority over the Soviet
Union in this area.

Desirability of Mixed Arsenal

"We need a mixed arsenal of both missiles and bombers
as a hedge against missile unreliability or improvements in
Soviet ABM capability." It is true that the steps the Soviet
Union would need to take to degrade the effectiveness of
bombers differ from the steps needed to prevent unacceptable
damage from missiles. They are, however, no more complex.
They would appear to be less so, considering the fact that
even supersonic bombers travel much more slowly than ballistic missiles.

But in any case, the argument neglects the enormous internal insurance already present in the missile force which
has, with 656 Polaris missiles and 1,000 Minutemen, more
than four times the number of separately targetable warheads
needed for assured destruction. This calculation does not include the deployment of multiple independently-targetable re-
entry vehicles which produce a further vast multiplication in
deliverable warheads. There is no Soviet ABM on the horizon
that could adequately intercept MIRVs. If additional insurance
were to become necessary, it could be supplied much more

TABLE 7

Comparison of U.S. and Soviet Strategic Bombers

| | Bomber | | |
Items Compared	B-52	Tu-20 Bear	Mya-4 Bison
Origin	U.S.A.	U.S.S.R.	U.S.S.R.
Range	12,500	7,800	6,050
Mach No.	0.95	0.78	0.87
Maximum Weight	488,000	365,000	250,000
Became Operational	1955	1956	1956
Payload	75,000	40,000	20,000

Source: The Military Balance of 1969-1970 (London: Institute for Strategic Studies), p. 56.

quickly and inexpensively by simply adding to and improving the missile force.

The question of time is also important. No one can say with complete confidence that the Russians will never develop the ability to neutralize U.S. missiles. In view of the inherent advantages enjoyed by the offense, however, one might more plausibly predict U.S. development of new missile techniques to nullify any new defense. It is safe to assume that the Soviets will not accomplish the towering technological and and physical task of neutralizing U.S. offense by 1980 or in the succeeding several years. If the B-1 is insurance against such a risk, there is at least no need to hasten toward full deployment before the end of the decade.

Moreover, it must be recognized that discussion of the B-1 does not require refutation of the mixed-force concept. As noted above, the B-52 and FB-111 could remain in the force well into the operational time frame contemplated for the B-1. In combination, they possess nearly all of the important capabilities planned for the B-1. A determined effort to defend against U.S. bombers therefore would require development of similar defensive capabilities regardless of whether or not the B-1 is acquired.

In short, there is no persuasive evidence that a risk to the missile force is likely to develop. If it were to develop, the B-1 would make little difference in the overall U.S.

capability to respond--in fact, it might weaken the response
by diverting funds and energies from more promising alternatives within the missile field.

Flexibility

   "Bombers have a greater flexibility than missiles. " A
classically cited demonstration of the superior flexibility of
bombers is the case of a bomber and a missile being dispatched simultaneously. The bomber can be recalled, it is
said, but the missile cannot. On the surface, this scenario
is accurate. Under close scrutiny, however, its flaw becomes
apparent. Any bomber is going to require several hours to
arrive at its target, whereas a missile will take half an hour
at most. Thus with a missile, especially a submarine-based
missile, one has the luxury of waiting several hours before
deciding whether or not to fire. If the decision is made to
fire, the missile will still arrive far ahead of the bomber
which had to be dispatched hours before. In the context of a
threatened nuclear war, such time can be crucial. Here the
strength of the bomber is in fact a weakness; its much longer
delivery time is what accounts for its "recallability. " Furthermore, Robert McNamara has pointed out that once a bomber
crosses what is variously known as the "HR line" or "fail-safe
point, " recallability is an illusion:

      There is not a darn thing you can do to change its
      course. From that moment on until the time it
      drops its warhead on the target, your enemy is
      warned. That period of warning which the enemy
      obtains from the airplane is far greater than the
      period of warning he obtains from the missile,
      and during that period your Nation is in danger. [24]

   Another weakness of long-range bombers is that they
generally depend on at least one refueling. They depend upon
the successful performance of aircraft tankers like the KC-135.
Mishaps in tanker performance, due either to mechanical
problems or interference by the enemy, could jeopardize a
bomber's entire mission. The B-1 is no exception. It requires one refueling before it arrives at its target.
   Significantly, this tanker requirement raises another grave
problem with the B-1. Its rapid take-off is cited as a major
advantage, in that it reduces vulnerability on the ground to

low-trajectory missile attack. But the KC-135 tanker upon
which it would rely for refueling is not blessed with a similar
capability. If the adversary destroyed the tankers on the
ground, the bomber's talent for quick take-off would, of course,
be useless. Thus we have the likelihood of massive new expenditures for a new short take-off tanker.

Given the disadvantage of the KC-135 as a tanker for the
B-1, it is not unlikely that the Air Force will attempt to purchase C-5s with tanker modifications. This would dramatically
increase the overall cost of the manned bomber program.

The main remaining attribute listed under "flexibility"--
the use of bombers for show of force purposes during periods
of crisis--is also questionable. It could as well be interpreted
as a "show of fear," causing doubts about U.S. intentions when
such doubts can increase the danger of miscalculation.

Diversion of Soviet Resources

"Bombers require the enemy to mix his strategic defenses,
thus diverting his funds from ABM." As stated above, present
U.S. bombers force the enemy to mix his strategic defenses
just as the B-1 would. Indeed, in 1968, our then-current
bomber force required the Soviets to spend a full 10 per cent
of their military budget just on bomber defenses. [25] Inasmuch
as many of the penetration aids of the B-1 either can or will
be on our present bombers, the Soviets would have to have the
same degree of bomber defense sophistication in any eventuality.
Also, as Robert McNamara has stated, the goal of mixing the
enemy's defenses does not take into account the size of the
opposing bomber force:

> The requirement for air defense is more a function
> of the number of targets to be defended than of the
> number of attacking bombers. Since the enemy
> would not know in advance which targets our bombers
> would attack, he would have to defend all the targets.
> Accordingly, his expenditures for air defense are
> likely to be the same regardless of whether we have
> a relatively small bomber force or a large one. [26]

Thus a fleet of 250 B-1s would seem unwarranted.

Potential of Conventional Use

"Bombers, unlike missiles, can be used conventionally. "
No one will argue the fact that, in a strictly conventional war,
bombers are far more useful than missiles, which would be
of virtually no value. The worth of the B-52 in Viet-Nam has
been substantial, judging from military opinion. It is questionable, however, whether a plane as sophisticated as the
B-1 is really necessary in a conventional war effort. American
air power has dropped about one million tons of bombs during
the course of the Southeast Asian conflict without losing a
single B-52 in action. Even earlier aircraft, such as the
B-47, may have been qualified for such missions.

Thus, in situations of limited enemy anti-aircraft capability, our current bombers appear sufficient. On the other
hand, against a highly sophisticated anti-aircraft capability
posture in a conventional war, aircraft having much greater
performance characteristics than those of strategic bombers
will be required, [27] since the damage done to strategic bombers
would not be offset by the destructiveness of their non-nuclear
payload.

Also, studies reported three years ago by the Department
of Defense show that "advanced defenses [to be] effective
against an equal-cost AMSA (B-1) force"[28] even against a
greater-than-expected Soviet threat. All these considerations
only underscore the point that what is needed is better penetration aids, not a new bomber.

COST AND DESIRABILITY

Certainly where the defense of the United States is vitally
concerned, survival must take precedence over cost. But
there is a very real question whether the B-1 is indeed vital
to U.S. defense. The previous discussion, coupled with the
fact that current B-52 and FB-111 forces alone are sufficient
for assured destruction of the enemy, [29] indicates that the B-1
program is not crucial to the U.S. defense posture.

If the national defense is no longer vitally at stake, cost
becomes a quite valid consideration. The official estimates
for the cost of each plane vary from $25 to $30 million, with
the whole project cost estimated from $9 to $13 billion. These
figures are doubtful at best. Observers have endured far too
many cost overruns on various weapons systems in the recent

past to accept such figures unhesitatingly. In the words of
the Air Force Chief of Staff, "The important thing is to recognize that early in the history of any system, estimates are
just that--nothing more."[30]

What evidence is there that the costs might be higher?
One sign is the steady increase in the estimated total cost for
RDT&E. In 1968, the cost estimate was $1.7 billion.[31] In
1969, the figure grew to $1.8 billion. In 1970, the figure
jumped 28 per cent to $2.33 billion.[32] The trend of these
RDT&E costs is clear. We can expect them to increase again
and again over the next several years.

Given this ominous forerunner, what can be expected for
production costs? There are several ways we can examine
them. One is to observe what cost overruns have been in the
past. The F-111 unit cost was originally planned to be $2.8
million, but today unit costs run over $8 million,[33] an increase
of more than 280 per cent of the original estimate. If such a
yardstick were to be applied to the B-1, we would expect to
pay $70 to $84 million per plane! It would not be quite fair to
multiply these prices by the total fleet number of 250; one of
the reasons for the F-111 overrun was the fact that the total
number to be deployed was slashed from its original number.[34]
Even taking 200 per cent as our standard, however, would result in unit costs of $50 to $60 million, or as much as $15
billion for fleet production costs alone.

The C-5A's current unit cost of about $45 million[35] is
almost three times the originally projected cost of $16.5 mil-
lion,[36] and the plane's manufacturer claims to be losing money
on even that tripled figure. Were the B-1's cost behavior
similar, we would end up with unit costs of $75 to $90 million
and a total fleet cost of $19 to $22.5 billion. These two un-
fortunate histories alone are enough to cast grave doubts on
the currently anticipated program costs.

Another way to approach the cost problem is to compare
a current airplane against the proposed B-1. For example,
consider the Boeing 747 passenger plane. This aircraft is
well within the state of the art, it experienced no truly major
problems in its development, and it is now in service and
performing well. It is larger than the B-1 is expected to be
(500,000 pounds versus 380,000, unloaded),[37] but it is a much
less complex plane. The 747 is fixed-wing; the B-1 will have
a swing wing. The 747 avionics (electronics in the plane)
system has no exotic requirements, whereas the B-1 avionics
system must be concerned with forward-looking radar, advanced droppler radar, passive infrared surveillance, passive

location homing and warning of enemy radar, air-to-air search, ground mapping, target identification,[38] integrated controls displays,[39] and a host of penetration aids, including on-board chaff and flare dispensers, forward-firing chaff-dispensing rockets, and a variety of passive decoys, in addition to active electronic counter-measures.[40] The B-1 must survive surface-to-air missiles, interceptors, anti-aircraft fire, nuclear explosions, expensive bomber defense missiles, short-range attack missiles, and subsonic cruise armed decoys, while trying to deliver a payload of weapons.

The 747 has only to fly passengers and cargo safely from one place to another, its only hazards being mechanical problems, hijackers, and weather. The 747 does not have to be highly maneuverable, whereas for the B-1, this is a necessity in order to avoid interceptors and SAMs. The B-1 must be able to withstand nuclear attacks, requiring hardened electronics and a fuselage capable of sustaining limited nuclear overpressures due to blast effects.[41] The 747 has no such requirements. The B-1 must have the capability of becoming airborne on very short notice in order to avoid being destroyed by an incoming missile. The 747 needs no ready-alert capability. The B-1 crew compartment must have an ejection capability, unlike the 747.[42] The B-1 will be provided with a world-wide communications capability, with digital computers available for weapons delivery, engine and wing-position controls, and inertial navigation and flight controls, unlike the 747.[43] The supersonic capability of this B-1 will require more expensive structural materials than the subsonic 747.

And this relatively simple 747 costs $20 million per copy, leading one to expect a very much higher cost for the B-1.

The complexity, hence expense, of the B-1's avionics alone is attested to in a recent article in a trade journal:

> The avionics for the B-1 has undergone far more extensive advanced system analysis than that of any previous U.S. bomber, and possibly more than any previous U.S. military aircraft of any type.[44]

Indeed, the costs for the avionics package alone were becoming so large ($12 to $14 million per plane) that the Air Force had to adopt a two-stage system, whereby an Initial Avionics System, designed to meet B-1 needs early in its operational life, is later superseded by a Standardized Avionics System, an expanded capability version for use later in the bomber's life, although this growth requirement "is easier to state than to meet."[45]

The avionics package has not been the only sore spot in the B-1 program. The specifications for the plane were also downgraded in terms of the craft's performance at low altitudes. Originally, the B-1 was to have a supersonic capability (Mach 1.2) at low altitudes.[46] Such a dash capability, however, would have resulted in crew fatigue, reduced crew efficiency,[47] a "bone-jarring ride,"[48] and "the apparently involuntary reflex on the part of the pilot to pull up slightly on the stick."[49] Presumably these characteristics have been eliminated by scrubbing the supersonic dash requirement. Again, it is interesting to note that the FB-111A, unlike the B-1, does have a supersonic dash capability of Mach 1.2.[50]

There is also a question of indirect costs associated with the B-1. The costs of SRAM, SCAD, and BDM RDT&E, production, and maintenance, as well as costs of modifications in the KC-135 tanker or procurement of new tankers, have not been included in the Air Force's cost estimates. These would be sizable expenses.

The above considerations strongly indicate that the cost of the B-1 will be far beyond the $20 million 747 price tag, well beyond the $25 to $30 million range quoted by the Air Force, and probably double the original estimate, if past performance and present trends continue. This would suggest a cost of $50 to $60 million per plane or more. The total production cost of the B-1 would be at least $12.5 to $15 billion and quite possibly higher. Adding research and development costs and operating costs, one can foresee the total system costing in the neighborhood of $20 billion. Will the marginal increase in our defense posture justify this staggering cost?

Rather than strengthen our defense posture, deployment of the B-1 could actually weaken it by taking our defense dollars away from projects of more discernible merit.

RECOMMENDATION

The current estimate for total procurement of the B-1 is about $9.4 billion. The Administration has requested $100 million for R&D in FY 1971. We recommend that the $100 million request be denied, leaving the $80 million carry-over from 1969 to continue R&D.

NOTES

1. *Aviation Week and Space Technology,* March 17, 1969,
p. 17; Defense Marketing Service, [AMSA] Market Intelligence
Report, March, 1969; *Congressional Record,* Senate, September 3, 1969.

2. *Congressional Record,* Senate, September 3, 1969.

3. Defense Marketing Service, *op. cit.*

4. *Space/Aeronautics,* April, 1970, pp. 26-33; "Advanced Manned Strategic Aircraft Fact Sheet," Department
of the Air Force.

5. *Ibid.*

6. *Aviation Week and Space Technology, loc. cit.* ;
Congressional Record, Senate, September 3, 1969; *Washington Post,* June 1, 1969, p. A26.

7. Letter of Dr. John S. Foster, Jr., Director of Defense Research and Engineering, to Senator William Proxmire, May 27, 1969.

8. Hearings on Military Posture, Committee on Armed
Services, House of Representatives, February-April, 1970,
p. 7590.

9. *Congressional Record,* Senate, September 3, 1969;
Melvin R. Laird, Defense Program and Budget for FY 1971 (Wash
ington, D.C.: U.S. Government Printing Office, 1970); Report
of the House Armed Services Committee for FY 1971, pp. 38-39.

10. *Congressional Record,* Senate, February 19, 1965.

11. *Congressional Record,* Senate, September 3, 1969.

12. Hearings on Military Posture, House Armed Services
Committee, February-April, 1967, pp. 499-500.

13. Hearings before the House Armed Services Committee
on Military Posture, February-April, 1970, p. 6879.

14.　Technology Week, March 27, 1967, p. 39.

15.　Space/Aeronautics, June, 1969, p. 67.

16.　Melvin R. Laird, Statement before the House Armed Services Committee, March 27, 1969, pp. 32-34; Astronautics and Aeronautics, January, 1970, p. 1; Hearings on Military Posture, House Armed Services Committee, February-April, 1970, p. 7585.

17.　Aviation Week and Space Technology, March 9, 1970, p. 104.

18.　Robert McNamara, Statement before the Senate Subcommittee on Department of Defense Appropriations, January 22, 1968, p. 72.

19.　Hearings on Military Posture, House Armed Services Committee, February-April, 1967, pp. 499-500.

20.　Clark M. Clifford, The 1970 Defense Budget and Defense Program for Fiscal Years 1970-74, January 15, 1969, p. 58059.

21.　Melvin R. Laird, Statement before the House Armed Services Committee, 1970, p. 6876.

22.　Hearings on Military Posture, House Armed Services Committee, April-June, 1968, p. 9675.

23.　Hearings on Military Posture, House Armed Services Committee, February-April, 1969.

24.　Robert McNamara, quoted by the Washington Post, April 8, 1969, p. A8.

25.　Hearings before the Subcommittee on Appropriations, FY 1970, Senate, p. 104.

26.　Robert McNamara, quoted by Aviation Week and Space Technology, March 1, 1965, p. 65.

27.　Congressional Record, Senate, September 3, 1969.

28.　Hearings on Military Posture, House Armed Services Committee, February-April, 1967, pp. 501ff.

29. Ibid., pp. 499-500.

30. Hearings before the Subcommittee on Appropriations, FY 1970, Senate, p. 104.

31. Hearings before the Subcommittee on Appropriations, House of Representatives, FY 1969.

32. Hearings on Military Posture, House Armed Services Committee, February-April, 1970, p. 7590.

33. Ibid., p. 8175.

34. Ibid.

35. Hearings on Military Posture, House Armed Services Committee, February-April, 1970, p. 7470.

36. Hearings on Military Posture, House Armed Services Committee, February-April, 1967, pp. 499-500.

37. Astronautics and Aeronautics, June, 1969, p. 50.

38. Defense Marketing Service, [AMSA] Market Intelligence Report, March, 1969.

39. Aviation Week and Space Technology, January 26, 1970, p. 23.

40. Aviation Week and Space Technology, May 4, 1970, p. 71.

41. Space/Aeronautics, April, 1970, pp. 26-33.

42. Ibid.

43. Ibid.

44. Aviation Week and Space Technology, January 26, 1970, p. 23.

45. Ibid.

46. Technology Week, March 27, 1967, p. 39; Aviation Week and Space Technology, May 4, 1970, p. 53.

47. *Aviation Week and Space Technology,* May 4, 1970, p. 53.

48. *Technology Week,* March 27, 1967, p. 39.

49. *Ibid.*

50. *Space/Aeronautics,* June, 1969, p. 67.

The C-5A is the world's largest airplane. The Air Force's contracts for the plane specify the following:

Performance

High cruise speed: 470 knots

Long-range cruise speed: 400 knots

Aerial delivery drop speed: 130-50 knots

Rate of climb at sea level, standard day at basic mission weight: 2, 100 ft./min. (basic mission 100, 000-lb. payload, 5, 500 nautical miles)

Take-off distance over 50 feet with 100, 000-lb. payload at midpoint of 2, 500 nautical mile radius mission, sea level, 89.5° F, wet grass runway: 4, 000 ft.

Designed payload: 2.5 g., 220, 000 lb.; 2.25 g., 265, 000 lb.

Range with 220, 000-lb. payload: 3, 050 nautical miles

Range with 112, 600-lb. payload: 5, 500 nautical miles

Ferry Range: 7, 200 nautical miles

Weights

Flight design gross weight--2.5 g.: 728, 000 lb.

Flight design gross weight--2.25 g.: 764, 000 lb.

Basic mission weight: 712, 000 lb.

Maximum landing weight (9 feet per second sink rate): 635, 850 lb.

Operating weight: 323, 904 lb.

Personnel Capacity
    Crew: 6
    Alternate crew: 6
    Courier seating: 8
    Troops--upper troop compartment: 75.

The C-5A is, of course, remarkable for reasons other than its size. With the possible exception of the F-111, the C-5A acquisition program and its difficulties have been the most widely publicized of any military program of recent years. Despite this, it is remarkable how little is really known about this largely unclassified program.

The reasons for buying the currently planned C-5A force are obscure. Indeed, the size of the planned force itself is uncertain. It is generally believed that eighty-one aircraft (four squadrons) of C-5A aircraft will be bought. At the same time, Department of Defense sources indicate that the Joint Chiefs of Staff are still "validating" a need for at least 120 aircraft (six squadrons) of C-5As.*

The six-squadron (or more) force of C-5As envisioned at the time of the program's definition phase in 1964 and 1965 was based on a series of studies in the early 1960's. These studies projected airlift requirements to meet military contingencies then foreseen for the 1970's. Congress does not know whether the original assumptions were valid or how the changing view of U.S. world responsibilities has or should affect plans for quick military intervention in foreign countries.

COST GROWTH

Aside from support of contingencies, the C-5A was originally envisioned as an extremely economical air cargo transport plane for general use. As late as the 1969 Senate debate on the authorization bill for military procurement, the C-5A was touted by supporters as competitive in cost per ton mile with sea transport. This claim did not pan out. The cost per ton mile for the C-5A was stated as $0.029. It turned out that Navy estimates for transporting dry cargo in water carriers in FY 1969 were $0.005 per ton mile, or about one sixth of the claimed cost of $0.029 for the C-5A. Worse, it turned out that C-5A ton mile costs were vastly understated. The $0.029 figure

---

*Written before the release of Price Subcommittee Report on Military Aircraft.

assumed that C-5A aircraft were free, and made no provision
for amortizing acquisition costs, which, of course, must be
done if the costs are to be comparable to commercial rates.

It turned out that the Air Force did have a ton mile figure
at that time--1969--which recognized investment cost. In fact,
the Air Force had just raised its estimate of the C-5A ton mile
cost from $0.10 to $0.12 to recognize increases in investment
costs. Unhappily, the narrow Air Force definition of "investment" did not include research and development costs or costs
of initial spare parts. When these were added, the C-5A's ton
mile cost became $0.148.

The program cost figures on which the $0.148 ton mile was
based were derived from the October, 1968, C-5A program cost
estimate prepared by the Air Force. This estimate represented
an increase of $1,959,000 over the Air Force's independent
cost estimate for the program prepared in April, 1965. The
comparison of these two estimates is summarized in Table 8.

The November, 1968, program cost estimate of approximately $5.3 billion is the last formal and definitive Air Force
estimate for the 120-aircraft program to be widely dissemi-
nated. However, informal estimates were made shortly before
the reduction of the public consumption plan from 120 to 81 aircraft. Some of these estimates placed program cost as high
as $5.8 billion, a further overrun of $500 million.

More recently, statements in the press indicate that DOD
officials expect C-5A unit costs of about $55 million for the
currently planned 81-airplane program. This compares to a
unit cost of $44 million for the $5.3 billion, 120-airplane program used to calculate the $0.148 ton mile cost in 1969. As-
suming the same life expectancy and utilization rate used in
the 1969 calculations, an increase of roughly $0.03 can be
projected in ton mile cost for the C-5A. This new figure of
$0.178 per ton mile would make the C-5A the most expensive
cargo carrier outside the space program.

                         C-5A MISSIONS

There remain other arguments in favor of the C-5A, of
course. One of the arguments used with great effect in the
1969 Senate debate was the prospect of "bringing the boys
home, " especially from Europe, with the advent of operational
C-5As. Unhappily, this turns out to be a somewhat specious
argument. As indicated in the summary of specifications, the

C-5A's normal passenger capacity is seventy-five. It is primarily designed to carry heavy equipment. The C-5A can be used to carry large numbers of troops in emergencies, but other aircraft now in wide use do the job more safely and inexpensively, especially to NATO Europe.

It is also argued that C-5As could be flown to unimproved airfields unsuited to other transport aircraft. Originally, it was envisioned that the C-5A would be landed at the forward edge of the battle area (FEBA) on rough fields. The high-flotation, 28-wheel landing gear was intended for this use. Unfortunately, more than high-flotation landing gear is needed if the aircraft is to be used more than once on rough fields. Structural strength is also important. The C-5A's structural strength is suspect, especially so if it is to be landed at high gross weights on rough fields.

This last statement may seem questionable in light of repeated assertions by prestigious review groups that the C-5A is in good shape, technically at least, despite numerous structural failures in testing. The July, 1969, Air Force Review of the C-5A stated: "An extensive evaluation by Air Force and NASA experts has revealed no major design deficiencies in the aircraft or engines, and that there is a high probability that all range, payload, take-off and landing performance requirements will be met."[1]

This and similar statements have been reinforced by repeated assertions that "all contract specifications will be met." Suspicions have been voiced that such statements are made plausible only by reason of relaxed specifications. These suspicions tend to be confirmed by the small amount of factual specification change data made available on this unclassified program. The July, 1969, Air Force report listed the following specification changes:

a. Reduction in landing design gross from the weight associated with a maximum weight payload to a basic mission weight payload, plus fuel. The revised landing weight more nearly approached the extremes of normal operation as compared to emergency conditions.

b. Reduction in turning side load factor during taxi from 0.5 G side load to 0.4 G side load. The original MIL-A-8860 does not recognize limitations due to nose gear skidding. The effect of this change was to reduce maximum taxi speed from 20 to 18 knots for a 45° nose-wheel deflection (hard) turn.

c. Revision of criteria for horizontal tail airloads distribution from earlier arbitrary 75-25 unsymmetrical

TABLE 8

C-5A Program Growth
(in millions of dollars)

C-5A Program	Original Estimate[a]	October, 1968 Estimate[b]	Difference
R&D (5 aircraft)			
Lockheed	514.1	607.0	92.9
GE	242.7	285.9	43.2
Add	220.2	109.8	(-110.4)[c]
Total	977.0	1,002.7	25.7
Run A (53 aircraft)			
Lockheed	892.4	1,157.4	265.0
GE	216.0	236.7[d]	20.7
Add	101.6	157.0	55.4
Total	1,210.0[e]	1,551.1	341.1
Total R &D + Run A	2,187.0	2,553.8	366.8
Run B (62 aircraft)			
Lockheed	538.8	--	--
Add (5)[e]	61.0	--	--
Total Lockheed	599.8	1,404.3	804.5
GE	172.9	--	--
Add (5)[f]	12.5	--	--
Total GE	185.4	230.3[d]	44.9
Total add	105.8	173.7	67.9
Total Run B	891.0	1,808.3	917.3
Air Force Logistics Command investment	203.0	968.0	675.0
Total Program	3,371.0	5,330.1	1,959.1

Source: Statement and Submissions of A. E. Fitzgerald, Deputy for Management Systems, Office of Assistant Secretary of the Air Force for Financial Management, Committee on Armed Services, House of Representatives, 91st Cong., 1st Session, Part 2, 1969, pp. 2949-3037.

NOTES TO TABLE 8

ᵃTotal figures based upon April, 1965, independent cost estimate except as shown in Note "e." Contractor amounts are contract values as of October, 1965. "Add" is the residual between independent cost estimate and contract values.

ᵇTotal figures are obtained from October, 1968, C-5A cost trade summary. Estimated contractor prices to be paid by the government Aeronautical Systems Division (ASD) cost team estimate of October, 1968, which indicate anticipated Air Force price at that time, except as noted in Note "d." Add figures are a residual between cost tract and contractor prices.

ᶜInasmuch as the add figures are a residual between program cost estimates and estimated contractor cost to the government, they can be expected to decrease as the program progresses.

ᵈFigures for GE current estimated price to the government have been made to reconcile to $467,000,000 as shown on the C-5A program cost estimate October, 1968, funding requirements versus August, 1968, Program Change Requests (PCR) for production run A, run B, and 5 run C. This amount is $76,400,000 under what is shown as the price to the government at that time. As near as can be determined, the difference is the result of not including the sixty-nine spare engines which were one of the production options (i.e., 69/564 x $631,000,000), as shown on pp. 1-5 of the Whittaker Report, Review of the C-5A Program, Department of the Air Force, July 24, 1969.

ᵉRun A totals have been reduced from the independent cost estimate figure by $23,000,000--the average cost of one aircraft and one set of engines--because the independent cost estimate run A was for fifty-four aircraft rather than the present fifty-three aircraft.

ᶠ$61,000,000 and $12,500,000 have been added to the contract amounts to add in the last five aircraft which brings the total up to 120 craft. They were shown as run C at the time of the independent cost estimate.

distribution to a distribution based on C-141 test data, inasmuch as the C-141 has a similar aerodynamic configuration.

d. Revision of taxi criteria from earlier static criteria to later criteria based on dynamic taxi analysis.

e. Reduction in ramp gross weight for <u>full</u> ground handling from 769,000 lbs. to 732,500 lbs. (the basic ramp gross weights). This ground handling limitation parallels the rationale for the taxi analysis and reduction in side load factor.

f. Reduction in maximum speed for full flaps from 205 knots (1.82 Vs) to 180 knots (1.65 Vs) inasmuch as the flaps are not used as a deceleration device; maximum speeds for take-off and partial flap position were unchanged.

g. Reduction in gross weight for operation from substandard fields from 678,500 lbs. to 571,000 lbs. (the gross weight associated with the basic tactical mission for delivery of 200,000-lb. payload and 1,000 nautical miles flyback).

h. Sink rate reduction from ten feet per second (FAA certification requirement) to nine feet per second. The current standard MIL-8862 specifies ten feet per second, but does not specify design strength at 150 per cent of limit load without failure as used for the C-5A with nine feet per second sink rate.

i. Reduction in limit speed (vl) from 410 KCAS to a linear variation with altitude from 402 KCAS at sea level to 392 KCAS at 22,400 feet. This reduced criteria still satisfies the basic requirements for margin in the event of upset and resulting dive recovery.

j. Reduction in flutter speed from 1.20 V-limit (the FAA certification requirement) to 1.15 V-limit, the Air Force standard.

k. Adjustment of gust criteria from initial conservative criteria to a more realistic criteria based on accumulated data.

l. Increase in the guaranteed weight empty by 1,340 lbs. from 318,469 lbs. to 319,809 lbs. This change was made June 3, 1968, and was the weight increase associated with an improved and redesigned empendage "bullet" that reduced the drag by two counts, improving the cruise performance. Resultant payload/range performance was improved for all missions except one, which was unchanged.

In general, these changes indicate a lightening and weakening of the aircraft structure. Moreover, it appears that even
the reduced specifications are not being met by aircraft actually being produced, although it must be conceded that very little
hard quantitative data has been released.

The June 16, 1970, report of the Air Force Scientific
Advisory Board (Bisplinghoff Committee) on the C-5A did little
to increase confidence in either the candor of official statements or the integrity of the airplane. Among other things,
the Bisplinghoff report restated the following old litany: "It
is concluded that the Air Force has not granted specification
deviations which have reduced the flight-performance requirements of the C-5A airplane."[2]

This seems strange in light of the known relaxations and
deviations. However, this misleading statement can be
rendered accurate by a narrow definition of the phrase "flight
performance requirements." In the past, this phrase has
been defined as requirements for payload/range, take-off and
landing distance, and cruise speed. Therefore, it has been
argued, the airplane can fly the basic mission even though it
must be flown rather carefully.

Beyond the bureaucratic deceptions, the Bisplinghoff
report raises serious questions about the technical health of
the C-5A program. Even though the report is heavily qualified and replete with disclaimers, it is clear that the aircraft's
structural and avionics difficulties are major problems.

As a minimum, it appears that the originally envisioned
objective of a C-5A transport operating at the FEBA is not
likely to be attained.

In reality, the only major unique use of the C-5A which
can conceivably be defended is transport of outsized cargo--
that is, cargo which is too large or too heavy to be carried
in other available aircraft.

In answer to the question how many C-5As would be
needed to meet contingency plans if C-5As carried only that
necessary cargo for which they were uniquely suited, the Air
Force has informally stated that forty aircraft would be needed.
This would entail assigning other aircraft, including Contract
Reserve Air Fleet (CRAF) equipment, to supplement the C-5A
fleet.

It should be noted that this, too, is only an assertion so
far as the Congress as a whole or the public is concerned.
We do not really know all the premises on which the forty-
airplane minimum requirement is based. The nature of contingencies envisioned is not known. The degree to which

prepositioning and other deployment concepts were considered
is not known. It is not known whether the Air Force has considered modifications of existing aircraft, such as has been
done rather inexpensively to carry bulky NASA equipment. Assuming it is really necessary to airlift fully assembled bridge
launchers and similar equipment, this last possibility becomes
a viable alternative now that the possibility of bouncing heavily-
loaded C-5As over hummocks at the FEBA has gone glimmering.

CONTINGENCY FUNDING FOR LOCKHEED

A final point that needs exploring is the ultimate use of
the contingency funding the Department of Defense requested
on the C-5A. In addition to funding the enormous overruns,
Congress also was asked to provide a $200 million down pay-
ment on a contingency fund of indefinite but unprecedented
size. This fund, primarily for Lockheed Aircraft Corporation,
could grow to $1.2 billion for a full bail-out situation, includ-
ing alleviation of possible financial problems on Lockheed's
commercial work.

Congressional staff specialists have long suspected that
Lockheed's commercial airplane problems were at least
partially to blame for that company's financial difficulties and
may have contributed, at least indirectly, to the huge overruns
on their military programs. Under questioning, assistant
secretaries Moot and Shillito of the Department of Defense
conceded that Lockheed's immediate cash problems were
primarily attributable to their commercial program, the
L-1011 airbus. [3] Although they have stated that the contingency
funding was not intended for Lockheed's commercial program,
they conceded that in fact there were no positive protections
against use of the military money to alleviate Lockheed's commercial cash problems. Moreover, the DOD has refused to
furnish a cash flow analysis of Lockheed's programs, explain-
ing that Lockheed objects to revealing this information. This
has disturbed some Senators to whom it appears that the Congress is expected to vote money without assurances of what
it will be used for.

Table 9 shows Lockheed's C-5A cost growth by cost element, illustrating some of the reasons for concern regarding
migration of costs.

The category "Other" includes charges from Lockheed
divisions other than the Georgia division where the C-5A is

TABLE 9

Lockheed C-5A Cost Information[a]
(millions of dollars)

Category	Government Preliminary Cost Estimates, April, 1965[b] (116 Aircraft) Low	Government Preliminary Cost Estimates, April, 1965[b] (116 Aircraft) High	Contractor Original Price Proposal, April, 1965 (115 Aircraft)	Original Price Negotiation Memorandum, August, 1965[b] (115 Aircraft)	Government Current Estimate, February, 1970[c] (81 Aircraft)
Direct Labor					
Engineering	.....	.....	130	.....	205
Manufacturing	.....	.....	108	.....	277
Other[d]	.....	.....	95	.....	134
Subtotal	.....	.....	333	.....	616
Material & Purchased Parts	.....	.....	470	.....	634
Subcontracts	.....	.....	355	.....	539
Other[e]	.....	.....	72	.....	550
Overhead	.....	.....	350	.....	682
General and Administrative Expenses	.....	.....	76	.....	143
Total Cost	2,097	2,432	1,656	1,703	3,164
Profit (or Loss)	210	243	166	170	-648
Total Price	2,307	2,675	1,822	1,873	2,516

[a]This functional break-out reflects Lockheed accounting practices and also the large amount of out-plant effort. There is no comparable break-out in the preliminary cost estimate or price negotiation memorandum. These two cost estimates were aligned, based on the Air Force's material program code, which is principally hardware- or product-oriented. The preliminary cost estimate is the Air Force's April 1, 1965, independent cost estimate and was based on all work done in-plant and was also based on an aircraft count of 116 vs. the 115 that went on contract for R&D, Run A, and Run B.

[b]Based on 85/15 cost-sharing arrangement.

[c]Based on 70/30 (over) and 50/50 (under) cost-sharing arrangement.

[d]Tooling, logistics, and quality assurance.

[e]Interdivisional charges for feeder plants, etc.

Source: Air Force Submission of April 10, 1970.

assembled. It shows the largest increase, both in absolute amount and percentage. DOD analysts have long believed that the largest source of interdivisional cost increases has been Lockheed's California Division, where the L-1011 commercial airplane is being built. If these charges include California Division overhead expense, as they presumably do, overhead absorption alone could benefit the L-1011 program substantially without actual migration of direct charges. Similarly, the increase in general and administrative expenses absorbed by the C-5A program could benefit the commercial programs. In addition, it is possible that the commercial program could be the prime beneficiary of the activities whose costs are charged to overhead and general and administrative accounts, notwithstanding the fact that such expenses are allocated in proportion to direct costs of the various programs.

RECOMMENDATIONS

1. Delete the $200 million Lockheed contingency fund.
2. Congress should take action to ensure that the acquisition of military equipment does not become a form of relief funding for private enterprises.
3. No C-5As should be accepted by the Air Force until original design specifications are met and the plane can carry out its originally designated missions. Under no condition should the Air Force accept defective planes.
4. Delay all funds for C-5A pending answers to the specific questions raised in the body of this section.

NOTES

1. Department of the Air Force, Review of the C5-A Program (July 24, 1969), pp. 1-5.

2. Congressional Record, Senate, August 13, 1970.

3. Meeting of Senator William Proxmire, Howard Shuman, Richard Kaufman, Ernest Fitzgerald, Robert C. Moot, and Barry J. Shillito, May 18, 1970, New Senate Office Building, Washington, D. C.

8

The ULMS program, as presently planned, is a successor to the Polaris/Poseidon fleet involving the development of a more efficient, highly survivable sea-based strategic deterrent capable of launching missiles of ICBM range from quieter submarines of improved design. The concept grew out of the Secretary of Defense's STRAT-X study in 1968, which assessed various strategic systems for basing advanced ICBMs.

Unlike the Polaris or Poseidon ballistic missile submarines, ULMS will be designed as a complete system. The missiles, hull, propulsion, and other subsystems will be integrated into one entire system. Thus, in the design stage, a significant change in size or capability of one component would have some effect on the others.

The major difference in ULMS is the increase in range of the missile from the present 2,000 to 3,000 miles to 6,000 to 7,000 miles. In addition to the longer range of the missile, the submarine will have a longer cruising or on-station time.

The number of missiles per boat probably will be greater than the sixteen presently installed on each Polaris submarine. The number of MIRV warheads also probably will be greater than the ten planned for each Poseidon missile. The program has not yet reached the contract definition stage, so decisions such as the total number of warheads have not been made.

ULMS will be designed for ease of maintenance and shorter in-port time for repairs relative to the time on patrol. It will be a quieter and possibly deeper-diving boat that together with its vast oceanic range will enormously complicate detection.

No technological breakthroughs are deemed necessary to construct the hull or build the propulsion plant. To achieve

the desired missile range, the Navy is seeking either a new
missile or a modification of the Poseidon, possibly using the
latter as a first stage. Emphasis seems to be on a new
missile system.

If sufficient funding becomes available, the Navy looks
for prototype construction to start in 1972 with delivery of
the first models in the late 1970's and a complete system on
station by the early 1980's.

The total number of boats or force level has not been defined, but, given the increase in range and the probable increase in the number of missiles and warheads, it is estimated
that the number would be significantly less than the forty-one
Polaris/Poseidon fleet that ULMS is designed to replace. The
number of ULMS submarines could be as small as half the
present figure.

COSTS

The budget request for FY 1971 was $44 million for re-
search and development. In FY 1969, $5.4 million was spent
on a study of the ULMS concept. During 1970, the Navy received an appropriation of $10 million--one half of the amount
requested. An overall figure, unclassified cost estimate, for
ULMS has not been given.

There are unresolved questions regarding ultimate force
levels for Congress to consider and influence. Also, the
Secretary of Defense declared 1970 a year of transition. Presumably, in 1971, five-year projections again will be given.
At that time, the strategic priorities of the Administration
will be more clearly determined and the Navy will have a
firmer idea of what portion of the nuclear deterrent will be
sent to sea.

Unofficial cost estimates have been supplied for ULMS:
$1 billion per boat, missiles, and ten years of operating cost.
Senator Stennis put a $25 billion price tag on ULMS for an
unspecified number of boats. Navy officials have objected to
the $25 billion figure and to the amount of $1 billion per system
plus ten years of operating costs. The actual cost is probably
in the $10 to $20 billion range for a fleet with warheads numbering between 5,000 and 10,000. This cost would include ten
years of operation.

In any event, the total cost is meaningful only if it is compared with the cost of land-based offensive and defensive

systems, because a case can be made for ULMS ultimately to
replace Minuteman, Safeguard, and the B-52s, as well as the
Polaris/Poseidon fleet.   It is believed the Administration
eventually will set strategic priorities and make trade-offs
encompassing the entire strategic nuclear force.

THE CASE FOR ULMS

Polaris A-3 and Poseidon vessels are limited to cruising
within an 800-mile belt off the Eurasian continent in order to
be within range of their targets with the existing 2,000 to
3,000 mile missiles.   The Navy fears that the Soviet Union
could improve their anti-submarine warfare capability in this
limited area of operation.   This could seriously impair the
U.S. undersea nuclear strike force.   Although no threats are
on the horizon, the Navy reasons that long lead-times are
needed to develop higher-performance submarines and efforts
must begin now even in the absence of a perceived threat.

The 6,000 to 7,000 mile range of the ULMS missile would
virtually give the Navy freedom of cruising in the seven seas
and still be within range of their targets.   In addition, the
greatly increased range would open up almost the entire 360-
degree perimeter of the Soviet Union to a second strike by
U.S. missiles.   This would, therefore, make suicidal (because of the invulnerability of ULMS) any Soviet first strike
on the United States or on ULMS.   The greater range of the
missile would allow ULMS to depend on logistic support from
the continental United States.   Bases in foreign countries
would not be needed.   Less anticipated maintenance would
give each sub more time on station.

By the late 1970's, the Polaris/Poseidon fleet will begin
to deteriorate and enter the replacement phase.   The Navy
could replace these ships with identical copies, assuming
force levels and capabilities were to remain constant.   If this
were not necessary, ULMS, a new generation of missile submarines, would phase out the present fleet.

ULMS would be specifically designed to incorporate new
technologies developed since Polaris construction was completed.   With the employment of a systems approach, total
costs including operation will be roughly comparable to the
costs of building more Poseidon boats.

THE ARGUMENT AGAINST ULMS

The main advantage of ULMS is its greater range and much greater invulnerability. ULMS could be such a credible deterrent or second strike force that the argument for land-based offensive and defensive systems would become extremely tenuous. Yet, the Navy, perhaps out of courtesy to her sister services, which could stand to lose strategic missions, frames its justification in terms of a mythical Soviet threat, described by the Secretary of Defense in his 1970 posture statement:

> According to our best current estimates, we believe that our Polaris and Poseidon submarines at sea can be considered virtually invulnerable today. With a highly concentrated effort, the Soviet Navy today might be able to localize and destroy at sea one or two Polaris submarines. [1]

He continued that it is conceivable that if the Soviets were to undertake a major world-wide anti-submarine warfare program, the result might be a slight increase in the vulnerability of Polaris/Poseidon in five to seven years.

If the present system is such a credible deterrent that the Soviets could never orchestrate a first strike against it, then why do we need a new generation of ballistic missile submarines? The argument in favor of ULMS seems ultimately to hinge on whether the nation decides to maintain its land-based system as the primary nuclear deterrent. The increasing vulnerability of Minuteman and the B-52s has been demonstrated by the admitted need for a Safeguard defense system. If the sea-based force were officially to become the first line of deterrence, then gradually the land-based deterrents could be phased out. Under these conditions, ULMS could be justified more easily. On the basis of a hypothetical Soviet threat, a few more Poseidon boats would seem to suffice.

STRATEGIC ROLE

The ABM debate of 1969 revealed to the public many of the assumptions from which strategic doctrine is derived. ULMS presents the question: Is there an absolute deterrent? Seeking an absolute deterrent in the form of an invulnerable

second-strike capability, the United States has invested billions into bombers and land- and sea-based ballistic missiles.
Together they form a strategic mix. Yet, the arms race continues and stability and sufficiency always seem just beyond
reach.

The United States has denied any intention to go for a first
strike against the Soviet Union. Also, the President has stated
that we could never protect our cities against a strike by the
Soviets. We, therefore, intend to maintain an invulnerable
second-strike capability. The land-based deterrent is vulnerable; the sea-based deterrent is virtually invulnerable.

Two questions present themselves. (1) Is a strategic
mix necessary and desirable? (2) Is a credible deterrent
against the Soviet Union also credible against a third power?

The concept of a strategic mix, like so many other
doctrines, seemed to evolve after the technology was developed
rather than before. The policy boils down to a matter of redundancy. More is better than less. However, some would
maintain that certain nuclear forces are more provocative
and less stabilizing than others. The intense concern by those
for and against the ABM contrasts sharply with the low-keyed
discussion of security of the Polaris/Poseidon fleet. The
almost total invulnerability of this force together with MIRV
yields a high rate of overkill or assured destruction capability
and combines to give the submarine-based ballistic missile
a credibility and a degree of stability to wind down the arms
race. The quantum jump represented by ULMS would greatly
increase this insurance.

At the same time, the Soviet Union knows that it cannot
destroy more than one or two submarines even in its most
sophisticated first-strike attempt. Now under these circumstances there is little weight to the argument that the Soviets
would not be deterred by one element of the strategic mix, the
sea-based missile system.

Conceding that deterrence would work for the Soviet Union,
the Administration contends that it might not against a third
nation such as Communist China.

There is no international definition of credible deterrence.
Deterrence is as much a psychological matter as it is one of
capabilities. Each country would perceive the credibility of
the same nuclear force differently. However, it is a long
jump in logic for anyone to maintain that a third power would
allow itself to be completely destroyed for the sake of some
political adventurism. The United States is perhaps taking a
risk if it assumes a third country will not be deterred by our

nuclear force. The reference by the Administration to a
surgical first strike of the Red Chinese nuclear capability can
give them little confidence in our intentions.

In summary, the ULMS would be the epitome of the "blue
water option." If our land-based deterrents are so vulnerable
and by necessity draw fire close to metropolitan areas, then
send the deterrent to sea, so the argument goes. Because the
sea-based force is virtually invulnerable and can be made increasingly so and because this force has an overwhelming
overkill capacity once MIRVed, we could clearly afford to rely
eventually on a sea-based deterrent. Under these circumstances, the nation could not afford not to deploy the ULMS.
Yet, if ULMS is not viewed within a broad context, it could be
demonstrated to be cost intensive rather than cost effective.

RECOMMENDATIONS

1. We should proceed with ULMS as part of a decision to
make a sea-based nuclear missile system the first line of
deterrence. This might require a redefinition of the concept
of "strategic mix," which has produced an expensive and excessive redundancy of strategic systems. ULMS is the
epitome of the "blue water option" at a time when the probable
obsolescence of fixed bases has become clear in the ABM debate. When viewed as a successor to land-based missiles and
their requisite defense systems, the ULMS, with proper
management, could be cost effective.

2. The FY 1971 request was for $44 million in R&D. We
recommend a low-profile no-cut position, authorizing the full
$44 million.

NOTES

1. Melvin R. Laird, Defense Program and Budget for
FY 1971 (Washington, D. C.: U. S. Government Printing
Office, 1970), p. 40.

9

**ADVANCED
ICBM
(WS 120-A)**

The Advanced ICBM is to be the strategic missile for the
late 1970's. It is the Air Force's concept for a silo-launched
missile with a greater payload capacity and a greater range
than the Minuteman III. Nonetheless, the Minuteman III is
expected to be the primary missile far into the future, according to statements made at the hearings on defense appropriations for 1970.

As currently defined, this program represents DOD's
decision to develop high throw weight missiles in superhard
silos, rather than the alternative scheme of emplacing more
missiles, each with less payload, in more numerous but
softer silos.

Like the Minuteman III, the Advanced ICBM is envisioned
as a three-stage, solid fuel, MIRV-carrying missile. It will
have a "hotter" propulsion system, incorporating a quasi-fourth-
stage Post Boost Control System (PBCS).

Development of this missile began in 1963. In November
of 1966, DOD contracted with the Institute for Defense Analysis
(IDA) to determine alternative basing schemes. A final decision was made to base the missiles in silos. Initial procurement was scheduled for FY 1973, and the system was to be
operational by FY 1976. The requirement was estimated at
500 deployment missiles, with the first ten by FY 1974.

The cost estimate for deployment of the Advanced ICBM
in the late 1970's in 1970 dollars is in the magnitude of $20
billion. From FY 1963 to FY 1969, the Advanced ICBM program
cost $105.5 million. For FY 1969, the Advanced ICBM Tech-
nology Program was funded at $56 million. The Air Force had

intended to initiate Contract Definition in FY 1969, but DOD
disapproved and directed the Air Force to continue the program
as a technology development effort. It should be noted that only
the most preliminary studies have been done on the Advanced
ICBM. Development of the missile itself is being held in abey-
ance with activity limited to subsystem advanced development.

PROGRAM COMPONENTS

The Advanced ICBM program consists of several components:

1. High-Performance Solid Rocket Motor. This was
funded at $1 million in FY 1969. The development program
has an estimated value in excess of $23 million.

2. Self-Aligning Boost and Re-entry (SABRE). This was
funded at $3 million in FY 1969, and an estimated $40 million
was funded for this aspect of the program through FY 1968.
In July, 1968, the Air Force awarded $2.8 million to IBM-
OWEGO for development of an Advanced Radiation Hardened
Computer to work with the new guidance system. However,
it should be pointed out that SABRE is not the only candidate
for the missile's guidance system. It was noted in the hearings
on defense appropriations for 1970 that funding for Advanced
ICBM technology for FY 1969 was $10 million (this figure does
not include hard rock silo development, which, as will be seen,
represents the largest share of the cost of the program), and
the amount requested for FY 1970 was $20 million. In explain-
ing the increase, the Air Force said that it was necessary for
the development of a hardened and survivable guidance system.
Survivable Radio Guidance System (SRGS) is an in-flight cor-
rection system for improved accuracy which can be used for
both the Minuteman III and the Advanced ICBM.

3. Advanced ICBM and Basing. This was funded at $6
million in FY 1969.

4. Hard Rock Silo Development (see Chapter 10). This
was funded at $38 million in FY 1969. These silos, emplaced
in hard rock, will be usable for both the Minuteman III and the
Advanced ICBM. This will involve the construction of all new
silos, rather than an upgrading of existing silos. TRW has
been awarded a $6.3 million contract to perform system engi-
neering and technical direction for the hard rock silo. The
superhard silo development is the pacing item of the overall
Advanced ICBM program.

In evaluating this program, a number of considerations should be made. Most basically, there is the question of whether or not we want to continue to develop, expand, and improve a land-based deterrent system.

Second, there is the question of fewer missiles with a high throw weight in superhard silos versus more missiles with less payload in more numerous but softer silos. The former appears to be less cost effective than the latter, and the Minuteman III can be sufficiently improved by increasing the weight of its first stage. Third, the arms race impact of any program involving new silo construction must be considered. The mere fact that brand new silos will be built will be provocative; the Soviet Union might assume that the old silos are still occupied.

Finally, there is serious doubt that the multi-billion dollar hard rock program for the Advanced ICBM would provide more than several years protection against the ever-improving accuracy of Soviet missiles.

RECOMMENDATION

No further funds should be appropriated for the Advanced ICBM until it is determined whether or not land-based missiles will continue to play a role in our deterrent posture.

Secretary of Defense Melvin Laird said in his posture statement on the FY 1971 Defense Budget that, given the magnitude of the current Soviet missile threat, and given the fact that the defense of the U.S. population against that threat is not now feasible, we must rely on our retaliatory power to deter a first strike. However, it is now the feeling, with regard to our land-based deterrent system, that the increasing accuracy with which the Soviet Union can pinpoint the locations of the ICBMs by satellite reconnaissance has made the land-based ICBMs vulnerable to a first strike.

In light of this, there are a number of possible courses of action. One approach, which apparently has been given little consideration by the Department of Defense, is simply to abandon our land-based deterrent systems and depend instead on submarine-launched missiles. Other responses are the ABM system, the mobile Minuteman, and the superhardening of silos. For FY 1971, $77 million is proposed for research and development on Minuteman hardening and rebasing concepts.

EVALUATION OF SUPERHARDENING

Superhardening involves strengthening the silos that house the missiles so that they will be able to withstand all but a direct or very close hit. The feasibility of this course depends on the degree to which a silo can be reasonably hardened, what the cost would be, and the degree of accuracy of the enemy's missiles. Unfortunately, much of the information needed to adequately evaluate these questions is classified--namely, how "hard" the silos are now (in terms of the amount of over-pressure they can sustain), the accuracy of enemy missiles, how "hard" the silos can be made, and how close a hit would destroy the effectiveness of the missile.

The silo hardening program was conceived in late 1966 and early 1967. The final decision on its need was made by the Joint Chiefs of Staff, and in November, 1968, the decision was made to fund this program. Originally, the program was to be part of the Advanced ICBM program. However, when it became clear that the Air Force would not be able to move ahead with the rapid development of the Advanced ICBM, the decision was made to harden silos to house the Minuteman II (which could also house the Advanced Minuteman if and when it was deployed). At present, silo hardening involves building underground silos embedded in bed rock (hard rock silos).

In the hearings on defense appropriations for 1970, the Air Force testified that the ABM system and hard rock silos are complementary, and are intended to be used together, as neither would be a sufficient defense alone. The Air Force asked for a balancing of ABMs and hard silos in order to minimize the cost of protecting our retaliatory capabilities. They said that without the ABM, all 1,000 of our Minuteman missiles would have to be housed in hard rock silos. The silos are viewed as a back-up defense against the missiles that might succeed in penetrating the ABM shield. It is felt that although larger numbers of direct hits by the Russians are unlikely, there will be more near misses, which would destroy the present silos. Finally, it was argued by the Air Force at the hearings that the use of both the ABM and hard rock silos would force the Soviet Union to have both large and numerous re-entry vehicles, which are conflicting requirements, thus presenting them with an economic dilemma.

Ralph Lapp, in The Weapons Culture, disputes this approach, essentially because, given improved accuracy and MIRV, there is nothing that can be done to eliminate the vulnerability of our land-based missiles. He concludes that it is unwise to continue to invest heavily in a land-based system which can never be fully effective. Lapp also maintains that undersea-launched missiles like Polaris/Poseidon are a more cost-effective deterrent because they have the advantage of mobility and concealment. The force size of our present Polaris fleet alone is sufficient to provide an adequate assured destruction capability. [1]

At present, the Air Force is moving ahead with building
a prototype silo, which, if it tests out successfully, will be
made operational. The cost of the prototype is $278.4 million,
which includes the civil construction of the hole, development,
and modification of present equipment to go into the facility,
e.g., the mechanical equipment to support the missile, shock
isolation, shock suspended floors on which the equipment is
placed, and housing for the electronics equipment. In 1969,
the cost of the prototype was estimated at $152 million. The
Air Force explained the difference by stating that the initial
estimate was based on an incomplete understanding of the
components. Currently, the cost of additional silos is estimated at $6 million per silo, based on "x" number of silos.
This cost includes everything but the missile--the land, construction of the silo, roads, support facilities, and aerospace
ground equipment.

At one point in the hearings, the costs of putting the ICBMs
in hardened silos were compared with the costs of the Poseidon
program. Again, unfortunately, much relevant data was classified. Based on equal costs including RDT&E, investment,
and operating costs, twenty-one hard rock silos compare to
approximately sixteen Poseidon missiles.

Through 1969, $24.2 million was programmed for RDT&E,
plus $8 million for site surveys, which comes from operations
and maintenance funds. No funds for construction were pro-
grammed at all. In the revised FY 1970 budget, an additional
$4 million was requested for site surveys to reduce the opera-
tional lead-time.

A breakdown of the FY 1969 $23 million RDT&E spent on
hard rock silo development was provided, which gives some
idea of the components of this program:

$5.6 million: system engineering and technical direction
                and development of hard rock specifications
                (TRW).
$5.1 million: system definition and studies (Boeing).
$2.4 million: engineering design and development of
                hard rock silo equipment (Boeing).
$1.4 million: preliminary system concept and facility
                design (Bachtel).
$8.5 million: supporting technology, e.g., rock tests
                1 & 2, structures, closures, silos, antenna,
                cable.

For the High Explosive Simulation Tests (HEST), $7.1
million has been appropriated through FY 1969 and $0.9 mil-
lion in FY 1970, for a total of $8 million.

In conclusion, an article that appeared in the Washington Evening Star of April 14, 1970, should be mentioned. It discussed some of the ideas being considered by the Air Force to prevent the land-based Minuteman missiles from being destroyed in a surprise attack.[2]

Earlier, the Air Force had hoped to move the Minuteman missiles into new holes dug deep in solid granite, where they would be immune, even from very powerful explosions. But it is proving far more difficult than anticipated to construct such silos. Attention, therefore, has turned to ways of making the missiles mobile.

RECOMMENDATION

We recommend that the FY 1971 request for $77 million in R&D be denied until the role of fixed-base missiles is clearly defined.

NOTES

1. Ralph Lapp, The Weapons Culture (New York: W. W. Norton and Co., 1968), pp. 128-69.

2. Washington Evening Star, April 14, 1970, "Air Force Studies Barges for Missiles," p. 1.

III

TACTICAL
FORCES

The United States buys and operates tactical aircraft to fight in several contingencies. In order to plan for adequate tactical air forces within acceptable limits of risk, assumptions must be made about the size and simultaneity of these contingencies. Table 10 shows several options that could be used for force planning purposes.

The previous Administration planned for general purpose forces to fight simultaneously (1) a major non-nuclear war in NATO against the Warsaw Pact, (2) a major war in Asia against Communist China, and (3) a minor contingency elsewhere, presumably of Dominican Republic proportions. Although we needed to use general purpose forces in other areas (e.g., as in Southeast Asia), these assumptions provided a hedge against the worst case.

The current Administration has modified the planning assumptions used by the previous Administration. Forces are now planned to be able to fight simultaneously (1) a major non-nuclear war in NATO or in Asia against the Soviet Union or Communist Chinese augmented forces, (2) in support of an Asian ally against a non-Communist Chinese aggressor, and (3) in a minor contingency elsewhere.

These changes were made for two reasons. First, the changes bring our planning assumptions in line with the new Nixon Doctrine. The Nixon Doctrine calls for our Asian allies and not the United States to provide the major share of manpower (land forces) in meeting the allied defense needs. The United States will stand ready to provide material, tactical air, and naval force support. Second, a re-evaluation of

TABLE 10

U.S. Contingency Planning

| | Simultaneous Contingencies | | |
	Major[a]	Assistance	Minor
Previous Administration	NATO and Asia	None	Elsewhere
Current Administration	NATO or Asia	Asian Ally[b]	Elsewhere
Alternative	NATO or Asia	None	Elsewhere

[a]Against forces including Soviet or Communist Chinese forces.

[b]Against forces not including Communist Chinese forces.

general purpose forces for different strategies and the associated costs indicated that, at least in the Administration view, these planning assumptions produced the best balance in terms of the fiscal constraints and political requirements.

An alternative to the current strategy is to eliminate the planning requirement to provide assistance to an Asian ally simultaneously with a major war in NATO or Asia. Some think that it is unrealistic to assume we would fight anywhere else in the world if we were heavily engaged in Europe.

The assumption of simultaneity requires that we plan for a costly increment in tactical air and naval forces, and in mobility and stand-by support and training bases. In effect, tactical air and naval forces remain close to the level maintained under the assumptions of the previous Administration. For the additional capability obtained, the costs are disproportionately high due solely to the simultaneity requirements.

Under the alternative strategy, the United States would not be prepared to fight a major war in the Middle East and at the same time a war elsewhere of Viet-Nam proportions. But neither is the current Administration's strategy likely to provide forces sufficient for two such simultaneous major contingencies.

DETERMINATION OF FORCE LEVELS
AND COMPOSITION

For a given strategy, the number and mix of tactical aircraft to be bought depends, for each theater, on (1) our evaluation of the threat, (2) the types of missions planned, and (3)
the estimates made about U.S. and allied capabilities during
combat.

The Threat

In Europe, the United States plans capability to fight with
NATO allies against the Soviet Union and its Warsaw Pact
allies (East Germany, Poland, Czechoslovakia, Hungary,
Rumania, and Bulgaria). Soviet aircraft are primarily light
interceptors with short range and limited weapons capability.
It is anticipated that they will fly primarily air defense missions using ground control radars. They are not likely to
emphasize offensive strikes because their aircraft are not well
suited to this mission.

The aircraft predominating in Soviet/Pact inventories is
the MIG-21. The aircraft design is older than the F-4. However, like the F-4, it has gone through many model changes
in arriving at the current all-weather version. The MIG-17
and MIG-19 are still older and less capable due to shorter
range and weapons capabilities.

Pact tactical aircraft are protected on the ground at major
bases by heavy aircraft shelters and at austere grass fields by
camouflage and dispersal. These measures improve aircraft
survivability but tend to reduce sortie rates and maintenance
efficiency. In addition, Pact bases are generally well defended
by anti-aircraft barriers.

NATO is considered to have a large offensive payload advantage over the Pact forces, especially when we consider the
new generation of U.S. attack aircraft such as A-6, A-7, and
F-111. However, NATO's advantage over the Pact in air-to-
air combat capability is uncertain, especially in light of U.S.
Southeast Asian experience. In many cases, Soviet-built aircraft performed very well in air combat against U.S. fighters.
Inasmuch as Pact's interceptors will be used to prevent NATO
from flying ground strikes, an effective air-to-air combat
capability to counter Pact interceptors appears to dominate
NATO tactical air requirements.

In Asia, the United States plans capability to fight against the Communist Chinese and the North Koreans. The Chinese have approximately 2,900 aircraft composed mostly of older MIG-17s and MIG-19s. They have some earlier version MIG-21s. However, it is unlikely that the Soviets are providing additional aircraft. The North Koreans have approximately 500 tactical aircraft of similar mix. Comments on air-to-ground and air-to-air capability for Pact aircraft apply here as well.

Unlike the Soviets, neither the Chinese nor the North Koreans have many large bombers for attacking targets on the ground or in the fleet.

The United States has a large payload advantage over the combined Chinese/North Korean tactical air forces. However, the same uncertainty surrounds the U.S. air-to-air combat advantage in Asia as in Europe. There simply is no way of predicting the success of either side in air-to-air combat.

In recent years, the Soviet Union has developed and flown several new interceptors believed to be superior to the MIG-21 in sophistication of radars and weaponry, speed capabilities, and high-altitude capabilities, but not necessarily superior to the MIG-21 in air-to-air combat. These follow-ons are unlikely to soon find their way into the inventories of client states due to their cost--several times that of the MIG-21-- and their complex maintenance requirements. On the other hand, an improved MIG-21, maximized for air-to-air combat, would be less costly and, if produced, might well be transferred to client states.

Tactical Air Missions

Four major missions are performed by tactical aircraft. Although tactical aircraft are designed for use in conventional (non-nuclear) conflicts, many could be used in tactical nuclear strikes. The emphasis placed on each mission will depend upon the expected returns relative to the other missions.

Close-Air Support

Tactical aircraft provide close-support to troops engaged with enemy land forces. This mission is especially important in Europe where the Pact has a large amount of armor. Close-support strikes prevent troops from amassing, armored vehicles from breaking through the lines, and friendly troops

from being overrun. Large loiter and payload capabilities
are important characteristics for aircraft used in close-support. In addition, survivability against ground fire is important.

Interdiction

Interdiction missions are of two kinds--battlefield interdiction and deep interdiction. When tactical aircraft strike
supply concentrations, vehicles, and lines of communication
in the vicinity of the front, these attacks are called battlefield
interdiction. They disrupt troop and armored column movement and prevent the enemy from stockpiling supplies near
their front lines. Deep interdiction missions, on the other
hand, aim at reducing the flow of troops and supplies to the
front by striking far behind enemy lines at communications
and industrial facilities. These deep strikes tend to have a
less immediate effect on the enemy troops at the front than
close-support or battlefield interdiction, due to the availability
of optional lines of communication and to the short repair/
reconstitution times for roads, bridges, factories, etc. In
addition, losses on deep interdiction strikes tend to be higher
because of the higher density of enemy anti-aircraft missiles
and artillery and interceptors. Pilots lost on these missions
have a very low probability of being recovered.

Thus, it is questionable whether we should continue our
present great emphasis on deep interdiction. The payoff is
low relative to other missions (close-support and air superiority) and attrition will be high. These missions require high
payload and long-range characteristics. In addition, mission
success requires large numbers of escorts and support aircraft. An important target on interdiction missions is an
enemy airbase. However, aircraft sheltering greatly reduces
the vulnerability of aircraft on the ground.

Air Superiority

Tactical fighters are used to protect ground attacks by
escorting strike aircraft, by flying protective cover (combat
air patrol), or by sweeping the front before strike aircraft
arrive. In view of the large number of interceptors in Pact
and North Korean tactical air forces, this is likely to be the
highest priority mission in the event of war. Air superiority
missions require an aircraft with high concentration, low

wing loading,* good controls response, and good visibility
out of the cockpit.

Airbase Defense Interception

Fighters are also used for point defense of airbases and
infrastructure. Navy fighters fly fleet air defense missions
to protect the carrier and its task force from enemy bombers
and cruise missiles. Assuming the carrier survives, these
same fighters must be able to fly air superiority missions and,
particularly, to escort the carrier's attack aircraft against
their targets.

Important capabilities for performance of the fleet air
defense mission are high speed dash, long loiter time, and a
long-range mission/fire control system. The Navy has assigned a high priority to these capabilities in the design of its
tactical fighters. But these capabilities are costly in terms
of dollars, and other fighter capabilities are compromised.
Moreover, other means of defending the carriers are avail-
able--for example, electronic counter-measures and surface-
to-air missiles. Regardless of the quality and variety of airborne and shipborne defenses provided, however, it is doubtful that carriers can survive against saturation attacks from
submarines, bombers, and cruise missiles. For the marginal
security achieved, the high priority assigned to the fleet air
defense mission in the design of Navy fighters is difficult to
justify.

U.S. Capabilities

Air Force

The basic Air Force tactical air structure will consist
of twenty-three wings of F-4s, F-111s, A-7s, F-105s, and
F-100s, reflecting "little changes through FY 1971."[1] This
force structure is being maintained despite what has been presented as a major change in strategy and sharp reductions in
the budget.

Fighters: F-15 and others. The highest priority mission in
Europe and Korea is close-in air-to-air combat. The F-4

---

*Determined by the ratio of aircraft weight to wing area.
Wings must be large enough for stability in turns but with low
drag.

is the only aircraft in the Air Force suitable for air-to-air combat with MIG-21 interceptors. The F-15 is intended to replace the F-4 in close-in visual and long-range missile encounters. However, the F-15 cost is expected to be four times that of the F-4. In view of the limited resources available through FY 1975 and beyond (see the 1970 Economic Report of the President), it is questionable whether the Air Force can buy enough aircraft to count on defending against even the older, but more numerous, MIG-21s, let alone possible new generation Soviet aircraft.

As in the past, the Air Force has frozen the design of an expensive aircraft without examining the implications of its cost and of budget limitations for future force structure. Once the aircraft goes into production, there is no choice but to buy the expensive version even though budget priorities may dictate otherwise. But if the cost of the F-15 (and Navy F-14) means that we cannot replace the Air Force (and Navy) F-4s on a one-for-one basis, our future force structure will be much smaller and may be weaker than the present one.

We do not know with certainty those factors that most influence air-to-air combat success. Numerical advantage, high acceleration, low wing loading, high thrust-to-weight, good cockpit visibility, superior tactics, longer and more realistic training, simple-launch weapons, a good detection capability, and high fuel capacity are important factors. But any aircraft design is a trade-off among these factors. Each factor contributes to aircraft cost and weight. The F-15 in its present configuration may be an excellent aircraft for "close-in visual and long-range missile encounters." However, the fact that it costs four times the F-4 indicates that it has undergone little scrutiny with regard to trading off extra nice-to-have capabilities for cost savings.

A simple example will show the effect of buying an expensive aircraft of our force size. Assume we have the option of buying these aircraft: the F-4, the current F-15 design, and a lighter and avionically simpler F-15 not designed for long-range missile engagements. Assuming costs for procuring and operating these aircraft, Table 11 shows the number of aircraft $5 billion would buy and operate for five years. The table suggests that unless we impose now a rigid design discipline upon our new fighter aircraft, we will not be able to buy enough to have a credible force. In addition, if we assume modest cost overruns of 25 per cent, this consideration becomes even more urgent.

One final point with regard to the F-15 design. It corrects major deficiencies on the F-4 design which were experienced

TABLE 11

Comparative Fighter Costs*

Aircraft	Unit Procurement Costs	Unit Annual Operating Costs	Number of Aircraft Available for $5 Billion
F-4	$ 3 million	$0. 50 million	910
F-15	$12 million	$0. 75 million	320
F-15 Mod	$ 5 million	$0. 60 million	630

*Estimated and intended only to indicate the order of magnitude of the quality/quantity problem we face. Actual costs should be requested from the Air Force.

during close-in visual combat with MIG-21s in Southeast Asia. For example, it has improved wing loading, acceleration, thrust-to-weight, visibility, fuel, and handling qualities. In addition, it provides a stand-off missile capacity which is assumed to be within the grasp of Soviet technology also. Although we know very little about Soviet intentions, we do know from our experience in Southeast Asia that the best counter to an opponent's stand-off missile capability may well be a high maneuvering capability.

The F-4 used in Southeast Asia had a stand-off missile capability, but the MIG-21 was still able to force it to close-in engagements due to the MIG's maneuverability and tactics. The new Soviet interceptor FOXBAT (MIG-23), shown at the 1967 Soviet air show, is believed to have a stand-off missile capability. However, scenarios of future battles in which stand-off missiles are used and are used decisively are problematic at best.

In Southeast Asia, the tactical advantage of using stand-off missiles has not proven to be worthwhile. And again on the basis of experience, missiles and their fire-control systems have proved to be less reliable than originally postulated. For example, component reliability has been a problem in friend-foe identification outside of friendly Ground Control Intercept areas. Even assuming solution of these problems,

it is probable that the enemy will develop counter-measures,
bringing the combat back to heat-seeking missiles and guns
in close-in visual engagements.

The most reliable counter to the hypothetical FOXBAT,
therefore, is to build the most maneuverable fighter possible.

Our recommendation for F-15, therefore, is to defer or
cut F-15 funds, pending submission of a design with costs between those of the F-4 and current F-15 design. Information
should be sought detailing force structure implications for
future years with total force costs.

Attack Aircraft: A-X. The Air Force will continue to have a
payload capability advantage for a long time. New Soviet
aircraft designs have shown some improvement in bomb-car-
rying capability but have not approached even that of 1960
vintage U.S. aircraft.

The United States has developed a substantial radar capability by investing heavily in the avionics of the F-111 (and
the Navy A-6). No other country has such radar bombing
systems. However, there is some question whether the great
expense involved in obtaining these systems is justified by the
low priority need of interdiction at night relative to air superiority and close-air support in Europe and Korea. Radar bombing does also provide an all-weather capability. But we already
have enough assets in existing F-111 wings to meet this mission.

The Air Force has proposed a new aircraft for providing
close-air support--the A-X. It is encouraging to see the simple
design of the A-X as this should result in a very low-cost
aircraft, to buy as well as to operate. However, in light of
our current large payload advantage, can we justify spending
any additional funds for a new close-support aircraft? There
are several advantages to buying the A-X.

First, Air Force studies show that although large bomb
payloads are effective against large point or area targets,
they are not effective against armored vehicles--a major concern in Europe. An internal machine gun with suitable ammu-
nition can be a more effective weapon against these targets
and one is being developed for A-X. Thus, the A-X will be
optimized against the most likely, as well as most difficult,
close-support targets.

Second, a major problem in Southeast Asia has been the
vulnerability of our attack aircraft to ground fire. The A-X
would incorporate many features to improve its survivability
by an order of magnitude over existing aircraft.

Finally, a contracting procedure that will ensure low-cost

development and production is intended for the A-X program. Unlike the F-14 and F-15 programs, the final A-X design will be selected after a prototype fly-off. This reduces the likelihood of non-essential components getting into the design.

In considering development options for future aircraft, Congress should examine the A-X and the F-15, along with alternative force structures. There may be fewer resources available in the future. If the Air Force emphasizes a high-cost replacement for the F-4, we may not be able to afford the A-X, and in any case, force levels will be eroded. If a cheaper replacement is found for the F-4, then procurement of the A-X looks more feasible and we can hope to maintain the force levels and mix of aircraft that the commanders say are necessary.

We recommend approval of A-X R&D funds, but request details on the force level impact through 1980.

Navy and Marine Corps

The number of fighter squadrons remains the same as 1969. It appears the number of attack squadrons remains the same also, although the addition of more A-6s and A-7s adds substantially to capability. Secretary Laird has stated, "With the increase in A-7 squadrons in FY 1971, the number of A-4 squadrons will be reduced."[2] These squadrons will continue to operate with a carrier force of fifteen Attack Aircraft Carriers (CVAs) and one Anti-Submarine Carrier (CVS). Like the Air Force, these levels are being maintained despite a claimed change in strategy and budget pressures.

Fighters: F-14 and accessories. The highest priority mission in Europe and Korea is close-in air-to-air combat. The F-4, currently our best air superiority fighter, was designed by the Navy for a different mission--fleet air defense. This accounts for many of the F-4's deficiencies in close-in air-to-air combat in Southeast Asia.

The principal mission of the now defunct F-111B (the Navy version of the F-111) was also to be fleet air defense. To perform this mission, it was to carry six long-range air-to-air PHOENIX missiles and sophisticated avionics to counter Soviet bomber and cruise missiles.*

---

*The PHOENIX and its AWG-9 avionics are still in development after experiencing technical difficulties, numerous delays, and cost increases over an eight-year period. Sources

The F-111B was scrapped after it encountered delays and cost increases, and weight and size problems in connection with heavy components such as engines, avionics, and PHOENIX, and with the airframes.

The Navy describes the new F-14 as a "multi-mission fighter," designed to provide air superiority, fleet air defense, and also an air-to-ground capability. The F-14 is to carry one or more weapons systems in varying mixes--internal cannon, PHOENIX, SPARROW, and SIDEWINDER missiles, a new short-range missile for air-to-air combat (AGILE) not yet off the drawing boards, and conventional air-to-ground ordnance-- depending on which threats materialize and which seem most important in any given situation.

The first model F-14A--present plans call for procurement of sixty-seven or fewer of this model--will use engines and avionics adapted from those of the F-111B.

The second model, F-14B, will have new higher-thrust engines. F-14As will be retro-fitted with new engines. The F-14C, expected in the late 1970's, will have improved avionics. Even if the Navy and Marine Corps should somehow find the resources to replace over 1,000 F-4s with F-14s, the unit cost of the F-14 under the most optimistic assumptions will be at least three times that of the F-4. Buys of fewer F-14s mean still higher unit costs.

Despite Navy statements, the fleet air defense mission still appears to be dominant in the design of the F-14, and to entail compromises in the potential air superiority performance. In terms of cost alone, fleet air defense requirements account for as much as one half of the F-14's cost. The aircraft design is clearly oriented toward accommodation of the PHOENIX and its weapons control system. Even though PHOENIX is partially "palletized"--i.e., carriage of the missile itself is optional, and it can be jettisoned if a "dog-fight" looms--the airframe must still gain in weight and size to have the option of carrying PHOENIX. A high percentage of titanium is being used to offset gains in weight. But titanium is expensive. The F-14's swing-wing (also used in the F-111) provides increased range and speed and is useful chiefly for fleet air defense. Additionally, the complex and costly radar and panel displays of AWG-9 avionics, as well as the second pilot, are associated with the fleet air defense mission.

indicate that unit costs of the PHOENIX missile could vary between $200,000 and $800,000, depending on the number of F-14s procured.

Fleet air defense requirements also account for many of the uncertainties in F-14 performance in all missions and models. Weight, size, and complex controls and weapons detract from the F-14's performance in air-to-air combat. Some reliable sources indicate that the F-14A will be less capable in air-to-air combat than the F-4. The F-14B, even with higher thrust engines, may not be a match in close-in combat for the as yet undisclosed follow-on to the MIG-21. The claim for the PHOENIX system of a capability of firing six missiles almost simultaneously is unsubstantiated to date. In addition, reliability and other problems associated with shorter-range stand-off missiles may well trouble the performance of the PHOENIX system and follow-on avionics as well.

Engineering experience with the F-111's swing-wing indicates that problems of wing structure and carry-through box have not been definitively solved. The position of the F-14's swing-wing will be automatically adjusted for optimum performance during mission. But clearly this feature will not be responsive enough in dog-fights and may not be sufficiently reliable or speedy for effective performance in other situations. The Air Force and Navy technical experience with the F-111 should be carefully examined before the current F-14 program proceeds beyond the point of no return. The extensive use of titanium, and of relatively new welding techniques, raises questions about the ultimate strength and endurance of the F-14 airframe.

If we assume that protection of the carrier task force is the highest priority mission for a new Navy fighter, the F-14 in its current design might be a suitable fighter to defend against non-maneuvering targets in low numbers incapable of saturating fighter patrols. The carrier, however, is valuable chiefly because it provides an offensive air strike capability. It must survive to provide this capability. Equally if not more important, its attack aircraft must also be able to penetrate hostile environments with F-14s as escorts and patrol aircraft. But the F-14's reliability in the performance of this mission through the early 1980's--chiefly its maneuverability for air-to-air combat--has been seriously compromised by fleet air defense requirements.

The Navy indicates that a major role of the attack carrier is to meet the "war at sea" requirement. In fleet air defense for war at sea, the F-14 primarily protects merchant ship convoys from submarine- and bomber-launched cruise missiles.

The first problem with this mission, and with the whole fleet air defense requirement, is its dubious necessity. Two Congressional committees have recently probed the bomber threat and have concluded that it is minimal. Chairman George H. Mahon of the House Appropriations Committee has indicated that the bomber threat to our fleet simply has not developed, a point reinforced by the Senate Armed Services Preparedness Investigation Subcommittee in its 1968 Report on U.S. Tactical Air Power Program.

Even if we assume the bomber threat, however, there is some question whether F-14s could protect against a heavy cruise missile attack which saturates the fighter network by using simple decoys and other devices to confuse our radars. In respect to sub-launched missiles, our anti-submarine warfare (ASW) capability may not be adequate to detect submarines in time to warn our fighters.

If we assume that the war at sea is a contingency we must prepare for, there is no justification for having the present large numbers of A-6 and A-7 attack aircraft on board carriers assigned to meet this contingency. Attack aircraft do not help in the war at sea since none of the targets are for bombs.

If we now consider the high projected cost of the F-14 and the PHOENIX missile system, we are faced with the same problem the Air Force has with the F-15--we cannot replace all Navy F-4s on a one-for-one basis with F-14s. There seems to be little point in spending large sums to maximize the F-14 to defend carriers against the worst possible threat (intensive bombing and cruise missile attacks)--which is improbable in most areas of the world, and where probable is likely to doom carriers despite the F-14 and other defenses. This concern becomes more telling if preparations for the extreme but improbable threat reduce the plane's other capabilities and promise uncertain performance against the more probable and more counterable threats posed by Soviet-built interceptors to carrier attack aircraft on mission. Eliminating the PHOENIX missile or reducing the number procured would reduce the total cost and provide funds to procure more aircraft.

If the PHOENIX is retained, however, care must be taken that enough can be bought to assure a balanced mix of weapons, and that adequate support can be bought for them. If funds are pinched, the tendency of the services too often is to cut back on weapons such as PHOENIX and especially their support while continuing to procure a system designed to carry them. In the case of the F-14, this would mean higher unit costs and reduced effectiveness for PHOENIX and reduced return from investment in an airframe designed for PHOENIX.

Without more details on future year program costs and force structure, particularly with regard to carriers, Congress is not in a position to approve continuation of the F-14 program. Approval now locks us into an expensive procurement program with no alternative for a cheaper F-4 replacement. There are several alternatives:

1. Approve F-14 R&D funds as requested. But in view of budget stringency, provide procurement funds for fifteen F-14s in FY 1971 rather than for the requested twenty-six. The contract with Grumman Aircraft has an option for a minimum buy of fifteen during this time period.

2. Approve F-14 R&D funds but defer all procurement funds and request future cost and force structure implications for given budget levels.

3. Defer all F-14 funds pending receipt of an alternative fighter design commensurate with European and Korean theater requirements and between F-4 and F-14 costs. Show the effect of both aircraft programs on future force structure and costs.

Attack Aircraft: A-7 and HARRIER. The Navy is completing a modernization program with the procurement of A-7s in FY 1970. These aircraft are replacing A-4s currently in Navy wings. FY 1971 procurement is to allow replacement of older A-7s in future years due to attrition. Although the A-7E provides a significant increase in capability over the A-4, Congress should be concerned about continuing to purchase this aircraft under the assumption that the fifteen carrier force structure will remain intact. Until we complete the land-based/sea-based study currently under review and tactical air studies currently in progress in Congress and the National Security Council, we cannot reasonably approve the purchase of additional A-7s. Our recommended alternative is to defer funds for Navy A-7s in FY 1971 pending completion of the tactical air carrier studies. Air Force A-7 procurement sufficient to maintain the FY 1971 production base should continue.

The Navy has proposed procuring additional A-6Es. The new radar system for radar bombing and new engines offer substantial improvement over the A-6As they will replace. However, inasmuch as the attack carrier study may indicate a Navy tactical air force reduction, there are grounds for deferral of these expensive aircraft. More important, we already have a substantial radar bombing capability and this procurement will not add significantly to it. For double the cost we do not yet double the present capability. Continued production of other A-6 type aircraft (EA-6B, KA6 conversions) might be used to maintain a production base if deferral of A-6E procurement were desirable.

Finally, the Marine Corps proposes the procurement of additional British HARRIER aircraft in order to complete one squadron. The new V/STOL close-support jet is designed to operate from amphibious ships and forward sites near the troops. The aircraft does not provide a significant improvement in payload capability over existing attack aircraft. Procurement of these aircraft will allow the Marine Corps to fully test the "forward operating" concept before buying additional aircraft after FY 1971.

In view of pressures to "buy American," the Marine Corps has included $24 million extra to have these aircraft assembled in the United States. The Marine Corps has proposed shifting the production capability to the United States over a period of four years. If it is decided to procure a large number of HARRIERs, there would be a more favorable balance-of-payments impact by shifting production from the United Kingdom to the United States. However, the Marines have not fully tested the aircraft or the "forward operating" concept, and there is some question about planning now for a large production of HARRIERs.

In addition, if only a limited number of aircraft are bought, $24 million is a high price (especially in view of other priorities) to pay to achieve a small reduction in gold flow. Furthermore, it may be possible to make a different arrangement with the United Kingdom to reduce gold flow while purchasing the FY 1971 production aircraft (for example, in exchange of F-4s). There are several alternatives. We recommend the third.

1. Approve the HARRIER funds as requested.

2. Approve the HARRIER funds, but assemble the aircraft in the United Kingdom (saving $24 million); follow-on aircraft procurement deferred pending Marine Corps test results.

3. Defer the HARRIER funds pending test results of FY 1970 production aircraft by the Marine Corps.

There is only a limited amount of information available on our major allies' tactical air capability in Europe and Korea. It is in the best interests of the Congress to request information about our allies' capabilities so that adjustments in U.S. forces can be made with full knowledge of attendant risks.

RECOMMENDATIONS

1. Cut F-15 funds, pending submission of a design costing between F-4 and current F-15 costs. Request detailed force structure implications for future years with force cost. The current estimate for the total F-15 program is $7.4 billion. The House has authorized the $470 million for R&D that the Administration has requested. We recommend allocation of $185 million for R&D.

2. A decision on a close-support aircraft (A-X) must carefully consider cost effectiveness. Data on an alternative existing fixed-wing aircraft should be requested. The administration requested $27.9 million for R&D for the A-X. The House authorized the full amount. We recommend authorizing the full $27.9 million.

3. The projected high unit cost of the F-14 and weapons has critical implications for the size of the force. Congress should defer all or part of F-14 funds pending recommendations on the role of the carrier fleet and pending receipt of an alternative simpler fighter design suitable for the European and Korean theaters, and costing between F-4 and current F-14 costs.

The current estimate for the total F-14 program is $8.3 billion; the Administration has requested $274 million for R&D and $658 million for procurement. The House authorized $658 million for procurement and $324.2 million for R&D. We recommend approving $274 million for R&D, but allocating no funds for procurement.

4. Defer funds for Navy A-7s in FY 1971 pending NSC review of attack carrier force levels, but allow Air Force A-7 procurement to maintain the FY 1971 production base. The Administration requested $118.3 million for the HARRIER; the House authorized this full amount. We recommend deleting all HARRIER funds pending a review of the flight tests by the Office of the Secretary of the Marine Corps and the General Accounting Office.

5. Continue full R&D on the F-111A, but delete the requested procurement of $515 million.

NOTES

1. Melvin Laird, Defense Program and Budget for FY 1971 (Washington, D. C. : U. S. Government Printing Office, 1970), p. 134.

2. Ibid., p. 138.

12

MISSION AND COSTS

The MBT-70, now known as the XM-803, is the new "dream" tank designed for use in Europe. It represents a "quantum jump" in tank technology and incorporates a number of sophisticated and extremely expensive features. The Department of Defense argues that it is necessary in order to counter the numerical tank superiority of the Warsaw Pact countries.

Whether this tank is called the MBT-70 or the XM-803, it serves as an excellent example of the Pentagon's problems in controlling cost and assuring performance in RDT&E and it illustrates the momentum a project gains once initiated. Cost overruns and schedule slippages have hindered this project from its inception.

The per unit cost of the tank has skyrocketed. Originally, the tank was to be produced for $420,000 per unit. The cost estimates then rose to $520,000 in Pentagon planning. When a DOD study of the tank began in the fall of 1969, its per unit cost was estimated to be $620,000. In mid-December of 1969, when the study ended, DOD announced a "re-designed" tank that would save $200,000 per unit, and placed the cost at $640,000; while acknowledging a real dollar increase of $20,000 per unit, the Department of Defense claimed a saving for the American taxpayer of $200,000 per unit. DOD explained that the tank and all its components had never been priced out before the study, almost five years after it was initiated, and that when it was, the price tag came to more than $800,000 per unit. Thus, according to Pentagon arithmetic, a real dollar cost increase of $20,000 per unit became, in Pentagonese, an enormous saving.

Decisions to proceed on the MBT-70/XM-803 have always been based on low-cost estimates and high-performance assurances. In fact, however, as cost increased, performance decreased, and now we have a tank well over original cost estimates and well below performance specifications.

One might reasonably ask why no one had ever accurately priced out a major weapons system that will eventually cost the American taxpayer over $8 billion. In fact, even DOD officials now admit that increases in cost have made the MBT-70/XM-803 less cost effective than alternative approaches. However, they continue to push for its development, procurement, and deployment.

Further, it appears the most recent cost estimates are just the beginning of the real cost. Hearings held by the Armed Services Committee in 1970, suggest that more funds will be required to improve the MBT-70/XM-803 tank. One knowledgable source stated that the eventual cost will probably run to $1 million per tank. [1]

The question is not whether the United States has need for a tank in the 1970's and early 1980's, but rather what kind of tank, at what cost, to fulfill what role. The MBT-70/XM-803 is the dream tank, designed to win World War II. But the role of the tank on the modern battlefield has been gravely affected by the development of long-range, accurate, and inexpensive anti-tank weapons.

In the modern battlefield environment, a $5,000 anti-tank weapon has a good probability of killing any tank, including the $650,000 MBT-70. Changes in the battlefield environment and upward revisions in the tank's cost mean that the MBT-70/XM-803 as presently configured is not cost effective.

The Department of Defense has argued that it must have tanks with which to counterattack, to penetrate the enemy's position, and to exploit such penetrations. This is not disputed, at least not in the time frame of the 1970's and early 1980's. The argument is over the extreme cost of the MBT-70/XM-803. The present tank, the M60A1, costs only $220,000 per unit; the "Chieftain," $240,000 per unit; the "Vickers," $264,000 per unit; and the "Leopard," about $300,000 per unit. The DOD has failed to respond satisfactorily to charges that the tank's degree of sophistication may lead to breakdowns on the battlefield. Nor has DOD adequately considered the

possibility that the role of tanks has been altered by a probable
battlefield environment in which anti-tank weapons are becoming more and more prevalent.

RECOMMENDATION

The funds requested by the Department of Defense for
FY 1971, a total of $77 million, including $36 million for
RDT&E and $41 million for production engineering, should
not be authorized until the recommendations of the House
Defense Appropriations Committee report for FY 1970 are
implemented by the Department of Defense. That report
stated:

> In its present design, the MBT-70 tank is over-
> sophisticated, unnecessarily complex, and too ex-
> pensive for a Main Battle Tank. . . . The most
> prudent use of funds provided for the MBT-70
> this year could be for the U.S. to design a tank
> with far less sophistication, a tank that can be
> produced at about a third of the cost now estimated
> for the current design. [2]

NOTES

1. Department of Defense, <u>Appropriations Committee
Hearings Report No. 36-735,</u> Senate, 1970, p. 468.

2. Department of Defense, <u>Appropriations Bill Report
No. 90-698</u>, Senate, December 3, 1969, p. 73.

13

ENVIRONMENTAL WARFARE: ANTI-PLANT CHEMICAL WEAPONS

According to a recent Army training manual, anti-plant agents for military application are:

> . . . chemical agents which possess a high offensive potential for destroying or seriously limiting the production of food and defoliating vegetation. These compounds include herbicides that kill or inhibit the growth of plants; plant growth regulators that either regulate or inhibit plant growth, sometimes causing plant death; dessicants that dry up plant foliage. . . . Military applications for anti-plant agents are based on denying the enemy food and concealment.[1]

Anti-plant chemical agents developed for the military defoliation program include the following: "Orange," a mixture of 2,4-D and 2,4,5-T; "White," a mixture of 2,4-D and picloram; and "Blue," an aqueous solution of cacodylic acid. Collectively, these agents have commonly been called "herbicides" and "defoliants." Technically, Orange and White are "growth-regulating compounds" and are directed mainly against forest vegetation; Blue is considered a "dessicant" and used primarily to destroy crops. Each of these anti-plant chemical agents have been used as a weapon of war in Viet-Nam.

U.S. USE OF DEFOLIANTS

Use of defoliants by U.S. forces began on December 4, 1961, when President John F. Kennedy authorized the Department of Defense to test the military effectiveness of defoliation on several lines of communication in South Viet-Nam. Since that time, the United States has spent over $96 million to defoliate over 5 million acres of forest and cropland in South Viet-Nam. The primary target has been forest areas. Roughly 13 per cent of South Viet-Nam's forest areas have been sprayed at least once and 15 to 20 per cent of this sprayed forest area has been subject to repeated sprayings. Regarding crop destruction, it is estimated that 7 per cent of Viet-Nam croplands have been sprayed. Table 12 illustrates the extent of spraying on a year-to-year basis.

Objectives of this environmental warfare program are to deny the enemy food and concealment. According to the Defense Department, the purpose of the herbicide program is to protect friendly forces, conserve manpower, and deny food resources to the enemy.

The most widely publicized aspect of U.S. defoliation activities in South Viet-Nam has been the use of an estimated 40 million pounds of Agents Purple and Orange, the most widely used general defoliant. These two herbicidal mixtures contain a large proportion of 2, 4, 5-trichlorophenoxy-acetic acid, better known as 2, 4, 5-T. Shown to cause birth defects in mice and rats,[2] 2, 4, 5-T has also been linked to bizarre congenital human damage in South Viet-Nam. A previously unknown abnormality called "egg bundle-like fetus," attributed to the spraying by many doctors, was frequently reported in 1967 at the end of the first year of widespread Allied defoliation.[3] As a result, Deputy Secretary of Defense David Packard suspended the use of 2, 4, 5-T in Viet-Nam "pending a more thorough evaluation of the situation."[4]

Although 2, 4, 5-T has caused the most controversy, Agents White and Blue, the other two defoliants widely used in Viet-Nam, may have equally deleterious or teratogenic (birth-defect producing) effects.[5] Neither the Department of Agriculture nor the Food and Drug Administration ran tests on them before they were requested for use in Viet-Nam, and there is no public record that teratogenicity tests have even been run on cacodylic acid.[6] The major ingredient of Agent Blue is 54 per cent arsenic and is listed as extremely poisonous by the Merck Index.

TABLE 12

Chemical Defoliation and Anti-crop Operations
in South Viet-Nam, [*]
1962 to July, 1969

Year	Defoliation (acres)	Crop (acres)	Per Cent Crop vs. Defoliation
1962	4,940	741	15
19(,3	24,700	247	1
1964	83,486	10,374	12
1965	155,610	65,949	42
1966	741,247	103,987	14
1967	1,486,446	221,312	15
1968	1,267,110	63,726	5
1969 (Jan.-July)	797,180	38,819	5
Total	4,560,719	505,155	

[*]The total land area of South Viet-Nam is approximately 42 million acres. Of this, about 7.6 million acres are reported to be under intensive cultivation and about 14 million acres are forested.

Source: Data supplied by the Defense Department to the National Security Policy and Scientific Developments Subcommittee of the House Foreign Affairs Committee (December, 1969).

135

Those chemicals which often fall on food or water supplies of "friendly" civilians are used in high concentrations in Viet-Nam.[7] Agent Orange, for example, was applied in Viet-Nam at a rate that is thirteen times as high, and Agent Blue at a rate that is seven and a half times as high, as the recommended concentrations for domestic use.[8]

But whatever the damage to the civilian population, it may be minor compared to the massive and irrevocable harm these chemicals are doing to soil, vegetation, and wildlife. Defoliation is rarely a temporary process. The vegetation often dies, sometimes disrupting patterns of nature for generations. Because no nation has ever been sprayed with such high concentrations of herbicides over such a wide region, the long-term effect in Viet-Nam cannot be judged from past experience. First-hand observation, moreover, is restricted because much of the affected land is in enemy or combat zones. Nevertheless, the available reports give some idea of the kinds of problems we are creating.

INVESTIGATION OF ANTI-PLANT ACTIVITIES

The first of these reports was written by Dr. F. H. Tschirley, a Department of Agriculture scientist who worked under contract to the Defense Department for three years to find more efficient defoliation methods. He showed that on experimental plots in Puerto Rico and Texas, most of the species studied, which were chosen for their resistance to defoliants, had regrown less than half their original leaves a full year after treatment. When one less resistant species was treated with Agent Orange, 98 per cent of the trees died within fifteen months.[9] A later check by Gordon H. Orians and E. W. Pfeiffer showed that visual observation tends to overestimate refoliation because the plots involved had been invaded by vines that climbed the trunks of the dead trees and spread over the former canopy. On some of the plots, nearly all of the greenery above three meters was contributed by vines and not by refoliation of the original trees. The vine-choked plots will not return to their former state as rapidly as they might otherwise because the dead trunks will probably collapse under the weight of the vines in a few years, creating a low vine-covered mat through which regeneration could be very difficult.[10]

An excellent summary of the ecological problems caused

by defoliation has been given by Dr. Arthur W. Galston, Professor of Biology and Lecturer in Forestry at Yale University.
Testifying before the Subcommittee on National Security
Affairs and Scientific Developments of the Committee on
Foreign Affairs of the House of Representatives, he cited one
example of the type of ecological havoc defoliants can wreak
on an area. Citing Tschirley's report that mangrove associations around the Saigon River were effectively killed by one
application of Agent Orange, [11] Galston pointed out that the
mangroves lining estuaries are crucial for the completion of
the life cycle of certain shellfish and migratory fish. He concluded that the result would be both increased erosion along
the estuaries and loss of needed foods for the protein-poor
Vietnamese. [12]

Tschirley feared that the mangrove association would not
be able to re-establish itself for twenty years or more. [13]
But Orians and Pfeiffer's later study indicated that "re-estab-
lishment of the original forest may be impossible except along
the edge of the river channels and backwaters." [14] Other ecol-
ogists have pointed to the danger that before the mangrove associations can re-establish themselves, the region will be invaded by almost ineradicable growths of bamboo--thus perma-
nently depriving the Vietnamese fishermen of a part of their
livelihood. [15]

The effects of defoliation on the mangroves may or may
not be typical. There have been verified reports of extensive
damage to rubber trees, [16] a major part of the economy of
South Viet-Nam, although according to the Department of
Defense these trees have never been intentionally defoliated. [17]
No thorough studies have been made, and one can only guess
what damage our defoliation efforts are doing to other wildlife
associations found in Indochina.

Exactly how soil is affected by chemical spray is difficult
to determine at this time. Some of the herbicides used, however, are quite persistent. Studies done on picloram, the
main ingredient of Agent White, showed that it remains in the
soil in relatively high concentrations for at least a year. [18]
Cacodylic acid also may remain in sprayed rice paddies to
poison with arsenic farmers who try to replant the next year.

Even if non-persistent defoliants were used, moreover,
the life-supporting bacteria in the soil may be killed, thus
making the soil sterile for years to come. [19] A further point,
raised by Galston and others, [20] is that about half of the soil
in South Viet-Nam is laterizable. These soils, when deprived
of the shade and organic matter foliage provides, may turn

into a brick-like substance that may not support life for hundreds of years. The United States could create a barren wasteland in part of South Viet-Nam that will be unfit for habitation for years after hostilities cease.

FOOD DENIAL PROGRAM

One aspect of allied defoliation activities that deserves careful consideration is the "food denial program." Under the pretense that this program hampers enemy troops, the United States has dropped herbicides, including the arsenic-containing cacodylic acid, on approximately half a million acres of South Vietnamese croplands.[21] This operation effectively hurts only civilians, women, children, and the aged because, as Dr. Jean Mayer, who is now President Nixon's special advisor on nutrition, said in a 1967 article in Science and Citizen, "Vietcong soldiers may be expected to get the fighters' share of whatever food there is."[22] Although the Department of Defense claims that this program has forced Vietcong troops to abandon combat operations for food gathering, it has also been pointed out that destroying their crops frees the Vietcong from harvesting duties to fight.[23]

The main result of the food denial program seems to have been the creation of thousands of refugees. When their crops turn yellow and die, the peasants are forced to leave their homes and travel to the cities or to refugee camps maintained by the Saigon Government at American expense. Food may be available here, but the living conditions are less than desirable.

The creation of refugees, in fact, seems to have been one goal of the program. Representative Richard D. McCarthy quotes ex-Presidential Science Advisor Donald F. Hornig as saying that the program is designed to force farmers outside of American- or South Vietnamese-held areas to abandon their farms and move into our sphere of influence.[24] The Defense Department denies this intention,[25] but cannot deny this effect. In any case, this method of waging a war makes us many enemies among the farm population of South Viet-Nam.

One of the most cogent arguments against the use of defoliants in the war in Indochina is that they are, as Dr. John Edsall of Harvard University has said, barbarous because they are indiscriminate. The bullets and bombs of conventional warfare have effects that may be limited in space and time to a specific target and a specific instant of contact. Defoliants,

on the other hand, produce secondary effects that will harm
many unintended victims for years after these effects have
ceased to be advantageous to the user.

Despite the precautions the military takes to avoid the
spraying of friendly areas, there have been many accidents
reported. For example, Representative McCarthy reveals
that the experimental station of the College of Agriculture of
the University of Saigon has been defoliated several times,
resulting in the repeated destruction of their crops.[26] He also
states, "U. S. AID officials have complained bitterly that
friendly villages have had their crops completely wiped out by
mistake";[27] and Galston at Yale reports, "We know that most
of the truck crops grown along roads, canals, and trails and
formerly brought into Saigon have been essentially abandoned
because of the deliberate or inadvertant falling of these defoliant sprays: many crops in the Saigon area are simply not being harvested."[28] Although the Department of Defense says
that great care is taken to avoid friendly territory,[29] whole
regions of the III Corps and other areas have been designated
as "free fire zones"--assuming that everyone in the area is
unfriendly.[30]

Needless to say, as with the food denial program, such
approaches must be making the allies many enemies. In addition, they cause severe long-term damage to the economy of
South Viet-Nam.

THE CAMBODIAN INCIDENT

One recent incident exemplifies the shortcomings of the
defoliation program in Indochina. This is the American defoliation in April and May of 1969 of 173,000 acres of then
neutralist Cambodia, including croplands and rubber and ban-
ana plantations.[31] Four important accounts of this action have
been published, each of which deserves consideration.

The first is in the letter of protest to the United Nations
from the government of Cambodia. In part, it reads:

From 18 April to 2 May 1969, aircraft of the United
States-South Vietnamese air forces continually scattered defoliants every two days over a vast area of
Cambodia stretching along the Khmer-Vietnamese
frontier and extending to a depth of twenty kilometers
from the frontier, in the districts of Krek and Mimot,

province of Kompong Cham. These defoliants caused
great havoc to rubber plantations, to orchards and to
forest. The damage surveyed up to 2 May 1969
amounts to 7,000 hectares of rubber plantations destroyed, of which 4,500 hectares are owned by the large
companies (mostly French) and 2,500 hectares are
indigenous family plantations. Five thousand jack
trees were killed and a vast wooded region was seriously damaged. The losses are extensive and seriously affect the national economy of the Kingdom.[32]

The Department of Defense, however, first denied that
any direct overflight occurred and then claimed that Cambodian
territory was never deliberately sprayed.[33] A Pentagon spokesman stated the following:

In situations such as this where you know there are
enemy base camps, enemy forces operating in the
jungle, and from which heavy fire may be coming,
spray operations close to the border have been conducted. It would appear that in one of these cases
either the spray plane was in an area that was in
dispute or was not clearly marked.[34]

To try to resolve these conflicting stories, the Depart-
ment of State sent four American scientists to investigate the
affected region.[35] This team consisted of Dr. Charles E.
Minarik, the Director of Plant Sciences Laboratories of the
Department of Defense; Dr. F. H. Tschirley, who had for
years been under a Defense Department contract to discover
more efficient defoliation methods; and the two men from the
Saigon office of the Agency for International Development
(AID). The group confirmed the essentials of the Cambodian
Government's claims. Three of the findings of the team are
of particular interest:

[1] The total area on which damage occurred
was approximately 700 square kilometers or 70,000
hectares (173,000 acres). The Cambodian Government claimed damage on about 15,000 hectares,
which represents the area in rubber and fruit.[36]
[2] Defense Department officials suggested that
the Cambodian defoliation was the result of drift
from operations in adjoining Tay Ninh province of
South Viet-Nam. The Minarik commission found

that these missions probably resulted in defoliation
of the area immediately north of the border. We
do not feel, however, that drifts from the Tay Ninh
missions caused damage to a distance of eighteen
to twenty kilometers above the Cambodian border.
If spray drift were responsible for all the damage
observed, one would expect to see a reduction in
severity of plant response with increasing distance
from the point of application. This was not the case
because rubber varieties fifteen kilometers north of
the border were as severely affected as similar
varieties closer to the border. Tapering off of effects was noted east and west of the severely affected area.[37]

    [3] Our second hypothesis was that of a direct
overflight made of the Dar-Prek Chlong plantations
for the purpose of defoliation. The pattern of extent and degree of herbicidal effect fits this hypo-
thesis more closely than any other.[38]

These findings were part of the evidence that led the
Minarik team to conclude the following:

> Herbicide damage in the southeastern part of
> Kompong Cham Province, Cambodia, was extensive
> due to a combination of two factors: (a) defoliation
> of fruit trees on the Cambodian side near the border
> was a result of drifts from spray operations in Tay
> Ninh Province, and (b) defoliation of rubber, fruit,
> and forest trees farther north was probably caused
> by a direct spray application by an unknown party on
> a north-south line running through the plantations
> of Dar and Prek-Chlong.[39]

This theory was confirmed and extended by the Westing
Commission, an ad hoc international scientific commission
that examined the damaged areas six months after the State
Department team.[40] In agreeing with the Minarik Commission
that the damage to the rubber plantations was almost certainly
due to a direct overflight, the Westing group elaborated on
Minarik's attribution of the spraying to "some unknown party":
"There is, of course, no question that the responsibility for
the extensive herbicidal damage we have observed rests upon
the United States. Only the United States has the ability and
material locally to carry out such operations."[41]

It is interesting to note the conclusions of this commission, the only one not sponsored by one of the governments involved in the dispute:

> it is highly likely that the overflights were a de-
> liberate violation of the frontier. The border is
> recognizable from the air and both the United States
> air and ground forces seem to be intimately familiar
> with its location. Although U. S. aircraft violate
> Cambodian territory daily for purposes of recon-
> naissance, the daily military combat activities in
> the region (a number of which we observed at
> rather close hand) are for the most part strictly
> limited to the South Vietnamese side. The fact that
> rubber plantations (which are readily distinguishable
> from the air) were so heavily hit (one-third of all
> this major Cambodian crop), suggests an attempt
> at punitive action on the part of the United States.
> That U. S. pilots are, we are told, under routine
> standing orders in South Viet-Nam to avoid the
> spraying of rubber adds further support to the
> hypothesis that this particular action was deliber-
> ate. [42]

The Defense Department was asked if their position on the Cambodian sprayings had been changed by the evidence of the Westing and Minarik reports. In a letter dated May 22, 1970, the Office of the Assistant Secretary of Defense for Policy Plans and National Security Council Affairs replied, "Regarding the herbicide spraying in Cambodia, the Depart- ment of Defense still maintains that the use of herbicides in Cambodia has been contrary to our policy."[43] Surely a further explanation is due, an elaboration that will resolve the many discrepancies between the Defense Department version of the sprayings and the findings of every other group that has re- ported on the incident.

RECOMMENDATIONS

1. The present anti-crop and defoliation program should be terminated and stockpiles gradually eliminated.

2. The transfer of anti-plant chemical weapons for use by second countries should be prohibited.

NOTES

1.   Department of the Army Training Circular TC 3-16, Department of the Army, April, 1969, p. 62.

2.   E. M. Mrak et al., Report of the Secretary's Commission on Pesticides and Their Relationship to Environmental Health, p. 655-69. Also Bionetics Laboratories, Evaluation of the Teratogenic Activity of Selected Pesticides and Industrial Chemicals in Mice and Rats, as reprinted in Thomas Whiteside, ed., Defoliation (New York: Ballantine Books, 1970), pp. 69-71.

3.   Hearings before the Subcommittee on National Security Policy and Scientific Developments of the Committee on Foreign Affairs, House of Representatives, 91st Cong. 1st Sess., 1970, p. 113, Testimony of Dr. Arthur W. Galston (henceforth called Hearings).

4.   Letter from the Office of the Assistant Secretary of Defense for International Security Affairs dated May 22, 1970, signed by Col. James W. Butler, Policy Plans and NSC Affairs Staff (henceforth referred to as Butler Letter).

5.   Hearings, p. 113, presents this view. The controversy over 2,4,5-T confirms it.

6.   From telephone interviews with the following: Pesticide Regulation Division, Office of Pesticide and Product Safety (Dr. Lamar Dale), Toxicology Branch of the same office (Dr. Thomas Collins), and Dr. Herbert Blumenthal of the petitions and review branch of the same office. All the above are in the Food and Drug Administration.

7.   A sample collection of the amount of a herbicide that could be ingested is in Whiteside, op. cit., pp. 30, 31.

8.   Ibid.

9.   Fred H. Tschirley, Research Report: Response of Tropical and Subtropical Woody Plants to Chemical Treatments, U.S. Agricultural Research Service, Publication CR-13-67, 1968.

10. Gordon H. Orians and E. W. Pfeiffer, "Ecological Effects of the War in Vietnam," Science, May 1, 1970, pp. 544-54.

11. Hearings, p. 109, citing F. H. Tschirley, "Defoliation in Vietnam," Science, Vol. 163, pp. 779-86.

12. Ibid., p. 109.

13. Ibid., p. 109.

14. Orians and Pfeiffer, op. cit., p. 546.

15. Hearings, p. 110, gives Galston's view. Whiteside, op. cit., p. 14, says that Tschirley agrees. The data from Tschirley, Research Report . . . , op. cit., p. 127.

16. A. H. Westing et al., Report on Herbicidal Damage by the United States in Southeastern Cambodia, p. 5. Also, Charles E. Minarik et al., Herbicide Damage to Rubber and Fruit Trees in Cambodia, limited distribution, Saigon, July 12, 1969, pp. 5-6. Also, Whiteside, op. cit., p. 12.

17. Butler Letter, p. 2.

18. Hearings, p. 110.

19. Galston brought this point up in Hearings, p. 109, and many other biologists have voiced similar concerns.

20. Ibid., p. 109.

21. Whiteside, op. cit., p. 3.

22. Reprinted in Whiteside, op. cit.

23. Butler Letter, p. 3.

24. Richard D. McCarthy, The Ultimate Folly: War by Pestilence, Asphyxiation and Defoliation (New York: Alfred A. Knopf, 1969), p. 88.

25. Butler Letter, p. 3.

26. McCarthy, op. cit., p. 82.

27. Ibid.

28. Hearings, p. 111.

29. Butler Letter, p. 3.

30. Whiteside, op. cit., p. 11.

31. These figures are given in both Minarik et al., op. cit.,
and Westing et al., op. cit., as cited in Whiteside, op. cit.,
p. 121.

32. Letter to the United Nations from the government of
Cambodia, dated May 5, 1969, and signed by Huot Sambath.
Reprinted in McCarthy, op. cit., p. 93.

33. Butler Letter, p. 3.

34. Hearings, p. 233. Testimony of Admiral William E.
Lemos.

35. Their report is Minarik et al., mentioned above.

36. Ibid., p. 4.

37. Ibid., p. 9.

38. Ibid., p. 10.

39. Ibid., p. 14.

40. This team consisted of Arthur H. Westing, an American
plant physiologist and the Chairman of the Biology Department
at Windham College; Dr. Egbert W. Pfeiffer, an American
animal physiologist and Professor of Zoology at the University
of Montana; Leon Matarasso, a French lawyer; and Jean
Lavorel, a French plant physiologist. Their report is Westing
et al., op. cit.

41. Ibid., p. 9.

42. Ibid., p. 11.

43. Butler Letter, pp. 2, 3.

14

GENERAL
PURPOSE
NAVAL FORCES

The United States procures and operates general purpose naval forces (excluding attack aircraft carriers and Polaris submarines) principally to protect merchant shipping from attack, to support amphibious landings, and to sink enemy merchant shipping and other surface ships. The missions, capabilities, and numbers of U. S. naval forces should be demonstrably related to contingency assumptions officially adopted by the Executive Branch and approved by the Congress. The "U. S. Contingency Planning" table in Chapter 11 presented alternative assumptions that could also be applied to naval force planning.

There is little in the official record to indicate that U. S. naval forces are justified in terms of the officially approved war plans. On the contrary, one leading naval expert, Dr. Arthur Herrington, has said, "Since World War II this country has not had a clear and consistent naval policy nor does it have one today."[1] During the past year, it has been demonstrated that the fifteen capital ship force level, maintained by the United States since 1921, is as thoroughly institutionalized as any dogma in any federal bureaucracy. Herrington also has pointed out that the size of the Mediterranean Sixth Fleet and the number of attack submarines in the U. S. inventory, despite radical changes in mission, wide variations in other-nation forces, the advent of nuclear weapons and propulsion, and vastly increased capabilities and costs, has remained unchanged for at least two decades.

Further manifestations of uncertain naval planning include the following:

1. The fast-deployment logistics shipbuilding proposal
was abandoned in face of political opposition and, some reports indicate, merchant marine industry lobbying.

2. Cost ceilings have been put on the DLGN and other
programs, resulting in lower force levels.

3. The anti-submarine carrier (CVS) fleet has been cut
from nine to four in six years, with no explanation, yet a $3
billion aircraft procurement for the remaining CVSs has been
undertaken as the carrier program seems to be grinding to a
halt.

4. Much has been made of the size of the Soviet Navy,
but many analysts point out that mere size of navies is not a
measure of force effectiveness. The House Armed Services
Committee Report on Sea Power cited a Soviet ship superiority
of 1,575 ships to a U.S. figure of 820, but these figures include a PT boat ratio of 505-7, and a 226-vessel Russian
superiority in nine-year-old mine-layers. These hardly tilt
the strategic balance.

5. The same criticism may be applied to current concern
with age of ships, which alone is not a measure of effectiveness. However, there is definitely a need for updating much
of our destroyer fleet.

6. Justification of U.S. naval programs frequently has
ignored the significant contribution our allies would make in
a naval war.

What is required of the Executive Branch is an unclassified
presentation of the Joint Strategic Objectives Plan and the Five-
Year Defense Program, as they affect naval forces. It should
explain U.S. naval warfare policy, the contingencies in which
we plan to use our naval forces, the program levels necessi-
tated by those contingencies, and the costs of these programs.
Only a thorough-going public review will restore the credibility
of naval force advocates and assure the Congress and the public
of the cogency of the multi-billion dollar expenditure the
Pentagon is requesting annually.

If the United States is planning for an overall capability
for 1-1/2 wars, general purpose naval forces are slated to
handle either a conventional war against the Soviet Union (in
the Atlantic, with some holding operations in the Pacific) or a
Pacific amphibious and aerial war against China, as well as
other minor contingencies. Short of general conventional war
with a major power, naval forces must plan to war with a minor
air and naval power, such as Egypt or North Korea, as well
as include provisions for counter-insurgency or interventions
against opponents with no air or naval capabilities.

WAR AGAINST THE SOVIET UNION

In the event of general conventional war with the Soviet Union, it is assumed that the major theater would be in the Atlantic, with some holding operations in the Pacific. The major naval problem for the United States would be to protect shipping in the Atlantic, both merchant and military, by preventing Soviet air and naval operations. Estimating the volume of shipping during such war is, of course, speculative, but there is reason to assume that merchant shipping would be reduced.

Marginal shipping would probably be automatically eliminated by increased costs, and non-essential trade would be cut by government action (for example, substituting U. S. for Swedish automobiles). Given existing stockpiles of foodstuffs and fuel oil in Britain and on the Continent, Europe's economy could presumably function for at least a month without shipments from the United States. This would allow time for reorganization and the establishment of convoys. Given existing Soviet forces, to protect shipping, U. S. and allied navies would be required to include capabilities for anti-submarine warfare (ASW), anti-aircraft defense, anti-shipping operations, and mine warfare.

For ASW against the Soviet Union, several types of forces could be used: (1) attack submarines, (2) surface escorts, and (3) carrier-based and land-based aircraft.

U. S. planned force levels provide for 103 attack submarines (of which forty-four are nuclear) by the end of FY 1970, and 105 (of which fifty-two will be nuclear) by the end of FY 1971. U. S. surface escorts could be supplemented by relatively large and efficient allied forces (mainly Royal Navy and Royal Canadian Navy). Allied land-based aircraft could also substantially increase available forces, supplementing the U. S. P-3 squadrons. The efficiency of allied aircraft could be greatly increased if provided with modern U. S. detection equipment. As for sea-based ASW, development of the S-3A carrier plane is being continued although the CVS force has been approximately halved. No significant loss of protection would result if the United States withdrew all its CVSs to inactive status.

For naval anti-aircraft defense against the Soviet Union, the following forces would be used:

1. The fighter component of carrier air groups, consisting of F-4 (Phantom), F-8 (Crusader), and F-14 (under development), which are flown from attack aircraft carriers (CVAs).

The United States maintains an average of ninety fighter planes
per carrier, with about five out of sixteen carriers deployed
at one time.

2.   The ships' anti-aircraft (AA) missiles.

3.   A marginal AA artillery capability; point-defense,
short-range missiles are under development.

Generally, for both ASW and close AA protection, carriers have to rely on screen warships (escorts).

In a war with the Soviet Union, the main threat from Soviet
surface forces would be represented by ship-mounted guided
missiles (surface-to-surface missiles). Specific counter-
measures, such as point-defense missiles to intercept the
relatively slow-breathing enemy missiles, or anti-shipping
missiles of our own, are not yet operational. At present,
reliance is put on the vulnerability of Soviet ships to our air
attacks. It must, however, be pointed out that the larger
Soviet ships have an AA missile component.

OTHER POSSIBLE CONFLICTS

It is reasonable to assume that a Pacific war with China
would require forces similar to those planned for a war against
the Soviet Union, although in reduced strength. At present,
China has considerably fewer submarines than the Soviet Union,
although enough to require some ASW deployment. Chinese air
power is less than that of the Soviet Union, although warranting
some AA operations. The Chinese surface force is largely
coastal and would pose little threat to military shipping or
trans-Pacific commerce (largely to Japan and the Philippines).

A conflict in the Middle East against enemies disposing
of moderate air and naval forces, presumably reinforced by
the Soviet Union, would present problems similar to those of a
war with China. Geographic conditions, however, would influence the situation. In particular, the confined Mediterranean
waters make the survivability of a carrier force more uncertain. On the other hand, carriers may be needed if the political situation does not allow the use of land bases, at least
initially. In later stages, land bases could probably be used.

Against an enemy having no air or sea power, or choosing
not to use it, naval operations could center around the use of
carriers for support activities. Naval strategy could thus exploit the sanctuary aspect of carriers; although there is some
question about the adaptability of current high-performance

carrier-based aircraft for counter-insurgency missions. If
other surface combat vessels are to be used, their conventional gunfire capability would be required, rather than their ASW
or AA capabilities. A portion of the riverine forces developed
for Viet-Nam may be usefully retained for this type of war.

PLANNING AND DESIGN PROBLEMS

A current problem for the Navy is block obsolescence.
A significant per cent of the present U.S. fleet is over twenty
years old, as compared with the relatively modern Soviet Navy.
Although the cost per ton of naval ships has remained more or
less constant for several decades, present ships tend to have
considerably larger tonnage and much more costly electronic
equipment than the ships they replace.

One approach to more effective replacement of large
numbers of ships is mass production in one shipyard. The
shipyard could thus specialize and benefit from economies of
scale. The Navy would benefit from standardization, for
savings would accrue from interchangeable spare parts. Strong
industry pressures, as well as the appealing argument for dividing work among all three U.S. seacoasts, have slowed the
application of this procedure. One solution is to standardize
design and arrange for close cooperation among shipyards.

In addition to these considerations of economy, two major
problems are met in naval force planning and in individual unit
design. The first stems from the fact that a naval task force
is an integrated complex of different units that must work together. Thus a change in the size of the carrier force would
affect the number of escorts which screen it and the underway
replenishment groups. Another aspect of the same problem
is unit homogeneity. For instance, it may be desirable that
the nuclear carriers be accompanied by similarly powered
escorts in order to take full advantage of their capabilities.
But this is open to question.

The main problem in unit design, apart from a tendency
to include non-essential features ("gold-plating") is the choice
between specialized and multi-purpose craft. Although a
general solution cannot be given, the problem can be illustrated
by specific examples. In the ASW field, patrol aircraft are
specialized ASW weapons, submarines have a more general
anti-shipping capability, destroyers, and to a more limited
extent destroyer escorts, also have an AA component and

some gunfire and support capability. It seems reasonable to suggest that flexibility should enter into cost-effectiveness calculations.

A final and critical problem for the Navy is posed by questionings of the value of its general purpose forces. For example, doubts have been expressed regarding the necessity for forces aimed at a protracted conventional sea war with the Soviet Union. Critics ask whether such a contingency would be approved for planning proposed after a serious White House effort to formulate a comprehensive naval policy. There is doubt about the vulnerability of all surface vessels. It cannot be assumed that they would survive against Soviet submarines or aircraft, for example. In confined areas, even less efficient forces such as the Chinese or the Egyptians may pose a significant threat. Only against an opponent lacking both air and naval forces would surface ships be invulnerable. As mentioned above, however, there is some question regarding the utility of surface ships for use against such opponents.

RECOMMENDATIONS

1. The Executive Branch should prepare and release a comprehensive White Paper drawing upon the Joint Strategic Objective Plan and the Five-Year Defense Program discussing U. S. postures related to naval forces. The various contingencies requiring naval forces should be detailed to allow Congress to determine what forces should be funded.

2. The "war at sea" contingency outlining a U. S. -Soviet non-nuclear naval war should be publicly re-examined.

3. When comparing U. S. and Soviet naval strengths to Congress, allied naval forces also should be examined.

4. The United States should enter Naval Arms Limitation Talks with the Soviet Union. It may be possible to negotiate agreements on shipbuilding or operational force strength that would provide more security than at present and save billions of dollars on both sides.

NOTES

1. Lecture delivered at the Naval War College, March 18, 1969.

The United States currently maintains about fifteen carriers on active duty. This force level is widely thought to have originated with the Washington Naval Disarmament Treaty of 1921, which allotted fifteen "capital ships" to the U.S. Navy. When the battleship became virtually obsolete in World War II, the carriers became the capital ship, and the Navy switched from a fleet of fifteen battleships to one of fifteen carriers.

This level--give or take a carrier--has been maintained ever since. The advocates of fifteen carriers, like their predecessors who defended the battleship, have cleaved to this tradition despite the changing role of the surface fleet and its increasing vulnerability to new weapons.

Since World War II, in fact, the attack carrier fleet has been a force in search of a mission. With no other surface fleets to engage, and new intercontinental nuclear bombing dominating strategic thought, the Navy first sought a role for the carrier in strategic nuclear warfare.

The advent of land- and sea-based missiles such as the Minuteman and the Polaris, however, soon eliminated this role. The Defense Department's posture statement of February 4, 1964, concluded that by 1966, the United States would "have a large enough number of strategic missiles in place" to relieve the carrier forces of any strategic retaliatory mission.

The Navy then shifted its emphasis to the carrier's tactical role in providing air support for ground troops, maintaining air superiority, and destroying supply lines. But changing political and military conditions raise doubts about the need

for fifteen attack carrier task forces even for this tactical
purpose.

The Navy now relies on the loss of overseas land bases
as a primary justification for a fifteen-carrier fleet, contend-
ing that there may be times, as in the early days of the Korean
War, when land bases are actually held by enemy forces, and
carrier-based air support may be a valuable temporary complement to nearly all land bases.

In 1969 Congressional testimony, the Chief of Naval Operations emphasized the value of carrier forces in areas where
land bases might not be politically feasible.

The question, however, is how much of our overall defense capability should be devoted to that unlikely contingency
in which we are called upon to defend a nation while being
denied the use of its bases. If the engagement arises from a
multi-nation treaty, such as SEATO, there should be land
bases available in at least some of the signatory countries.
If there are not, it may well indicate something amiss about
the commitments involved.

But regardless of the foreign policy implications of such
interventions, the possible loss of overseas land bases provides an argument only against elimination of all attack carriers. The case for reductions in the carrier fleet is virtually
unaffected. We acknowledge that some carriers are needed
to ensure flexibility in our overall tactical air capability.

COSTS

The most important arguments for reduction of the fleet
derive from the huge cost of carrier-based air power, estimated by the Navy to account for 40 per cent of its total budget.
The cost of building an attack carrier rose from about $83
million in World War II to $171 million during the Korean War.
The original end cost estimate for the first Nimitz-class carrier, the CVAN-68, was $427.5 million. That figure has now
risen to $536 million. The cost of the CVAN-70 is now esti-
mated at $640 million. The Administration has requested
$152 million for procurement in FY 1971.

But even this figure is still going up, as the Navy acknowl-
edges. And the cost of the carrier itself is just the beginning.
The Navy also operates the carrier with an air wing and with
a task force of various escort and logistical ships.

The Navy estimates a $1.4 billion procurement cost for a

nuclear carrier task force--consisting of the carrier and four destroyer escorts. The air wing costs an additional $409.5 million. This brings the total procurement cost for the task force, not including operating costs, to $1.8 billion. Considering inflation and cost overruns, these figures will often run a great deal higher.

But even this is not a complete picture. For the Navy normally maintains a continuous deployment of only two task forces "on station" in the Mediterranean and three in the Western Pacific. For every carrier task force on station, two must be held in reserve as back-ups, because the normal rotation time of a carrier is four months. Because each task force contains an air wing, the Navy must pay for three wings to keep one on station. The investment cost of maintaining one nuclear task force on continued deployment, therefore, amounts to a multiple of three times the cost of one carrier task force--or $5.4 billion. These, of course, are capital costs and do not include the operating cost of each carrier.

The attack carrier force level clearly is a major factor in the defense budget. If a smaller force level is adopted, we will save not only the investment and operating costs of additional carriers, but also the cost of numerous escorts, support ships, and air wings.

A land base is a far cheaper operation. According to the Air Force, a base in the Pacific can be built for $53 million; the Bare Base Support Program can convert an existing civilian runway for about $36 million.

The two carrier task forces on station in the Mediterranean are capable of providing a maximum of 150 offensive sorties per day. Considering that we are flying almost 1,000 offensive sorties per day in Viet-Nam, 150 sorties might well be insufficient in a conflict of similar size in Europe.

CRITIQUE OF CARRIER ROLE

The geographic spread of overseas bases either operated by or available to the United States gives us an impressive land-based tactical capability, especially in the Mediterranean and Western Pacific. In Europe, the United States alone--not including NATO forces--has bases in six countries, with over 400 tactical aircraft, and at least four of those bases are within striking distance of the Mediterranean. In the Pacific, we have bases in seven countries, with over 800 tactical aircraft.

Furthermore, our capacity for creating new land bases
as needs arise is almost limitless. There are at least 1,000
overseas civilian air fields that the Air Force claims it can
convert to fully equipped tactical airbases. Using the "pre-
positioned kits" of the Bare Base Support Program, the Air
Force estimates it needs just three days for the conversion
process.

These existing and potential bases for U.S. land-based
tactical air forces are made more effective by the increasing
range of modern tactical aircraft, now between two and three
times greater than in the past.

This increased range is expanded even further by the use
of mid-air refueling. Our overseas land-based planes are
now capable of reaching many more targets than they were
even ten years ago; and U.S.-based tactical aircraft can be
operational anywhere in the world in a short period of time.
Secretary McNamara, in calling for a reduced carrier fleet,
confirmed in the Defense Department's February, 1964,
posture statement that "the increasing range of land-based
tactical aircraft has reduced our requirement for forward
based air power." It is interesting that no other nation has
found it necessary to build carriers in the last decade. *

The Navy contends that the reduction in the number of
U.S. bases--from 119 in 1957 to 47 in 1970--justifies
continuation of a fifteen-carrier fleet. But the number of
tactical air wings has increased from sixteen to twenty-three
during the same period, and their greatly expanded range--
both from the United States and overseas--means that far
fewer land bases would suffice, supplemented as necessary
by the Bare Base Support Program.

The carriers' overlap and duplication of our land-based
capabilities was dramatically illustrated in a September, 1969,
letter and memorandum from the Air Force to Senator Mark
Hatfield of Oregon. Senator Hatfield had asked whether the
loss of overseas land bases had jeopardized the Air Force's
tactical air capability. The Air Force responded:

The capability of USAF tactical air has in no sense
been diminished by land-based activations. . . .
There are enough land air bases in Southeast Asia
and Europe to base all the tactical fighter aircraft

---

*The two Soviet "carriers" carry no fixed-wing aircraft,
only helicopters, and apparently are designed for ASW and
quick envelopment missions.

which the Joint Chiefs of Staff estimate are required
to meet a major contingency in those areas. [1]

It is true that where land-based air power is not easily
available or politically accessible, the carrier may serve as
a complement to our overseas bases. But where the carrier
clearly competes with land-based air power, the justification
of the carrier must be based on its comparative effectiveness
and efficiency.

By these criteria, the maintenance of fifteen-carrier task
forces for tactical air support around the world appears both
wasteful and ineffective.

First, the sustained use of carrier sorties duplicates and
overlaps existing and potential U.S. capability for providing
land-based tactical air power.

Carrier task forces are assigned to the two major
"trouble areas" of the world--nine for the Western Pacific and
six for the Mediterranean. But our capacity to deploy land-
based tactical air power seems more than adequate in these
areas, as well as in most other parts of the globe where peace
or U.S. interests may be threatened. The U.S. Air Force
maintains twenty-three wings of tactical fighters and bombers
in active forces at home and abroad.

The reliance upon carrier rather than land-based air
power is also made questionable by the carrier's high and increasing degree of vulnerability to modern weapons, including
submarines, aircraft, and ship-to-ship and air-to-air missiles.
Submarines pose a particularly ominous threat. Because of
the continuing ineffectiveness of anti-submarine warfare, a
carrier can do very little to defend itself adequately from submarine attacks.

Recent innovations in missile technology, moreover, have
made the carrier virtually unusable in all but the most limited
conflicts. The lethal nature of even the older missiles, such
as the Soviet STYX, was adequately demonstrated when an
Egyptian PT boat sunk an Israeli destroyer with a single STYX
in 1970. Both the Soviet and American arsenals contain far
more advanced anti-ship missiles, with greater range and
higher speed.

Unique to the Soviet inventory, according to the Chief of
Naval Operations, are the guided cruise missiles. The Navy
estimates that 16 per cent of the Soviet fleet carry 400 nautical
mile cruise missiles designed primarily for use against land
or sea targets. Other advances in missile technology have
produced other extremely swift and sophisticated anti-ship

missiles. A vessel designed for combat in World War II is
thus increasingly threatened. The implications of this threat
for carriers should be carefully reviewed.

The carrier is not completely defenseless against existing
threats. In fact, the ever-present fear of enemy attack causes
the carrier task force to concentrate its resources on defense,
thereby substantially reducing its offensive capability. This
idea was well expressed in a 1966 dissertation on attack carriers by Dr. Desmond Wilson of the Center for Naval Analysis:

> Most of the carriers' usefulness when functioning in
> support of a land campaign during a limited war ap-
> pears to be significant only under conditions of little
> or no submarine opposition. It is a matter of some
> doubt that the carrier force could continue providing
> combat sorties in support of a land campaign if the
> task force commander had to worry about air or
> submarine attacks. [2]

James Field, a naval historian, noted that a carrier task
force in fear of enemy attacks cannot successfully participate
in a campaign of interdiction. He wrote that in Korea, for
example, "logistic considerations and the dangers of air and
submarine attack made it undesirable for carriers to operate
for more than two days in the same location."[3]

Perhaps the most crucial limitation on the carrier's effectiveness is that the threat of attack diverts offensive sorties
to defense of the task force. Thus, during World War II and
the Korean War, 23 per cent of the total combat sorties flown
from carriers were defensive. This contrasts with 2.7 per
cent flown by planes from land bases during the Korean War.

Fears and uncertainties concerning an enemy's anti-
carrier warfare potential also affect the "rapid responsiveness" of the attack carrier, which is its strongest attribute.
Wilson noted that uncertainties as to weapons, belligerents,
and the "limits" of the war did in fact impede carrier deployment early in the Korean conflict.[4] Future limited wars will
also be surrounded by "uncertainties as to who will fight and
with what weapons."[5] The tremendous investment in a carrier
and its task force and the vulnerability of the carrier thus
makes the Navy hesitant to commit it to a conflict or potential
conflict.

The threats that have limited a carrier's responsiveness
and effectiveness in past wars are far more dangerous today.
And inasmuch as naval doctrine, Wilson points out, "as yet

says nothing about treating the attack carrier as expendable in a limited war, "[6] the carrier will be even less effective in future conflicts with a sophisticated enemy.

Naval planning does not fully recognize the vulnerability of carriers. The carrier is assumed to be a vital participant in the full range of conventional conflicts--the relatively minor Dominican Republic type, the "mid-range" Viet-Nam type, and the full-scale conventional war--whatever that would be in this nuclear era.

By allocating to itself such a comprehensive role, the Navy is refusing to acknowledge that events since 1945 have limited the "scenarios" in which carriers can be effective. Although the Soviet Union represents the greatest threat, other countries possess various weapons designed for anti-carrier warfare. Many of these weapons have been supplied by the Soviet Union, including such items as long-range bombers, MIG-21s, the STYX and other anti-ship missiles, and long-range conventional submarines.

Relatively few scenarios remain in which a carrier may be free from threats of enemy action and able to function effectively in an offensive tactical capacity. Although the carrier retains some utility in a conflict in which the enemy has a limited anti-carrier capability, carriers simply cannot operate effectively as the threat increases.

The Navy is quick to remind us that land bases for tactical aircraft are also vulnerable to enemy attack. Land bases are subject to attack by aircraft and missiles. In addition, they are uniquely exposed to ground attack and artillery, particularly in a guerrilla war as in Viet-Nam.

But in examining the relative vulnerability of land- and sea-based tactical air power, we must look at their relative effectiveness and repairability. Land bases are easier to repair, are less inhibited than carriers by the threat of attack, and are capable of delivering more offensive sorties.

Carrier vulnerability also makes this system less desirable from a cost point of view. It has been estimated that at least one half of the cost of a carrier task force is allocated for defense, thus sharply raising the cost of each offensive sortie. In return for this large defensive investment, we have carrier task forces that are inadequately defended against high-level threats and are overly oriented toward defense against low-level threats. Carriers, therefore, can serve as a useful complement to land-based air power primarily in limited conflicts where land bases are not immediately available. But despite the Navy's recognition that carriers should

be complementary to land-based air power, it has been un-
willing to accept the fact that the need for carriers is reduced
where there is ample land-based air capability.

Carriers, for example, were useful in the beginning of
the Viet-Nam conflict when land bases were still limited. But
a serious question can be raised whether the Navy's continuing
level of involvement in the Viet-Nam conflict once sufficient
land bases were constructed there reflects as much the need
to give the Navy a "piece of the action" as a reasoned military
judgment.

The designation of six carrier task forces to the Atlantic
and nine to the Pacific also attests to the Navy's unwillingness
to recognize the complementary nature of carrier and land-
based air power. Desmond Wilson commented on the Mediterranean task force:

> With the subsequent development of land-based air
> covering NATO's southern flank, and with the later
> introduction into the region and coverage of the re-
> gion by the sea and land-based missile systems,
> the Sixth Fleet may have become increasingly re-
> dundant. It almost certainly became increasingly
> vulnerable with the marked growth of the Soviet
> nuclear capability, along with submarine, aviation
> and missile delivery systems. [7]

But even the present level of fleet deployment can be carried out with less than fifteen attack carriers. To begin with,
the Navy claims that fifteen attack carrier task forces are required to keep five continually on station--two in the Mediterranean and three in the Western Pacific. Granting that the
rate of on-station deployment has occasionally been higher in
the past, the Navy continues to insist that because of the need
to rest the crew, make repairs, and maintain logistics, three
task forces are needed to maintain one on station throughout
the year.

The Navy does concede that but for the need to relieve
the crew, a carrier task force could remain longer on station.
However, they have never satisfactorily explained why the
relief of the crew should force the carrier to be withdrawn
from forward deployment.

The Navy itself has successfully dealt with this problem
in Polaris submarines by rotating crews. A Polaris sub is
thus able to stay on active duty longer than a carrier. Yet the
Navy has failed to adapt such a method to attack carriers,

although it would make it possible to keep five task forces on
station with a reduced carrier fleet.

The Navy's carrier fleet is not limited to attack carriers.
There are, in addition, four smaller carriers, used primarily
for anti-submarine warfare. These are capable of handling
several types of tactical jet fighters, and one of these smaller
carriers is currently being used in Viet-Nam in an attack
capacity.

Surely such carriers could be used to supplement the
existing attack fleet in many cases where limited tactical air
power is called for. And for the relatively minor missions
depicted in the Navy's list of "wars and near wars"--such as
evacuating citizens--these smaller carriers are in fact more
suitable than the modern attack carrier. It becomes all the
more difficult, therefore, to justify the beginning of a brand
new attack carrier in light of the overwhelming cost of a fleet
which actually numbers nineteen.

Increased capability of the carrier fleet, moreover,
means that today's fifteen attack carriers can deliver far more
tactical air support than the fifteen carriers in the fleet of the
1950's. Secretary McNamara relied on this increased capability as a justification for reducing the size of the carrier
fleet.

These questions about present U.S. carrier policy have
been expressed in the past by defense and other government
officials, as well as by military historians, but much of this
debate has been kept from public view. For example, the
Defense Department's Office of Systems Analysis has often
recommended cuts in the attack carrier fleet, but the studies
underlying these recommendations have not been divulged.
One such study by this office showed that over a ten-year
period, the carrier-based wing alone costs almost $1 billion
more than a land-based wing.

Criticism of present policy did come to light in the Defense Department's posture statement for fiscal 1965--presented
by Secretary McNamara on February 4, 1964--which called
for "some reduction in the number of attack carriers by the
early 1970's." McNamara cited the increased tactical air
capability of modern carriers and modern carrier-based aircraft, the end of the carrier's role in our strategic nuclear
forces, and the reduced need for forward-based air power as
a result of the increased range of land-based tactical aircraft.

Criticism of the carrier force level from within the Defense Department has persisted. Dr. Arthur Herrington, a
Department official, questioned the size of the carrier fleet
in a speech at the Naval War College:

Today we still plan a 15 (attack carrier) force for
the future. Yet over this 25 year period, we have
seen: a polarization of the world into Communist
and non-Communist camps, and lately an increasing
fragmentation of both; the development of the
Marshall Plan, NATO, the conversion of our enemy
in the Pacific, Japan, to an ally, and the conversion
of our old ally, China, to an enemy; a doubling of
the size of the attack carrier, nuclear propulsion;
jet aircraft and nuclear weapons. In truth, 15 attack carriers (or 15 capital ships in the U.S. Navy,
if you will) appears to be close to an "eternal
verity" in U.S. military planning. [8]

The most revealing admission of the Pentagon's own doubts
about the justification for fifteen attack carriers can be found
in a Departmental Statement filed in 1969 with the Joint Economic Committee. Representative William Moorhead of that
Committee had asked the Defense Department to explain the
necessity for a force of fifteen attack carriers. A Department
spokesman wrote in reply:

It is very difficult to determine the precise division
of effort between land-based and sea-based forces
which will meet our worldwide commitments at the
least cost. The program supported by the previous
administration included 15 attack carriers. In
response to a directive by the National Security
Council to examine alternative General Purpose
Force strategies, we are currently reassessing
both the total requirement for tactical aircraft
to meet each alternative strategy and the relative
costs and effectiveness of different mixes of land-
based and sea-based aircraft. Pending completion
of this study, we are not recommending any major
changes in the previous program.

Other high-level government officials directly responsible
for defense planning have also expressed doubts about our
carrier policy. Charles Schultz, a former Director of the
Bureau of the Budget, testified before the Joint Economic
Committee that the request for an additional attack carrier
was the first item to be examined in eliminating unnecessary
military expenditures. [9]

RECOMMENDATIONS

1. Because the cost for constructing new nuclear carriers is prohibitively high, no new nuclear carriers should be constructed. Moreover, the number of carriers on active duty should be reduced to ten or twelve as soon as practical. Some of the money saved in operating costs should be invested in updating our present carrier fleet.

2. The current estimate for completing the CVAN-70 is $640 million. We recommend halting construction on the carrier and deleting the $152 million requested for procurement in FY 1971.

NOTES

1. Letter from the Department of the Air Force to Mark O. Hatfield, September, 1969.

2. Desmond Wilson, "Evolution of the Attack Aircraft Carrier: A Case Study in Technology and Strategy," unpublished doctoral dissertation, MIT, February, 1966, p. 163.

3. James A. Field, History of U.S. Naval Operations in Korea (Washington, D.C.: U.S. Government Printing Office, 1962), p. 111.

4. Wilson, op. cit., p. 146.

5. Ibid.

6. Ibid., p. 147.

7. Ibid., p. 107.

8. Arthur Herrington, Naval War Review (September, 1969), pp. 47-63.

9. The Military Budget and National Economic Priorities, Joint Economic Committee, Publications Document No. 31-690 (Washington, D.C.: U.S. Government Printing Office), p. 53.

The DD-963, formerly the DX, is a 7,000-ton, 460-foot-long destroyer. It is the first large naval ship slated for mass production since World War II. A production contract was originally to have been let in mid-1969, but was delayed until late June, 1970, when $2.1 billion was awarded to Ingalls Shipbuilding, a subsidiary of Litton Industries, for the construction of thirty ships during the next eight years.

The DD-963 is planned to be powered by a gas turbine propulsion unit which will give the ship a 30-knot speed. The ships are to be outfitted with 200 tons of electronic equipment to protect them from air, surface, and submarine attack and to hunt and sink enemy submarines, and will carry "almost everything presently operational and many developments now in the test phase"[1] in the field of electronic warfare (ECM). *

The primary mission of the DD-963 destroyer is to upgrade U.S. anti-submarine warfare capability for both merchant and naval ship protection and hunter-killer operations. Its secondary mission is to provide support for amphibious assault operations through shore bombardment and to screen support forces against air and surface threats.

If properly integrated, the highly sophisticated subsystems planned for the DD-963 should provide increased ASW capability for our destroyer forces; many of the destroyers in the present

---

*It is reported, however, that many or all of these systems may be dropped from the destroyer as a means of cutting down on the cost growth that has thus far plagued the DD-963 program. At the very least, the government may have to pay an additional $455 million for the radar equipment.

fleet are quite old and not designed to absorb all the electronics necessary to improve their performance. In providing fire support for assault operations, the 963 does not appear to offer anything that is not now available.

COSTS

The Department of Defense request for FY 1971 is $506.8 million for six ships; the FY 1970 buy will be three ships at a cost of $308.6 million. In December, 1967, the total program of forty ships was estimated by the Office of the Secretary of Defense (OSD) to cost $1.364 billion. In late February, 1970, the Navy estimated the cost of thirty ships at $2.4 billion, and the General Accounting Office (GAO) has suggested that it may go as high as $3.35 billion (see Table 13).

The $2.4 billion figure would indicate an overrun of 135 per cent as of February, 1970. This figure does not take into account the fact that contractor tasks required in the original plan are not required in the present plan. For example, the new destroyer originally was to have an elaborate electronics warfare unit. But that unit is still being developed, so it has been dropped from the construction contract. The builder now will have to provide only the space and weight capability for the unit and the Navy will buy it later, under a separate contract. The contractors proposed that 80 per cent of the initial training for the vessels' operation and maintenance crews be done by the government and 20 per cent by the contractors. To reduce the contract cost, the Navy now proposes that only 10 per cent of the training be done by the contractors.

THE NAVY'S CASE

The Soviet Union now has deployed about 380 attack and ASW submarines, some twenty of which are nuclear powered, compared with our 105 attack submarines, of which about fifty are nuclear powered. The U.S. attack submarine fleet has stabilized at some 105 vessels, and the changes contemplated are related primarily to nuclearization rather than to a substantial increase in numbers. The Russians are continuing to stress conversion of their submarine fleet to nuclear capability. The reasons for the Soviet submarine buildup are not entirely clear.

TABLE 13

DD-963 Program Cost Estimates

Department	Cost
OSD-1967	$1. 364 billion for 40 ships or $34. 1 million each
Navy-1970	$2. 4 billion for 30 ships or $80 million each
GAO-1970	$3. 35 billion for 30 ships or $111 million each

Much of the present Soviet submarine fleet is convention-ally powered and relatively inefficient, so that comparisons between relative numbers of Soviet and U. S. submarines are difficult. The Russians are known also to be experiencing difficulty in maintaining enough qualified crew members to man their subs, so that it is hard to determine if their under-water forces are operating at an optimum level. Moreover, the Soviet boats are relatively noisy and therefore often lack the element of surprise which is so vital for successful sub-marine operations.

Soviet naval strategists have not yet responded to the U. S. submarine force by an extensive destroyer construction program. As of July 1, 1970, the United States will have thirty-four de-stroyers on order, eleven destroyers less than one year old, a 20:0 superiority in destroyers one to five years old, a 30:18 superiority in ships six to ten years old, a 27:92 inferiority in ships eleven to twenty years old, and a 133:0 superiority in ships twenty years or older.

In any case, the threat posed by Soviet submarines to U. S. naval forces, both surface and undersea, is clear. The DD-963 is a response to that threat.

THE CASE AGAINST THE DD-963

The DD-963 relies very heavily on highly sophisticated electronic equipment which has had a history of cost growth and poor performance. For instance, the SQS-26 long-range radar, one of the most important subsystems on the ship, has suffered from concurrent development and production and has not achieved the high performance expected of it. The systems slated for inclusion in the DD-963 are in various phases of research, development, and production, and it will be an extremely difficult task to synchronize their progress so that the ships can be operational on schedule. Both potential contractors for the ship, Bath Ironworks Corporation and Ingalls Shipbuilding Corporation, emphasized a modular design as a hedge against the virtually certain need for a major retro-fit program, much of which will be necessary even as the first thirty ships are being constructed. Ingalls subsequently was awarded the contract, totaling $2.1 billion.

It is not clear when the DD-963 will have all its subsystems in reliable working order and integrated well enough to achieve the ship's mission. It is possible that as one subsystem is achieving its optimum capability, another will be becoming obsolete, and still another might be requiring modification. The initial purchase price of the ships, high in any case, is not an accurate reflection of the costs required to keep them operating and up to date. A destroyer, like any other ship, cannot do its job effectively if it is in constant need of retrofit and repair.

The DD-963 will become operational only when enough of its essential component subsystems are reliable enough for deployment in the fleet. The interdependency of the various systems of the DD-963 multiplies the possibilities for delay in the production schedule. Delays in the production schedule, in turn, limit the utility of the ship when it is finally deployed by creating pressure for the incorporation of systems whose testing and evaluation is incomplete.

Congress should take the lead in requiring more thorough testing of subsystems and systems, mandating GAO to develop the capability to audit test programs and reports, ending concurrency between development and production, and generally moderating the pell-mell race to incorporate the least tried, newest systems in DD-963 and other procurement programs.

Performance data on the DD-963, as with most ASW systems, is not readily available. Such information is absolutely essential if the Congress is to be able to make a reasoned judgment whether or not the DD-963 is worth its high cost. Congress should require detailed comparative cost-effectiveness studies on DD-963, DLGN-38, P-3C, S-3A, and SSN-688, to determine which programs provide the greatest ASW capability for the tax dollar. It is quite possible that

DD-963, despite the problems it has experienced to date, should still be built--and the cost overruns paid for by canceling a duplicating ASW program, such as the S-3A.

Another matter to which the Congress should turn its attention is the lack of competition in ship procurement evidenced by the DD-963. There were six responses to the Navy's first Request for Proposal (RFP) in February, 1968. Three companies were selected for contract definition in July, 1968. The Navy eliminated General Dynamics in September, 1969. In 1970, however, the Navy reported that it was greatly simplifying the contract. Might one of the four eliminated companies have had the best proposal for the revised simplified contract? How much of the competition between the finalists is economic, and how much political? Once millions have been invested, how much control will the Navy really have over cost growth? Answers to these questions are not easily acquired. These are troubling questions, however, and they are symptomatic of the feeling that new solutions--such as construction in government-owned shipyards--may be necessary for the shipbuilding programs of the next decade.

RECOMMENDATIONS

The DD-963 should have close Congressional scrutiny and constant review. It is among the most overrun-prone systems on the current Pentagon shopping list, and the likelihood of cost growth must be taken into account in evaluating the priority to be given to the program.

1. Performance data on the DD-963, as with most ASW systems, are not readily available. The Congress must require adequate justification for the program in the form of validated test data before a commitment is made to full-scale production. The subsystems of the DD-963 are in various states of research and development and there will be considerable pressure to deploy some of them before they are ready for service use. Congress should require assurance that the subsystems are (a) fully tested, and (b) integrated to operate as a unit.

2. Programs such as the DD-963 have had a history of expensive retro-fitting as the state of the art advances and individual systems become obsolete. The retro-fitting requires considerable loss of time on station and much expense. Congress should have assurance that such retro-fitting will be kept to an absolute minimum. In the absence of such assurance the usefulness of the DD-963 becomes increasingly marginal.

3.   The Administration in 1970 requested $459. 5 million
for procurement of the DD-963.   The House authorized $406. 8
million.   We recommend that $100 million of the House author-
ization be deleted due to (a) concern over the extraordinary
cost overrun, and (b) a need to ensure that the necessary R&D
is completed before procurement.

NOTES

1.   "DD-963, " <u>Market Intelligence Report</u> (October, 1969),
p. 6.

CHAPTER

17

DLGN-38
NUCLEAR
FRIGATE

The destroyer was developed from the motor torpedo boat of pre-World War I days. Its primary mission was the destruction of submarines. With development of more efficient torpedoes, as well as the advent of seaborne air power, destroyers assumed an important role in the defense of military fleets and convoys.

In many respects, the DLGN program is a follow-on to the destroyer fleets of the past fifty years. It is designed to meet a number of requirements: (1) the need for defense of shipping against submarines, (2) the air defense of shipping, and (3) the retention of some surface-to-surface firing capability.

The DLGN-38 is a special class of destroyer. It was initially designated as an experimental guided missile nuclear powered frigate (DXGN), a follow-on to the DLGN-36 class destroyers. The DLGN-38 class ships will be smaller than the DLGN-36 class ships and will have only one missile system instead of the two-missile system. The Navy soon will have a total of five nuclear powered surface escort vessels (Long Beach, Bainbridge, Truxton, DLGN-36, and DLGN-37.)

THE CASE FOR THE DLGN-38

The Navy believes that the DLGN-38, with its high speed endurance, will be able to respond better to the threat of modern submarines than conventional destroyers. Although this question is largely tied to the escort situation, DLGN-38 will be able to participate in general ASW operations with greater likelihood of success than conventional destroyers. With the Mark 48 torpedo (now under development), DLGN-38 might prove to be a significant part of the answer to the ASW problem.

The second mission is defense of carriers from air attack. There are two distinct categories here--aircraft defense and missile defense. As for attack by aircraft, the DLGN-38 class will be armed with Tartar-D missiles, which have a range of approximately ten miles, and five-inch dual-purpose close-in anti-aircraft guns.

The primary role of these ships will be attack carrier defense; long-range protection of the aircraft carrier and its attendant escorts will be provided by the carrier's aircraft. Missile defense is another problem brought to the fore by the sinking of the Israeli destroyer Elath on October 22, 1967, by Komar-class torpedo boats using STYX missiles. The American response to this threat has been the development of Sea Sparrow III, an offshoot of the SPARROW air-to-air missile system. Another system, the AEGIS, is also under study. Neither system is operational now. It would probably not be necessary to arm the DLGN-38 class with either system because a carrier with these systems probably could defend itself and its escorts. If this were not considered feasible, the destroyers themselves could be so armed.

There are a number of reasons why nuclear powered escorts are preferred over their conventionally powered counterparts. A key reason is that the nuclear escorts can have far greater high speed endurance than the oil burners. Thus, they can provide protection to a carrier over a considerable period of time whether en route to station or conducting flight operations. A second factor is the necessity of oil burners to be refueled every three days if they are conducting operations with carriers. During these periods of refueling, they are themselves very vulnerable to attack and the carriers they are supposed to be protecting have less protection.

THE CASE AGAINST THE DLGN-38

DLGN-38 is not necessarily the answer to the ASW problem simply because of its high endurance rate. The ASW problem has a number of ramifications, the most significant

being the capability of recently developed Soviet submarines
to dive to considerable depths--depths at which ASW torpedoes
apparently cannot operate. It is probable that the real answer
to the Soviet ASW threat is the anti-submarine rocket (ASROC)
and the submarine-launched rocket (SUBROC), which are capable of attacking a submarine at fairly great distances. Inasmuch as this does not require sustained high speed, there is
no reason for development of a new destroyer for a function
that can be performed by existing ones. It would appear
prudent to await development of a Mark 48 torpedo before using
it as a rationale for the development of the DLGN-38.

Again, it appears to take five or six conventional destroyers to do the work of four DLGN-38 class ships. These
conventional destroyers, such as the DD-931, are already
available. There are also a number of other classes of ships
armed with missiles and ASW weapons that can provide the
same degree of protection.

The argument about the vulnerability of the oiler is of
doubtful validity. Aircraft carriers (even nuclear powered
ones) must carry fuel for their escorts. Often this is enough
and no oiler is necessary. In the event that an oiler is considered a necessity, five or six conventional destroyers are
sufficient to provide protection for it as well as the aircraft
carrier. In addition, all carriers must carry even more
volatile aviation fuel, and these supplies have to be replenished
periodically. Nuclear escorts will not solve this problem.

As the United States revises its plans for simultaneous
involvement in conflicts around the world, there are implications for the size and nature of U.S. naval requirements.
There seems to be considerable sentiment within the Executive
and Legislative branches for reduction in the number of attack
carrier task forces. As long as it is not clear what the out-
come of the current controversy will be, it is equally unclear
what investment in carrier escorts should be made. It would
seem prudent to defer these secondary decisions until the
overall decisions are made.

Again, in the minds of some analysts, it is a matter of
urgent concern that so large an investment is being made in
surface ships when the Soviet Union appears to be leading the
world in deploying anti-ship missiles, and when the American
ship defense missile, AEGIS, is only in the research stage.
According to press accounts, exercises in the Mediterranean
by the Sixth Fleet have indicated that small motor torpedo
craft are able to penetrate carrier defenses. Congress should
insist upon the development of high-confidence systems before

approving multi-billion dollar expenditures for military concepts which may be obsolescing.

Costs of the DLGN-38 program have soared. In the FY
1969 Posture Statement, it was estimated that five DLGNs
could be built for $625 million ($125 million each).[1] In the
FY 1971 Posture Statement, four are priced at $846 million
($211 million each), with a total system cost exceeding $4.9
billion.[2]

Congress should ask for very detailed explanations of
cost increases. If inflation is blamed, for example, the
Navy should state exactly what the old estimates were for
labor, materials, and subsystems, and which cost-price in-
dexes reflect the inflation rates asserted for these ships. Research and development on subsystems should be complete before the larger systems are designed--avoiding the pattern of
constant redesign and retro-fit of present ship procurement.

The most drastic step would be for types of vessels to be
funded once and only once. The Navy might have been given
all $625 million for five or more ships in 1969 and required
to spend the money as efficiently as possible. Only far-
reaching steps by the Congress will improve the quality of
management of these systems. Until such steps are taken,
ship procurement programs are going to see the same inflation
of prices and cuts in number of vessels procured as in the
DLGN-38.

RECOMMENDATIONS

1. Construction of DLGN-38 should be slowed until the
weapons it will use, the Mark 48 torpedo and the AEGIS anti-
missile, are tested. DLGN-38 will be only as good as its
weapons. If these programs are failures, there is little point
in a billion-dollar ship procurement to buy platforms for them.

2. Authorization of DLGN-38 should be postponed until
a comprehensive naval war policy for the United States is published. This alternative is akin to the recommendation of the
House Armed Services Committee that no funds be obligated
for any shipbuilding monies in the FY 1971 request until the
National Security Council makes its study of the wisdom of
going ahead with CVAN-70, the fourth nuclear carrier.

3. The Armed Services Committee should take immediate action to determine whether the DLGN-38 could be built
in government shipyards at less cost to the taxpayer. Industry

profits of 6 to 10 per cent might be saved by this device. Alternatively, enhanced cost discipline for this program could be devised by putting strict controls on change orders, compliance with cost and specification items, testing of all subsystems before final design of the larger system, and GAO participation and review of estimates, contracting, and testing.

4. The current estimate for the total program is $4.9 billion. This includes a request by the Administration for $221.3 million for procurement during FY 1971. We have recommended that the entire $221.3 million be deleted from the budget.

NOTES

1. Defense Program and Budget FY 1969 (Washington, D.C., U.S. Government Printing Office), pp. 97-99.

2. Defense Program and Budget FY 1971 (Washington, D.C., U.S. Government Printing Office), pp. 146-47.

18

The SSN-688 class is envisioned as a group of "superfast, superquiet" nuclear powered attack submarines, primarily designed to protect our Polaris fleet and to destroy Soviet sea-based missile systems. Preliminary studies by the General Dynamics Electric Board Division were ordered in October, 1964. Initial funding followed in November, 1966, for development of a successor to the SSN-671 Narwhal class and a variation on the Sturgeon class "fast" submarine.

The SSN-688 will be slightly larger than Narwhal and Sturgeon and will have a speed of over 30 knots. A hunter-killer, the new submarine will precede development of the SSN-685 TEDS superhigh-speed, "quiet" craft presently under design and will be capable of diving to an estimated 1,800 feet, armed with Mark 48 torpedoes and SUBROC. Costs for the SSN-688 do not include SUBROC or Mark 48, although for the purposes of competent analysis, their inclusion is necessary.

SUBROC is a 4,000-pound, twenty-foot-long missile with a range of thirty-five miles. After ejection from standard submarine torpedo tubes, the rocket motor ignites, propelling the missile out of the water. At a pre-set point in flight, the motor shuts off and separates from the warhead. The warhead, either conventional or nuclear, continues on a ballistic trajectory until it lands at a predetermined point on the water. Fifteen hundred SUBROC units procured through fiscal year 1969 are to be deployed, four to six each, on all thirty-seven SSN-637 class submarines and on SSN-688. The follow-on missile, called STAM, is in the study phase and will have both short- and

long-range capability as opposed to SUBROC's long range
only. Both these systems are tied to the submarine's sonar
capability, which is very limited in comparison with the range
of SUBROC. (For Mark 48 analysis, see Chapter 19.)

COSTS

For FY 1970, the Congress fully funded three ships and
advanced procurement for five more. In February, 1970, the
Pentagon stated that at least three or four SSN-688s (including
the five with advanced funding) should be authorized in FY
1971 and FY 1972. A final decision on how many SSN-688s will
be procured depends on delays in funding the successor ship,
SSN-685. Ship construction will begin in 1973 for first deliver-
ies in 1974, with deployment for the eight-ship fleet by 1979.

Cost for one SSN-688 is estimated to be approximately
$220 million, with additional submarines of this class to cost
$153 million each, for a total of $1.291 billion. The request
for fiscal year 1971 is $475.5 million, which is $135 million
less than was authorized for FY 1970. Total systems cost is
estimated to be in excess of $4.3 billion.

THE SSN-688 MISSION

The mission of the SSN-688 is to track and kill Soviet
undersea attack craft seeking to destroy American ballistic
missile submarines. It also will be designed to hunt Soviet
missile submarines. A portion of the U.S. attack submarine
fleet, predominantly older diesel-powered boats, would join
surface and air ASW forces arrayed in picket line barriers
off U.S. coasts to deny short-range firing positions to Soviet
ballistic missile submarines.

Although the Soviet Union is considered to be behind the
United States in current ASW capability, the Soviet Navy is
devoting increasing effort to development of such systems,
including nuclear attack submarines to counter the U.S.
Polaris fleet. Their submarine deployment, moreover, is
already impressive in quantitative terms.

At the close of World War II, the Soviet Union possessed
a fleet of 200 diesel-powered submarines. Since then they
have retired some and constructed hundreds of new submarines

of which sixty-five, and possibly more, are nuclear powered.
During the same period, the United States constructed ninety-
nine new boats, of which eighty-two were nuclear powered.
The United States presently has a fleet of over 150 submarines,
including sixty-one diesel-powered boats, compared to a Soviet
submarine force of about 380.

The increasing numbers of Soviet submarines, particularly
attack models, plus the possibility of a Soviet ASW technology
breakthrough, have led the U.S. Navy to press for production
of the SSN-688 and early development of its successors. The
long lead-times required to develop and produce ASW equipment, particularly a new submarine such as the SSN-688, are
said to dictate starting now without waiting for intelligence reports of Soviet initiatives in the field.

CRITIQUE OF THE SSN-688 PROGRAM

In his 1970 Posture Statement, Secretary of Defense
Melvin Laird said, "According to our best current estimates,
we believe that our Polaris and Poseidon submarines at sea
can be considered virtually invulnerable today. With a highly
concentrated effort, the Soviet navy today might be able to
localize and destroy at sea one or two Polaris submarines."[1]

Thus, at present, without the SSN-688, the U.S. ballistic
missile submarine fleet as a whole is relatively invulnerable.
The limited numbers of SSN-688s planned would provide little
defense against a concentrated attack on one or two U.S. submarines.

The same logic applies in reverse to use of the SSN-688
offensively to track and destroy Soviet missile submarines.
If concentrated, SSN-688s and similar craft may achieve some
degree of success attacking a limited number of Soviet missile
submarines. The Soviet boats are very noisy, and at present
only a very few of them have the range required to come within
striking distance of the United States.

Nonetheless, the Soviet missile submarines are capable
of traveling in depths approximating their U.S. counterparts.
The Soviet ballistic missile fleet thus would likely cruise into
position at considerable depth, approaching near the surface
only to fire. While cruising, the Soviet subs would be relatively invulnerable to SSN-688 using SUBROC, given SUBROC's
characteristics. SSN-688 would then be forced to rely on the
Mark 48 torpedo. The Mark 48 is designed to operate at great

depth but has encountered technical difficulties. As the SSN-
688 and related craft are only as effective as their weapons,
the problems in Mark 48 development (see Chapter 19) raise
questions concerning the effectiveness of the attack submarine
class.

As part of off-shore barrier arrays deployed to deny
Soviet submarines access to short-range firing positions, the
limited number of nuclear attack submarines planned would be
backed up by large numbers of older diesel submarines. The
barrier ASW defense is a mix of aircraft and submarines using
sonobuoys of indeterminable efficiency. Even if some future
breakthrough provided the United States with a near impene-
trable ASW barrier, a Soviet equivalent to the Undersea Long-
Range Missile System (ULMS) would give the Soviet ballistic
missile submarine the ability to clear Soviet ports and fire
without approaching the U.S. coast.

The strategic rationale for the SSN-688 is somewhat
analogous to the case for ABM. An assured second-strike
capability is presently the keystone of the U.S. strategic posture. As ABM is proposed as insurance for Minuteman, so
SSN-688 and similar attack submarines are designed to ensure
the invulnerability of the U.S. submarine missile fleet. There
the analogy ends, for even without SSN-688, the U.S. ballistic
missile submarine fleet is relatively invulnerable. It will provide an assured second strike for the next decade at least
regardless of increased numbers of Soviet attack submarines
or improved surface and air ASW forces.

In conclusion, if existing American ballistic missile submarine forces without the SSN-688 and similar craft do not
constitute a credible deterrent, the whole concept of credible
deterrence may be thrown into question. For the alternative
advocated by the Pentagon--rapid deployment of ULMS in addition to existing Polaris/Poseidon forces with MIRV warheads,
plus a large American attack submarine fleet--might give the
United States a posture that would be too credible. With
MIRVed land forces and ABM, it would be credible not for
deterrence, but for its first-strike capability. Three past
Presidents and their Secretaries of Defense have disclaimed
any intent to achieve that position, with its promise of either
an expanded arms spiral or war.

RECOMMENDATIONS

1. No further funding for procurement of the SSN-688 should be approved until a significant threat to Polaris submarines can be fully identified and the cost effectiveness of the Mark 48 torpedo system is clarified.

2. The current estimate for the total system cost of SSN-688 is $4.3 billion. Of this, $475.5 million has been requested for procurement in FY 1971. We recommend that these funds be deleted. However, $238 million should be allocated for continuing R&D, particularly in submarine-detection systems and undersea guidance technology.

NOTES

1. <u>Defense Program and Budget FY 1971</u> (Washington, D.C., U.S. Government Printing Office), p. 40.

The Mark 48 torpedo is intended to be a high-speed, long-range, deep-diving torpedo. It was originally designed to protect U. S. submarines from the latest high-speed Soviet attack submarines. Later it was modified for greater surface ship destruction capability.

There are three versions of the Mark 48. The Mark 48 Mod 0 is a nineteen-foot, 3,500-pound weapon with a range of twenty-five miles and a diving capacity of more than 3,000 feet. It is a highly complex weapon with acoustic homing features and the capability for mid-course guidance through a wire connecting it to the launcher. It can be fired from either submarines or surface ships.

The Mod 1 differs from the Mod 0 in the propulsion and homing systems and in a larger warhead designed to give greater surface ship destruction capability. The Mod 2 is also a dual-purpose version intended to provide greater surface destruction capacity. The Navy has begun some limited development to convert the Mod 0s to Mod 2s.

The precursor of the Mark 48 was the EX-10, an experimental torpedo designed under the Research Torpedo Configuration (RETORC) II-A program initiated in 1958 and conducted by the Naval Underwater Ordnance Station and the Ordnance Research Laboratory at Pennsylvania State University.

The development characteristics of the Mark 48 were prescribed in late 1960 by the Chief of Naval Operations, and the first technical development outline was issued in February, 1961. This plan estimated the time schedules and funding necessary to develop the system and produce approximately ten torpedoes for testing and approximately fifty (later

augmented to eighty-five) for technical and operational evaluation.   The Mark 48 development program was initiated in 1962.

In June of 1963, the Program Definition Phase began with
contracts on a cost-no-fee basis with two selected torpedo
contractors and two selected fire control contractors.   Evaluation of resulting proposals led to development contracts with
Westinghouse Electric Corporation for the torpedo and General
Precision, Inc., Librascope Group, for the fire control system.
By June of the following year, a revised Technical Development
Plan indicated that all major components of an operable EX-10
torpedo had been tested under the RETORC II-A program.   The
paper concluded that it would not be necessary to conduct major
applied research or exploratory investigations on the Mark 48.
Westinghouse was awarded a fixed-price contract for prototype
models of modification kits to transform the EX-10 into the
Mark 48 and for new equipment common to fire control systems
of the ships and submarines scheduled to use Mod 0 of this new
torpedo system.

COSTS

According to the House Armed Services Committee, "a
meaningful cost comparison cannot be made" between the Mark
48 and its predecessor, Mark 37, "unless the magnitude of the
difference in their intended missions and importance to the
security of the nation is appreciated." Unit costs for the
various versions of the Mark 37 ranged from $26,027 to
$38,585 over an eleven-year period.   The unit cost estimates
for the Mark 48 Mod 0 are now running at $1,087,577 each for
the initial buy of fifty-two weapons and about half that amount
if they go into full production.

By the end of June, 1969, the Mark 48 development program had involved twenty-five different companies under
contract with the Navy as well as forty-one non-contractor
activities directly or indirectly involved.   Estimated program
costs of the Mod 0 had increased from $682 million to about
$3.9 billion, an estimated growth of $3.2 billion.   Of this
increase, $245 million was in RDT&E and production proto-
types and $2.96 billion in total production costs. * Cost in-
creases in RDT&E generally represented effort not originally

---

*Not included in these figures are certain installation
costs, the magnitude of which could not be discovered.

anticipated when development began in 1964; reasons for the
increase in production costs have not been explained.

Mod 1 RDT&E costs in the June, 1969, Selected Acquisition
Report (SAR) were estimated at about $111 million, a $40
million increase over the original estimate. The GAO reported
that "the Navy's SAR does not adequately disclose reasons for
cost increases or include an estimate for Mod 1 production
costs in its current estimate of total cost." This lapse was
supposedly accountable to a failure to determine which version
of the Mark 48 (i. e. , Mod 1 or Mod 2) would be procured. But
it also may have been prompted by an expectation that the larger
Mod 1 would have even higher production costs.

The Navy claimed that $17 million of the $40 million cost
increase was for additional developments. The Mod 1 Project
Manager, however, said this $17 million represented estimated
costs for design and engineering services during the early
procurement phase. GAO analysis revealed that only $0. 5
million is for design and engineering services.

In its SAR of September 30, 1969, the Navy indicated that
it had reduced the cost growth of the Mark 48 Mod 0 to $2. 6
billion, instead of $3. 2 billion; however, the GAO noted a con-
comitant reduction in the total planned quantity to be procured.
The estimated cost overrun of the Mod 1 was at this time $62
million, an increase of $22 million over the June estimate, in
spite of a decrease in planned quantity of production prototypes
from sixty-five to thirty-six torpedoes.

The Navy had indicated that several "general factors" have
been involved in the increase of unit costs of the Mark 48:
(1) detailed changes in specifications, (2) increases in approved
rates of independent research and development, general and
administrative costs and fees, (3) unanticipated economic
inflation, and (4) greater sophistication than originally planned.

PROGRAM AND MISSION

Secretary Laird in his Defense Report of February, 1970,
stated the following:

The Navy plans to complete development, test, and
evaluation of all three versions of the Mark 48 torpedo; and then to choose one of the dual purpose
versions for procurement in quantity for the operational inventory. In the interim, the Navy proposes

to procure a limited number of Mark 48-0 and Mark
48-1 torpedoes to begin to meet urgent ASW requirements and to keep production lines in being until
evaluation of the Mods 1 and 2 has been completed
and the choice made between them, which the Navy
now expects will be in mid-1971.

The weapon the Mark 48 was designed to replace, the
Mark 37, was produced for use against "older" Soviet nuclear
powered and diesel electric submarines. Development on the
Mark 37 began in 1946; it was first produced in 1958. It is an
active/passive homing weapon with five versions, two of which
are wire guided. It is battery propelled, whereas the Mark 48
utilizes a liquid monopropellant fuel called OTTO. The Mark
37 has a range of twelve miles and a depth capability of 2,000
feet and can be fired from all submarines, with the exception
of a small number of the older diesel electric submarines
which cannot accommodate the wire-guided versions. Most of
the ships that use the Mark 37 will probably be converted to
use the Mark 48.

Anti-submarine warfare studies in the early 1960's disclosed that the conventional anti-submarine torpedoes and the
Mark 37 had unacceptably low effectiveness against hostile
submarines. The Navy was directed by the Department of
Defense to recommend a back-up program to expedite development of the new torpedo weapon system. By November of 1964,
the Chief of Naval Operations was calling for investigation of
the possibility of accelerating delivery to the fleet. In December of that year, Clevite and three other firms were awarded
contracts to assist Westinghouse in developing several critical
components.

The back-up program was approved by DOD in January,
1965, and additional contracts were awarded to several companies. In May, the Navy concluded that it was feasible to
provide the torpedo twenty-five months ahead of the original
date of November, 1969. In October, the Secretary of Defense
authorized program acceleration. The Navy was then expected
to go into production before technical evaluation was completed.
But as of June 30, 1969, no production contracts had been
awarded for Mod 0 quantities, with the exception of one contract
for fire control equipment.

In early 1967, a Naval review of the Mark 48 program
determined the need for an updated capability of the torpedo
against surface ships. Clevite was funded at $5.4 million for
research and development on the new test vehicle which

eventually became Mod. 1. Perhaps another motive for the
Clevite contract was Westinghouse's problems with the systems.
In addition to the cost overruns, the program was encountering
technical complications that delayed delivery of prototype hard-
ware for testing from August of 1967 to February of 1969.

This slippage has delayed the award of the first production
contract about two years beyond the original date of November,
1969. It was not until March 2, 1970 (a lag of over two years),
that a contract was signed with Westinghouse for procurement
of long lead-time items for a limited number of Mod 0 torpedoes, and the Navy has acknowledged that it will be several
years before the finished product will be deployed.

A report to the Secretary of the Navy resulting from a
review by the Chief of Naval Material placed the cause of delay on the type of contract (fixed-price-incentive). This contract, the Navy claims, precluded direct imposition of technical solutions upon the contractor. A comprehensive cost
analysis of the program by the Office of the Comptroller of the
Navy reached the same conclusion on the culpability for delay.

In October of 1967, a new Navy plan calling for continuation
of Mod 0, expansions of Mod 1, and development of an anti-
ship capability for the Westinghouse torpedo (later designated
as Mod 2) was approved by the Department of Defense.

In April of the following year, Mod 1 development was
initiated. Clevite's existing contract was modified for the
design, fabrication, and testing of twenty dual-purpose torpedoes. The cost of this development was then estimated at
about $45.8 million.

Schedule slippages with the Mod 1 so far have been much
less significant than those of Mod 0. By June of 1969, Clevite
had delivered four of twenty Mod 1 prototype torpedoes to be
tested. At that time, with most of the test vehicles yet to be
delivered, Clevite was awarded a contract for sixty-five production prototype torpedoes. No production prototypes had
been delivered by mid-1970; final delivery on the twenty prototypes was December, 1969.

CRITIQUE OF THE PROGRAM AND MISSION

Although some unanticipated costs may be understandable,
the astronomical increases in this program demand full investigation. The failure to anticipate inflation at all has no
legitimate excuse. The fact that a considerable portion of the

cost increase can be attributed to increases in the sophistication of the weapon raises the question of whether an adequate
basis was ever established for this weapon. For example,
in 1964, when the plans were given to Westinghouse, the Navy
was told they were unworkable because the torpedo itself generated so much noise the enemy submarine could not be detected. Additional contracts were let to alleviate the problem.
Moreover, it is difficult to understand why a torpedo designed
to dive in excess of 3, 000 feet with a range of twenty-five
miles needs much additional development to achieve the relatively simple anti-surface ship capability. The fact that the
Mod 1 has not only a larger warhead but also different homing
and propulsion systems would tend to support the view that the
additional development was not undertaken solely to adapt the
systems for surface attacks.

There is almost no unclassified discussion of the strategic
purposes of the Mark 48, but some possibilities are evident.
Inasmuch as it is designed primarily for use against "modern,
fast, deep-diving submarines" of a sort produced only in the
United States and the Soviet Union, one possibility is its employment to destroy Soviet ballistic-missile submarines. Although a first-strike move by the United States is contrary
both to our announced strategy and to the alleged defensive
purpose of the Mark 48, this possibility is not likely to be
overlooked by the Soviet Union.

The United States might also wish to destroy Soviet
ballistic-missile submarines in the unlikely contingency of a
nuclear exchange in which the Soviets did not use their entire
sea-based ballistic-missile force. Not knowing when the Soviet
Union would initiate such an attack, however, it would be
necessary to shadow every Soviet ballistic-missile submarine
on a twenty-four hour basis. This is not feasible.

A second use for Mark 48 might come in defense of U.S.
ballistic-missile submarines against a highly coordinated
Soviet effort to destroy them all simultaneously. To be effective as part of a first strike, such an attack would have to be
accompanied with attacks on bombers and land-based ICBMs.
But it is physically impossible to consummate simultaneous
attacks on all three elements, and virtually impossible to
achieve a successful simultaneous attack on the submarine
alone.

Beyond the difficulty of coordination is the ability of U.S.
missile subs to move so quietly that even our own ASW gear
cannot track them. Soviet submarines lag behind their
American counterparts, perhaps by more than a generation,

and they are even less able to carry out the necessary tracking
for a coordinated attack. Of course, it is very improbable that
the Soviets would attempt such an effort in the first place; for
if they were to miss just one ship, sixteen MIRVed weapons
targeted at the Soviet Union could be immediately unleashed.
In any event, if such a coordinated attack were attempted and
were to fail as all evidence suggests, deterrence could be
maintained. Unless it were Navy policy to destroy all submarines penetrating to within twenty-five miles of ours, a
successfully coordinated attack would provide no warning time
in which to employ the Mark 48.

There remains the possibility of a war of attrition to
destroy U.S. ballistic-missile-carrying submarines. It would
seem that only in this event would the Mark 48 actually be fired.
Such a scenario is highly improbable; for each "kill" the Soviets
attempt, they would risk provoking other retaliation.

There are a number of questions to be raised about the need
for the torpedo even within this highly improbable strategic
context. If the Soviet torpedoes have a range of less than twelve
miles, perhaps the Mark 37 is adequate for defensive weaponry
purposes. Also, given that U.S. Polaris/Poseidon-carrying
submarines have had a slow and silent capability for some time
now, could not the Soviets likewise soon develop a submarine-
quiet enough to elude the acoustical homing device of the Mark
48 and render it obsolete? The 1970 House Armed Services
Committee Report on the Military Appropriations Bill revealed
that Soviet submarines were appearing with silencing and
speed characteristics not expected until 1975.

These questions deserve an answer; they cannot be fully
treated here because of classification of relevant material.

RECOMMENDATIONS

1. The 1970 Defense Posture Statement indicated that the
Navy plans to complete RDT&E on all three versions of the
Mark 48 and then choose either Mod 1 or Mod 2 for procurement in quantity for the operational inventory, procuring in
the interim a limited number of Mod 0s and Mod 1s to meet
ASW requirements. This raises the question of why procure
any Mod 0s if the final choice is to be made between Mods 1
and 2? Or why waste any money on procurement and development of the inferior versions? The Navy should choose which
version to deploy before any further funds are authorized.

2. The current estimate for the total system cost is $2.57 billion for the Mod 0 and $185.4 million for the Mod 1. We recommend a cut in FY 1971 of $46.8 million for the Mod 0, a delay in the funding of $55.1 million for the Mod 1, and a delay in the funding of $8.7 million for conversion.

20

**S-3A
ANTI-SUBMARINE
PLANE**

The S-3A, formerly the VS-X, is an anti-submarine war-fare airplane that will operate from ASW aircraft carriers. There are four ASW carriers in service and each carrier would have approximately thirty-five S-3As.

The plane will carry a Sperry Rand computer, the Command Activated Sonobuoy System (CASS), the Low Light Level TV (LLLTV), and improved Magnetic Anomaly Detector (MAD), the AN/APS-116 front-viewing radar, the Carrier Airborne Inertial Navigation System (CAINS), Bullpup missiles, Mark 48 torpedoes, and mines. There is also speculation concerning the addition of forward-firing ordnance, a side-viewing radar, and a more advanced missile to take the place of the Bullpup.

The S-3A is scheduled to replace the S-2. The S-2 is a propeller-driven aircraft which has been in service over seventeen years. It is a good airplane; however, it cannot accommodate all the modern equipment the S-3A can carry.

The prime contract for the S-3A's airframe was awarded to the team of Lockheed/LTV/Sperry Rand. General Electric holds the engine contract. Lockheed's Burbank, California, division will be the site of final assembly.

The S-3A contract was awarded to Lockheed on August 2, 1969, well after the disclosure of cost overruns on the Lockheed C-5A and Cheyenne helicopter. Although the S-3A contract is written in such a way as to avoid cost overruns, it is curious that the ceiling for the program jumped from $2 billion, a figure mentioned repeatedly up to August 1, to $3.2

billion on the date the contract was awarded to Lockheed. Because Lockheed is also the prime contractor for the P-3C Orion, the S-3A contract gives it a monopoly of ASW aircraft.

The total systems cost of the S-3A, including RDT&E and procurement, but not including annual operating costs, is at least $2.9 billion. This does not include the operating cost of the carriers and their escorts. The Administration's request for FY 1971 was $207.8 million for R&D and $101.7 million for procurement. In 1969, no funds were allocated for procurement, and only $140.2 million was funded for R&D.

The original estimate for 193 planes was about $2 billion, or about $10 million a plane. The current estimate of $2.9 billion raises the per plane cost to $15 million.

S-3A PROGRAM JUSTIFICATION AND CRITIQUE

The S-3A is being developed to counter the Soviet's growing submarine threat. The Soviet Union now has more than 380 submarines, at least sixty-five of which are nuclear powered. This compares with the United States' 190 submarines, about half of which are nuclear powered. Eighty-eight of the Soviet submarines are armed with missiles; about eighty of these are armed with 300-mile cruise missiles. Only about four of the boats are even roughly equivalent to our Polaris ships. The Russians are currently producing seven Y class submarines per year, although Secretary Laird says they have the capability to produce twelve a year.

Until recently, most Soviet subs have been non-nuclear. Non-nuclear subs have to surface more frequently and can neither dive as deeply nor travel as far as nuclear subs. Thus, until recently, the threat has not existed on the present scale.

The S-3A is meant to counter the threat against our ships and coastal defenses posed by Soviet torpedoes and missiles. The S-3A is joined in its task by other naval forces such as destroyers and attack submarines, as well as by another aircraft, the P-3.

Even given an increased Soviet threat, however, the S-3A is redundant and expensive. The missions it is assigned can be carried out more efficiently and more cheaply by other elements of our ASW forces such as the P-3C and attack submarines.

S-3A and related investment and operating costs are so high that it would be 50 to 100 per cent more expensive to

provide equal area search capability using the S-3A than by
using additional copies of the P-3C, our land-based ASW aircraft.

Land-based ASW aircraft can cover 80 per cent of the
oceans' surface, and cargoes and naval forces in need of protection by such aircraft can be routed to areas where such
coverage is available.

The P-3C, for example, operates out of various bases in
the Pacific and Atlantic. At present, there are enough bases
available to cover nearly all of our convoy planes as well as
most of the approach paths of Soviet boats assigned to launch
missiles against the continental United States.

It also has to be remembered that the aircraft carriers
on which the S-3A would be based are highly vulnerable to
hostile submarine action which could put them and their S-3A
out of commission. In addition, the Navy's action of recent
years, reducing the number of ASW carriers in its inventory
from nine to four, is a tacit admission that these carriers and
their aircraft are not essential to counter the growing Soviet
submarine threat.

In order for the S-3A sensor system to be effective, the
aircraft's ability to navigate with respect to the sonobuoys,
which it drops in a pattern on the water, must be improved.
Difficulty in fixing aircraft position relative to these sonobuoys
results in distorted range and direction data. A further draw-
back of the S-3A is its limited night flying capability.

The development of the S-3A has been strongly resisted by
forces within the Department of Defense. Although the Navy
won out and Secretary McNamara ultimately gave the program
its go-ahead, he referred to it as very "marginal." Now, at
a time of much tighter defense budgets, its marginal benefits
are clearly not worth pressing.

The Navy is requesting $207.8 million of research and
development and $101.7 million of procurement funds in FY
1971 for the S-3A. This request should be challenged in that
the evidence available indicates that we have no need for this
new aircraft.

The most prudent course available would be to cut funds
for procurement and reduce the funds for research and development. However, inasmuch as the P-3C can handle the mission of the S-3A and the ASW carriers have yet to prove their
worth, it seems that even funding for research may be wasted.

RECOMMENDATIONS

1. The funds requested by the Navy in FY 1971 should be disapproved, the S-3A program canceled, and our existing ASW carriers phased down during the course of the next fiscal year.

2. The current estimated total RDT&E and procurement costs for the program are $2.9 billion. We recommend that the $309.5 million requested for FY 1971 be dropped entirely.

21

Despite an apparent intention to reduce American military manpower strength by over 400,000 between fiscal 1968 and a target date in fiscal 1971, the cost of maintaining more than 2.9 million men still will represent at least 15 per cent of the total defense budget. Potential savings from force reductions are being offset by higher pay scales and by increasing costs of support personnel.

The Viet-Nam buildup brought about a massive--and quick-- increase in American military manpower from around 2.7 million in 1965 to well over 3.5 million men in 1968. But the cost of manpower shot up even more rapidly--from $13.4 million in FY 1965 to over $21 billion in FY 1968.

The United States maintains one of the world's largest military organizations measured in both absolute and proportionate terms. The mid-1969 figure of nearly 3.5 million active U.S. forces, the world's biggest military personnel, comprises 1.5 per cent of the population, a percentage equaled, or topped, by only fourteen other nations.*

The figures in Table 14 are the latest available estimates and show active-duty military strengths of the United States, the Soviet Union, and Communist China in July, 1969.

American land forces total 1,824,000 and include the Army at 1,522,000 men and Marines numbering some 302,000. The

---

*Greece, Portugal, Bulgaria, Czechoslovakia, Albania, Cuba, North Korea, South Korea, Mongolia, North Viet-Nam, South Viet-Nam, Iraq, Israel, and Nationalist China (the highest).

TABLE 14

U.S., Soviet, and Chinese Military Manpower

Branch of Military	Country		
	United States	Soviet Union	Communist China
Army (mid-1970)	1,522,000[a]	2,000,000[b]	2,500,000[c]
Navy (mid-1969)	761,000	465,000	141,000
Air Force (mid-1969)	869,000	505,000	180,000
Other (mid-1969)	302,000[d]	330,000[e]	---
Total	3,454,000[f]	3,300,000[g]	2,821,000[g,h]

[a]About half are overseas.

[b]Only 400,000 are out of the country--in Eastern Europe.

[c]All are in China.

[d]Marine Corps

[e]Strategic Rocket Forces

[f]This figure is expected to be reduced to 3,161,000 by June 30, 1970, according to DOD estimates. This total would be composed of Army--1,363,000; Navy--694,000; Air Force--810,000; Marine Corps--294,000.

[g]Does not include "para-military" security forces and border guards.

[h]Increases during 1968 of up to 600,000 may have brought this total as high as 3,300,000, but no definite information is available.

Source: The Military Balance 1969-1970, (London: Institute for Strategic Studies, 1970).

National Guard and Army and Marine Reserves total 710,000.
The principal overseas deployments of American land forces
currently include the approximately 425,000 in Viet-Nam,
some 210,000 in West Germany and Berlin, approximately
55,000 in South Korea, and smaller contingents in other parts
of Europe, the Panama Canal Zone, Hawaii, and Okinawa. *

Some 100,000 combat troops, deployed in the continental
United States, are assigned to the Strategic Reserve and as
specific re-enforcement for Europe.

The remaining ground forces are deployed in the Army
Air Defense Command, seven Special Forces Groups, other
specialized units, the large support "tail" for combat available land forces, and some 230 Aviation Units operating nearly
11,000 aircraft, both overseas and in the United States.

By comparison, Soviet land forces number some two
million men, with about 400,000 deployed in Eastern Europe
and another 450,000 or 500,000 in the European U.S.S.R.
Various para-military organizations and reserves number
about 1,750,000 men. China's Army is estimated at approximately 2 1/2 million, deployed only in China, and para-military
militia estimated variously from 7 to 200 million. [1]

THE STATUTORY LIMIT THAT ISN'T THERE

The huge buildup of American military manpower is a
hard fact, yet all of it has been done in the face of statutory
constraints on the absolute size of U.S. forces. There are
now in the law comprehensive limitations on the total size of
the armed forces, as well as specific limitations on the sizes
of each of the individual services. These limitations, first
enacted in the Selective Service Act of 1948, were intended to
carry out Congress' responsibility to supervise and control
the size of the armed forces. The totals then enacted limited
the total size of U.S. active military forces to slightly over
two million men--in itself a higher number than ever before
sanctioned in peacetime.

In August of 1950, with international tensions increasing
and the shadow of Korea falling across the future, Congress
suspended the statutory ceilings on active military force levels
which had been enacted only two years before. The House
Armed Services Committee reassured the House at the time

---

*Figures taken as of mid-1970.

of this original suspension that "the subject will come actively
before the Committee again, of course . . . prior to July 9,
1951"[2] (the renewal date for the Selective Service Act). The
Committee also said, "The Committee reminds the House that,
in his message of July 19, 1950, the President specifically requested that the present ceilings on the Armed Forces be temporarily suspended."[3]

In 1951, however, the suspension of statutory ceilings did
not come before the Armed Services as automatically as anticipated. In fact, the original House-passed bill to extend the
Selective Service Act did not mention the statutory ceiling suspension at all. In the conference between House and Senate
managers, the 1950 suspension was renewed with only this
cryptic comment by way of justification: "The House and Senate
managers agreed to continue the present statutory limit on the
size of the Armed Forces, suspended until July 31, 1954."[4]

Despite the fact that continued suspension of statutory
military force ceilings received only cursory consideration by
the House and Senate Armed Services Committees, one new
provision was added to the 1950 act--an overall force level
limitation of five million. No mention of this new section was
made in either the House Report or the Conference Report.

Since 1951, the suspension of statutory ceilings has been
renewed by the Congress five times--in 1954, 1957, 1959, 1963,
and 1967. Despite the express Constitutional provision that no
appropriation for the armed forces would be for a period of
longer than two years (an indication that the Framers intended
at least biennial review for military force levels and commitments), the suspensions of statutory ceilings were for four
years each, beginning in 1959.

The justifications for continued suspensions in each year
they were approved were hardly illuminating. In 1954, the
House Armed Services Committee told the House, "It is obvious that the Armed Forces must be maintained at a strength
in excess of 2 million persons in the foreseeable future."[5]
In 1957, the need for continued suspension was also "obvious."[6]
In 1959, continued suspension of force ceilings was termed
"vital to the preservation of the American Way of life and to
our national security."[7] In 1963, the Committee told the
House that "it is clear that this section of the law must be extended" and that its enactment "is essential to our national
security."[8] In the 1967 extension of ceiling suspensions, the
House Armed Services Committee did not even offer a justification for the continuation. After describing the effect of the
statutory ceilings and noting that they were intended to apply

"in peacetime," the Committee said simply, "The ceilings
have been continuously suspended since the buildup of our
Armed Forces following the hostilities in Korea."[9]

POTENTIAL SAVINGS FROM
MANPOWER REDUCTIONS

American military manpower has fluctuated substantially
in recent years. But savings foreseen as a result of rather
large reductions have generally failed to materialize because
of inflation, pay increases, and other problems difficult to
appraise. Current DOD accounting methods create serious
difficulties in ascertaining potential savings from manpower
cuts.

An important step in estimating more accurately the cost
of various U.S. military deployments, both overseas and at
home, would be a comprehensive GAO study of military manpower, by rank--determining the total salaries paid and various
other fringe benefits and support costs accruing by grade. Such
a study could ascertain: (1) the total cost of various benefits
for dependents, (2) the cost of rental and construction of facilities, (3) the annual total transport costs, and (4) the costs of
forward-deployed equipment.

Such an accounting is badly needed, as DOD itself does not
keep records in this manner and must make cost estimates on
a geographical basis by various complicated factorings. Such
a study is clearly within the prerogatives of the Congress to
undertake and should be begun without delay.

One rough breakdown of potential manpower reductions and
the resultant savings has been done by the Congressional Quarterly[10] and is based upon extensive consultation with defense
experts both in and out of government. Its analysts found broad
agreement that the large "transient" category, those in transit
between assignments within the uniformed services, could be
the basis for substantial manpower reductions. Scrutinizing
manpower use in each service and eliminating the transient
category, they advocated a 10 per cent across-the-board cut
in support personnel, according to the following breakdown:

  1. Army: With a total manpower of some 1,550,000
  men, including 360,000 combat troops, 110,000 transients
  and 1,080,000 support personnel, the Army could cut a
  total of 218,000 troops at a rough annual saving of $2.2
  billion (using the crude average of $10,000 per man for
  total ascertainable annual support).

2. <u>Navy:</u> With a total manpower of 775,000, including 330,000 in combat units, 50,000 transients, and 395,000 support personnel, the Navy would cut some 90,000 men at a savings of some $900 million.

3. <u>Air Force:</u> The Air Force totals 900,000 men, with 270,000 in combat units, 5,000 in transit, and 625,000 in support. The <u>Congressional Quarterly</u> approach would decrease Air Force manpower by some 67,000, at a saving of $675 million.

4. <u>Marine Corps:</u> Currently numbering some 300,000, the Marine Corps contains 120,000 combat personnel, 25,000 transients, and 155,000 support personnel. The cut here would be some 40,000 men and save $400 million annually.

The total annual savings that could result, with no decrease in combat manpower (unless DOD chose to alter the mix) would be approximately $4.175 billion.

A possible European adjustment would enable still further retrenchment. For example, an agreement by the German Army to provide complete logistical support for an undiminished American combat force in the Federal Republic would permit an additional 95,000 American support troops to be brought back and demobilized, at a saving of nearly $1 billion annually. Such a support role is already well within the capabilities of the German Army.

The total decrease in U.S. military manpower would be on the order of half a million men. This would lower U.S. military manpower to just under three million, a level not much smaller than the 3.3 million Soviet armed forces.

Similar reductions could be pursued in other smaller U.S. military deployments at comparable savings. If South Korea were to be included, the total annual savings could amount to $5.5 billion.

Against such savings, it has been estimated that one must calculate such countervailing costs as a rise in retired pay and benefits as a result of demobilization and a conservatively estimated $1.5 billion per annum DOD pay increase.

The key to progress on this issue, however, lies in the effect of such recommendations and rough calculations in bringing into the open more accurate assessments of the costs and savings involved, and the reasons for and against such reduction

This analysis refers to manpower alone. It is not related even to conventional equipment of forces, for it does not address itself to combat elements. There is, however, substantial room for reductions even in combat forces, although this issue is far more a function of the U.S. Southeast Asian involvement.

CHANGING STRATEGIES AND
FORCE LEVEL PLANNING

Heretofore, military projections have been based upon the "2-1/2" war posture, which assumed that the United States might have to fight simultaneous conventional wars in Western Europe and Asia, and handle a minor contingency elsewhere. This planning basis has currently been revised downward to a "1-1/2" war level, creating the potential for substantial manpower cuts.

Among other, more costly implications of the move to a 1-1/2 war strategy is the increased need for long-range mobility. Consequently, any land force reductions that might accrue from the strategy switch may produce increased investment demands for sealift and airlift capabilities. The converse is also true; increased strategic and theater mobility permit a reduction in theater reserve forces.

All nations encounter serious difficulties in attempting to measure effectiveness or capability of land forces. For example, problems arise when land forces are cut in an effort to take advantage of the ostensibly greater deterrent effect of strategic nuclear forces. Land force reductions do not necessarily permit greater dependence on the nuclear deterrent.

The responsibility for determining the configuration and number of U.S. ground combat forces derives from Congressional powers (1) to raise, regulate, and support armies, (2) to relate force levels to national security goals, (3) to approve U.S. support commitments to other nations, and (4) to authorize deployment of land forces overseas.

As currently practiced, land forces are planned and raised according to an extended process, from force estimation through deployment.

"Force estimation" is a basic assessment of levels required to meet alternative military strategies drawn up by the Joint Chiefs of Staff and the services. This process relies heavily upon the threat projections contained in the Joint Intelligence Estimates for Planning prepared by the Defense Intelligency Agency, and it has been significantly affected by the switch to a 1-1/2 war concept. In addition, any re-examination of existing U.S. foreign commitments should have a major bearing. For example, if some of the post-World War II commitments or treaties were repealed, or vitiated by time and events, or modified, it should be possible to reduce land forces accordingly.

Alternative mixes of forces and weapons can be used to deter or defend against a given threat. Cost-effectiveness analysis of various mixes can well become a further economy in conventional force levels. Another key question concerns availability of units--whether they are stationed at home or abroad, are active or inactive. Annual operating costs of a reserve division run about 15 to 18 per cent below that of an active division, and the question of economy can usefully be balanced against lower levels of force readiness.

In a rough fashion, such considerations exemplify recent reviews of American military policy. Review documents themselves contain detailed examinations of alternative force levels and various budgetary impacts. Consideration of these analyses leads to the authorizations and appropriation requests given to Congress.

For the second step, after going over the reviews, the Secretary of Defense issues two further documents, a Strategic Guidance Memorandum and a Tentative Fiscal Guidance. The Secretary's decisions are combined in a series of publications done by the Joint Chiefs and the services. Together with the alternative level studies, these documents comprise the Joint Strategic Objectives Plan and cover the fiscal year starting one year from their publication.

These two steps take from October to June. Then the Secretary conducts a force apportionment review and makes budget guidelines for the fiscal year beginning one year later. From June to December, DOD concentrates on force development of the levels approved in the initial steps.

Decisions are related to current five-year defense programs at the strategic level, and program/budget aspects at the funding level. Budget figures are developed to correlate with the approved force decisions, and the five-year program is again altered to conform with any Congressional changes. From this point on, plans and proposals can begin to be turned into actual force management and employment--steps four and five.

The first four steps are planning stages. In the final step, DOD and the Joint Chiefs raise the forces, which are then deployed according to present and anticipated needs: (1) operations plans, i.e., strategies and tactics for dealing with existing situations--such as Viet-Nam and Southeast Asia; and (2) contingency plans for dealing with anticipated situations--such as a possible Egyptian invasion of Israel.

MANPOWER PROBLEM AREAS

Changing strategies and conditions affecting the size and shape of American military manpower also have substantial impact on other current manpower problem areas. This section concludes with analysis of eight of those areas. Action to alleviate these difficulties can aid transition to a volunteer system.

Draft Reform

Rapid and extensive draft reform is in order. The Nixon Administration proposals to modify the draft are steps in the right direction and could well serve as the basis for a more extensive Congressional program were further changes not forthcoming from the Administration.

The executive order eliminating occupational deferments and deferments for fathers serves to make the draft more equitable. The proposals to end college and apprenticeship deferments and to improve the lottery should be enacted by Congress. Eventually, all but a small number of hardship deferments, sole surviving sons, ROTC candidates, etc., could be eliminated. Alternate service for conscientious objectors, however, should be retained.

A thorough reorganization of the Selective Service System along the lines of the Marshall Commission Report is also necessary. Uniform national standards ought to be ensured and due process guaranteed. Loop-holes that may emerge in the lottery should likewise be eliminated.

According to military recommendations, eighteen- and nineteen-year-olds are preferable to older draftees. Furthermore, the high school graduate drafted before he begins college is disrupted least in his career patterns.

Military Pay

By law, DOD is required to undertake studies and report back to Congress in 1970 on a series of military pay recommendations. A complete review is ordered every four years, and although initial recommendations have been ready since 1967, they have yet to be submitted to Congress.

The first report--called the Hubbell Plan-- was approved by service chiefs but never got past the Secretary of Defense,

and was not sent to Congress. As expected, the Plan's impact
on a wartime defense budget was drastic, and, at last report,
it was still undergoing extensive study within the office of the
Secretary.

Even though President Nixon did not mention military pay
in his April 23, 1970, message, the need for pay reform is
urgent, and DOD should make recommendations to Congress
in the near future. Key areas of reform include:

1. Conversion of the antiquated pay system of basic pay
plus a myriad of allowances and fringe benefits into a salary
system.

2. At the same time, provision to ensure that military
personnel are paid as much as civil servants doing comparable
work.

3. Increased pay for lower enlisted ranks, counting cash
and kind, at least to earning level of peers outside the military.

Prepaid Medical Care

The military requirements for doctors could be reduced
by requiring dependents and retirees to use some form of pre-
paid medical care rather than requiring drafted doctors to
provide this service.

As in civilian facilities, military hospitals should be
managed by professional administrators. Instead, according
to one report, over 2,500 physicians in the military establishment manage, but do not practice, medicine.

According to a Pentagon survey, over 9,000 military doctor positions could be filled by civilian doctors under contract;
this would obviously decrease dependence upon the "doctor
draft."

Minimizing the use of conscripted doctors involuntarily
assigned to non-defense duties and using non-doctor profes-
sionals in administrative positions should improve the efficiency
of facilities and the quality of treatment available. Savings
should be on the order of $130 million annually.

Civilianization

Civilian-type jobs in non-combat units should be performed
by civil servants or contractors. Because of greater specialization and no necessity for frequent rotation, civilians would
probably be significantly more efficient in certain occupations

than military personnel and could therefore allow a cut in total
manpower. Studies repeatedly point to net savings in civilianizing military jobs. Under Secretary McNamara, 113,000
"military" jobs were civilianized, but the program stalled because Congress set a low ceiling on civilian manpower, while
the ceiling on military manpower remains far higher than existing requirements.

Government manpower experts estimate that if total armed
forces were cut to 2.1 million, it would still be possible to
civilianize 101,000 Navy, 130,000 Army, and 179,000 Air Force
military jobs, for a total of 410,000. This could lower the size
of the uniformed services to less than 1.7 million.

Congress should insist that detailed review be made of all
military jobs with an eye toward isolating those that can be
civilianized. Moreover, a detailed explanation should be de-
manded whenever positions are designated as not appropriate
for civilianizing. However, the question arises whether a large
civilian military bureaucracy is not perhaps as undesirable as
a large military one.

Greater Management Efficiency

The Defense Department accounting system known as
"Project Prime" (PP) should be fully implemented. PP calls
for application of a number of modern management techniques
to military units and would significantly improve the quality
of resource-management information available from installation
levels on up. At present, individual installations have ceilings
on civilian manpower, supplies, and military manpower, but
budgets are required only for the first two. Project Prime
would provide a commander with a military budget.

Such budgetary controls, however, need not be applied in
such a way as to deny a commander the flexibility necessary
in combat or in an emergency situation. Present budgetary
controls over military supplies might be taken as a model for
the controls created for manpower.

Strong incentives for efficient management of manpower
at the installation level must be created. Post commanders
should have to budget for troops, and military salaries should
be paid from that budget. Should assigned manpower be larger
than the budget calls for, reassignment should be requested.
Such awareness of dollar costs would contribute substantially
to more efficient management and use of manpower.

Training costs should be billed to operating commands,
and training commands should be made self-supporting through

these payments. Training for particular jobs should be con-
solidated under single managers, as suggested by the House
Appropriations Committee last year. Degree-holders educated
at government expense should be used in jobs requiring those
degrees. Combat training for Army soldiers who will not be
assigned to combat duty should be minimized; this is a vestige
of University Military Training costing $50 million annually.
As mentioned above, many of these jobs can be civilianized.

Modernization of Assignment and Promotion Policies

The flexibility to enter the services at the rank and pay
of the recruit's civilian competence, after suitable military
orientation, would be a substantial improvement.

When a military job is civilianized, it can be performed
by a new employee; until it is civilianized, regulations prevent
its being filled by anyone other than a soldier who has reached
a certain rank. Eventually, many jobs susceptible to lateral
entry should be civilianized.

To the maximum practical extent, military personnel
should be able to select training, assignments, jobs, and tour
lengths, especially when such choice would enhance specialization and length of service.

Promotions are often too highly centralized. Those who
are responsible for promotion only rarely have had personal
contact with those whom they promote. Within guidelines concerning minimum time in grade and quotas on rank, promotions
should be less centralized so that the quality of the work performed by the promotee will have a direct impact on the quality
of the organization commanded by the promoter.

Reassignments are also too highly centralized. A man who
desires to work in a specific command, or a commander who
desires to have a certain individual assigned to him, is usually
without formal means of doing so. Within guidelines setting,
among other things, minimum tour lengths, assignments should
be decentralized so that men may apply for the commands and
jobs in which they want to work and the commander can select
from among the applicants.

Separating rank from pay would enable pilots, nuclear
technicians, doctors, etc., to keep their traditional ranks
while receiving competitive salaries. The special bonuses
now paid such personnel could then be adjusted or eliminated.

Increasing separation of pay from rank will probably be
necessary in the 1970's and 1980's because at present, promotions to captain or Navy lieutenant or sergeant are made

within as little time as twenty-four months. The vast majority of career soldiers are never promoted beyond lieutenant colonel or platoon sergeant, which means that a majority of lower-ranking uniformed personnel can look forward to only one or two more promotions. What is more, in the case of officers, promotions to the grade of captain (0-3) are automatic; this means that in the entire course of a twenty-year military career, the average officer really "earns" only two promotions.

Retirement

Another vital area of concern is the increasing cost of retired pay. This is a direct result of the twenty-year retirement policy for all military personnel. This system is not the result of a coherent plan, but rather of a series of uncoordinated revisions in military personnel legislation.

According to one estimate, by the year 2000, the total number of retirees will be 1.6 million, with 2.8 million dependents, receiving $17.4 billion annually, not including fringe benefits. In the FY 1971 budget, retirement costs increased by $0.3 billion; the thirty-year cost will total approximately $260 billion.

This whole system must be analyzed and modified. The goals of redesigning retired pay should be: (1) to maximize the number of full careers the military can offer, (2) pay a full pension to those who serve a full career, (3) provide a partial pension after five or more years of service, (4) guarantee the right to "cash in" amounts contributed (in which case no pension would be payable), and (5) change the definition of "full career" from the present twenty years' service to a more equitable figure, such as that in the civil service.

Moreover, retirement pensions should include the value of fringe benefits--such as medical care--and, until the retirement system is reformed, costs of retirement should be charged to the services to present a more realistic picture of the costs of the services' policies.

Reserves

An area requiring fundamental re-examination is that of the reserve forces. Some of the more interesting proposals for reform involve making reserve positions analogous to part-time jobs, with regular hours; making reservists' active-duty

periods fewer and longer, such as one or two months annually,
as is done in the Soviet Union, Sweden, and Italy; establishing
permanent ties between reserve and active units, as in Israel,
Britain, France, and some U. S. Air Force units; and trans-
ferring active-duty personnel to the reserves to enhance their
possibilities for promotion and eventually allow them to retire,
while opening up slots in the active forces to younger men, as
is done in the Soviet Union.

Such measures increase the equity and competitiveness
of military salaries. The military today is overcentralized
and overbureaucratized, and under-uses the skills, ambitions,
and creativity of the young men who enter it. One result is
the decreasing percentage of junior military personnel who
decide to make the military a career. Only with substantial
reorganization of personnel and career management practices
will the armed services be attractive to the high-quality personnel needed to manage the huge defense budget efficiently and to
provide the streamlined military force which national security
requires. And only such reorganization can make possible an
orderly and economical transition to a volunteer force.

RECOMMENDATIONS

1. The Administration should submit to Congress an
annual manpower authorization request. This request should
specifically relate DOD requirements to the State Department
Foreign Policy Posture Statement. The magnitude and deployment of land forces should be justified in terms of U. S. foreign
policy goals and treaty obligations.

2. During termination of the Viet-Nam War, the armed
forces should be reduced by 800, 000 men--the manpower increase generated by the conflict. Additional cuts can be gradually made over several years, returning manpower levels to
the currently suspended statutory ceiling of 2. 3 million men
or less.

The shift to a 1-1/2 war planning base and elimination of
Viet-Nam mobilized forces could well permit a 15 or 20 per
cent reduction in land forces. Potential savings from such a
move might range from $4 to $8 billion.

3. The General Accounting Office should undertake a
comprehensive study of military manpower by rank, determining total salaries, fringe benefits, and support costs accruing
by grade.

4. An integrated manpower management program should
be created by DOD. Management by the separate services is
inefficient and redundant. Many jobs and managerial techniques
are the same throughout the military.

5. Congressional Armed Services Committees should
proceed with draft reform hearings focusing on the recommendations of the Gates Commission. At the same time, the
Committees should act to reform the Selective Service System
as part of a phased program leading to ultimate adoption of a
volunteer military. Initial reforms should include measures
to apply uniform standards, plug lottery loop-holes, rationalize
the drafting of physicians, and provide right to counsel.

Requirements for drafted doctors can be drastically reduced by requiring non-combatant military personnel and all
dependents and retirees to use some form of pre-paid medical
care rather than inducted doctors for non-military work.

6. DOD should present its pay reform recommendations
to Congress. A salary system with room and board should be
introduced, and present retirement provisions should be replaced. Retirement income available to military retirees
should be reduced during the years they could still work if they
were civil servants. Improvement and rationalization of pay
and retirement scales are important intermediate steps if a
transition to a volunteer military is to be efficiently accom-
plished.

7. DOD should continue its "civilianization" program,
which was abandoned during the Viet-Nam buildup. This program would create new civilian jobs, produce some budgetary
savings, and free some military personnel to return to civilian
life.

8. Project Prime, a modernized accounting system for
the entire defense establishment, should be implemented.
Congress should receive quarterly reports on operating costs
and efficiency.

9. All reserve units should be assigned mobilization missions or affiliated with active units. Training and preparation
of reserve units could then be integrated with active training.
In addition, Congress should require regular reserve forces
readiness indicators and reports on operating costs.

NOTES

1. Data in this section taken from The Military Balance
1969-1970 (London: Institute for Strategic Studies).

2. House Rep. 2719, 81st Cong., 2d Sess., p. 2 (1950).

3. Ibid.

4. House Rep. 535, 82d Cong., 1st Sess., p. 22 (1951).

5. House Rep. 1104, 83d Cong., 2d Sess., p. 1 (1954).

6. House Rep. 390, 85th Cong., 1st Sess., p. 2 (1957).

7. House Rep. 27, 86th Cong., 1st Sess., p. 10 (1959).

8. House Rep. 58, 88th Cong., 1st Sess., pp. 13, 14 (1963).

9. House Rep. 267, 90th Cong., 1st Sess., p. 38 (1967).

10. See Hearings before the Subcommittee on Economy in Government of the Joint Economic Committee, June, 1968, Part I, pp. 104-12.

22

There is currently a great deal of controversy in the
United States concerning American force levels in Europe.
This concern is related to the war in Viet-Nam and to the general questioning of American military activities which is caused
by that war.

The American force deployments in Europe have fluctuated
substantially in the past two decades, ranging from the Berlin
Crisis high to the current low of some 315,000, with 220,000
in Germany (see Table 15). Over the past eight years, there
has been a reduction of nearly 100,000 in American force
levels. But the basic assumptions underlying the presence of
a substantial U.S. conventional "war fighting" capability in
Europe and the current nature of the NATO relationship have
not been re-examined.

Widely accepted "revisionist" history indicates that there
has been a gross overestimate of Soviet power, if not Soviet
intentions, during the past twenty years. Yet American policy
continues to be based substantially upon some of the assumptions of the past.

A dispassionate and thorough official assessment of
American interests and capabilities in Europe is therefore
long overdue.

There are varying assessments of the balance of conventional forces in Europe, but most recent data indicate a rough
parity (see Table 16).

TABLE 15

U.S. Forces in North Atlantic Area

Location	Number
West Germany, including Berlin	228,000
Mediterranean, afloat and ashore	28,000
Britain	22,000
Turkey	10,000
Canada, Greenland, Iceland	10,000
Atlantic, afloat	20,000
Subtotal	318,000
Spain	10,000
Middle East and Africa	10,000
Total (excluding dependents)	338,000

Source: William W. Kaufman, The U.S. Contribution to NATO, unpublished paper, 1969.

THE CASE FOR LARGE-SCALE U.S. PRESENCE

Perhaps the best recent expression of the assumptions underlying this force deployment came from the Administration in a speech by then Under Secretary of State Elliot L. Richardson in Chicago on January 20, 1970:

> American conventional forces are . . . in Europe . . . to resist possible attack by Warsaw Pact formations. They are meant also to deter piecemeal aggression which an enemy might be tempted to conclude he could get away with if the only alternative to our capitulation were the unleashing of nuclear war. . . . The U.S. military presence in Europe . . . continues to be taken as tangible evidence of our commitment. . . . Any sudden or dramatic reduction would have unpleasant consequences. . . .
> 1. NATO's conventional defenses would be significantly weakened.
> 2. Other NATO members might be tempted to follow suit.
> 3. A less powerful NATO would be driven to nuclear weapons sooner.

TABLE 16

Conventional Forces in Europe:
NATO and the Warsaw Pact

Country	Total Military Forces	Army	Forces on Central Front[b]	Reserves & Para-military
NATO Countries[a]				
West Berlin	465,000	328,000	328,000	780,000
France	503,000	328,000	52,000	470,000
Britain	405,000	198,000	48,500	125,000
Italy	420,000	313,000	--	741,000
Portugal	182,000	148,000	--	515,000
Greece	159,000	110,000	--	223,000
Turkey	483,000	400,000	--	560,000
Netherlands	124,000	82,000	82,000	20,000
Belgium	102,400	78,000	78,000	13,000
Canada	98,300	37,300	5,400	26,000
Denmark	45,500	28,000	28,000	120,000
Luxembourg	560	560	560	350
Subtotal	2,987,360	2,050,860	622,460	3,593,350
U.S.	3,454,000	1,522,000[c]	200,000[d]	660,000
Total	6,441,360	3,572,860	822,460	4,253,350
The Warsaw Pact Countries				
Poland	275,000	185,000	185,000	45,000
Czechoslovakia	230,000	175,000	175,000	135,000
Rumania	193,000	170,000	--	110,000
Bulgaria	154,000	125,000	--	165,000
East Germany	137,000	90,000	90,000	427,000
Hungary	97,000	90,000	90,000	140,000
Subtotal	1,086,000	835,000	540,000	1,022,000
Soviet Union	3,300,000	2,000,000	400,000[e]	1,750,000
Total	4,386,000	2,835,000	940,000	2,772,000

[a]These include the total forces of the NATO countries, on the assumption that an attack upon them would invoke a response from all forces and not merely from those assigned formally to NATO--likewise for the Warsaw Pact.
[b]The Central Front is taken to include West Germany, Denmark, and the Benelux countries on the NATO side, and East Germany, Poland, Czechoslovakia, and Hungary on the Pact side.
[c]Airborne and airmobile forces are included with those on the Central Front, except for those based in the United States; this includes an airmobile division and regiment based in France and part of the French Strategic Reserve.
[d]There are an additional 100,000 or so American troops in Europe and surrounding areas.
[e]There are an additional 450,000 in the European U.S.S.R.

Source: Data taken from The Military Balance 1969-1970 (London: Institute for Strategic Studies).

   4.   Distinctly destabilizing effects on the European
        scene. [1]

Military consensus seems to be that current NATO deployment is somewhat weaker in conventional terms than the
Warsaw Pact, or, at best, is at the minimum force level
capable of a conventional resistance to the largest feasible
Pact attack.
     Conceding the basic assumptions concerning Soviet capa-
bilities and intentions underlying the current American/NATO
deployment in Europe, several points remain about which extensive inquiry is required.
     Given a current rough numerical parity between NATO and
the Warsaw Pact--leaving aside entirely the questions of relative effectiveness, firepower, support capability, etc.--the
traditional military rule of thumb that offense requires substantial superiority over defense (at a ratio of 3 or 4 to 1) may well
still apply.
     Another crucial variable is the presence in Europe of some
7,000 tactical nuclear weapons. These weapons are not irrele-
vant to conventional troop levels, despite arguments that they
should not have to be used in the event of a Warsaw Pact
aggression. Pursued to its logical conclusion, this argument
tends to assure the Pact that a relatively low-level aggression
will be met conventionally, thereby diminishing the deterrent
value of the tactical nuclear capability.
     A third important consideration concerns the impossibility
of hiding a mobilization adequate to move successfully against
Western Europe. The mobilization and training preceding the
Czech invasion were followed for many weeks in NATO headquarters. Nothing was done on NATO's part because the
maneuvers simply were not perceived as a threat to the West.
The truth of the situation is that NATO could very rapidly reinforce its forces in Central Europe in response to an
aggressive-appearing mobilization. One-shot mobilizations
are, in the long run, substantially cheaper than large standing
armies.
     Lastly, perhaps, Warsaw Pact effectiveness must be
examined with an eye to the composition and capabilities of
forces involved. The Bulgarian or Rumanian forces are not
as well equipped or well trained as the Soviet forces, nor are
the Czech or Hungarian forces as reliable. It is inconceivable
that Soviet planners do not assess such factors; it is misleading
for NATO or American planners to fail to do so.

DETERRENCE AND NATO POLICY

Deterrence is not a direct function of the deployed war
fighting capability of NATO.   Rather, it is an indirect and only
partial function.   The Soviet planner, contemplating aggression
in Western Europe, must perceive risks of an "escalatory
confrontation" with the United States as sufficiently small, and
the potential gains from aggression as sufficiently large, before he can act.

The risk of escalatory confrontation results not from the
size of forces so much as from their presence.   It is crucial,
furthermore, to realize that, in strategic planning, nuclear
war is assumed to be most probably a result of escalation from
lower conflict levels rather than a spontaneous occurrence.
This assumption may be shared by Soviet strategic planners.
If no aggression can be completed "bloodlessly" and quickly,
leaving NATO to face a fait accompli, then the risk of escalatory
confrontation is high.   This is the "trip-wire" notion.   Conceivable situations in Europe in which a Warsaw Pact aggression
could pose NATO with a fait accompli rank high in the primary
considerations that should determine NATO troop deployment.

The second part of any Soviet calculation of aggression in
Western Europe must be a feeling that potential gains would be
great.   A small piece of bordering territory--thinly inhabited
and unlikely to be defended--may be clearly insignificant; a
"significant" objective is unlikely to be attainable without substantial resistance.

To maximize deterrence, NATO forces must be so deployed
that any movement toward a worthwhile objective guarantees
substantial NATO resistance.   Ultimately, it is perception of
the risk, coupled with potential gains, which determines whether
or not aggressive action is taken.   Wise policy is to deploy
forces so that anywhere potential gains from an aggression are
great, risks of escalatory confrontation also are very high.
The level of response, then, need not be massive, as long as
its probability is sufficiently great.

Such calculations should underlie NATO military policy
and should be augmented by a thorough and dispassionate re-
reading of Soviet military and foreign policy history.

WESTERN EUROPEAN STABILITY
AND SOVIET INFLUENCE

A more compelling argument for maintenance of current force levels is that a substantial imbalance between NATO and Pact forces would give the Soviets leverage upon the foreign and perhaps even domestic policies of Western European nations. The Europeans might be forced to accommodate themselves to the Soviet presence on their borders, and the ties between Western Europe and the United States would be eroded.

It is important to ask certain questions of proponents of this theory. (1) In what sorts of situations could the Soviets gain significant leverage over Western Europe, and (2) what kinds of leverage and how much? With the exception of West Berlin, the possibilities for change inimical to American interests are probably small. (3) Under what conceivable circumstances could the Soviets pressure the West Germans, for example, into actions against German or American national interests? The Federal Republic is the fourth largest industrial nation in the world, and satisfactory trade relations with her are manifestly of increasing interest to both the Soviet Union and Eastern Europe. (4) What kinds of leverage could the Soviets bring to bear against France or Italy? Could they influence the electoral processes there in favor of the domestic communist parties?

Serious difficulties of this sort become probable only if the United States were to repudiate completely its commitment to Europe and withdraw all forces, and perhaps not even then, given Soviet and East European internal difficulties. As for the West Europeans having to make some modifications in their rhetoric and some of their policies toward the Soviet Union and Eastern Europe, this need not prove inimical to American interests unless future American policy so defines it. A more comfortable Soviet Union might very well worry less about liberalization in Czechoslovakia or Rumania.

All possible concessions should be sought from the Soviets before cutting American force levels. It is important to see what they would be willing to pay in exchange--perhaps a reduction in their force levels to the minimum required only to police the East Europeans. On the other hand, Soviet unwillingness to make such trade-offs is not sufficient cause, alone, to maintain current American force levels in Europe. This is likely to be the case, and it is probably an indication that the

Soviet Union is very seriously concerned about the implications
for control over Eastern Europe inherent in European force
reductions by both sides.

What sorts of reactions might American reductions cause
in Western Europe? Sudden and dramatic reductions would be
irresponsible, and could well unsettle things seriously. There
is no persuasive reason to think, however, that the well-planned
and orderly reduction of American forces, within the context of
a general consultative review in NATO of its role in European
defense, would substantially worsen the American relationship
to Western Europe or Western European internal relationships.

The Federal Republic of Germany is neither Finland nor
Austria in terms of geopolitics, size, or economics. It is unlikely that the European Economic Community (EEC) would be
hurt or Britain or other applicants kept out. On the contrary,
such an eventuality, if well planned, might well hasten European
integration rather than impede it, in response to the growing
significance of the Federal Republic in European affairs. In
short, a new status quo might soon find supporters in all the
camps.

Another point that might be made on this issue deals with
predictions that American reductions in NATO would probably
lead to similar actions by other NATO members. Although in
the extreme case of a total demobilization this might well be
unsettling, no one is proposing such measures. In the presence
of perhaps 100,000 American troops, it is highly unlikely that
NATO nations would as much as halve their forces or, under
certain circumstances--a credible multi-year commitment for
an American presence of some substance, for example--cut
them at all.

On the other hand, if consideration of American reductions
in troop levels in Europe were to lead to substantial reductions
on the part of other NATO members, the United States should
certainly re-examine the proposition that American interests
in Europe require actions which our allies--the purported
beneficiaries of those actions--are not interested in performing
for themselves.

Benefits accruing to the United States could include a substantial budgetary saving, as well as improve the balance of
payments. Both would, in turn, create effects beyond American
borders as well as in the reallocation of resources to pressing
domestic needs.

If the units brought back from Europe were not completely
demobilized, savings still could be made. As Congressman
Henry S. Reuss has pointed out on more than one occasion,

there is additional room for substantial savings in stream-lining and eliminating functional duplications. In terms of the balance of payments, troop cuts in Europe would be a healthy influence and would have significant international economic effects benefiting both American and, in the long run, the international economy as a whole.

It is unlikely that current levels and kinds of American influence in Europe could be maintained intact in the face of substantial troop withdrawals. Yet it is equally clear that no substantial political withdrawal is possible in the face of the historical ties between Europe and the United States, as well as the large and growing economic interdependence.

The beneficial results of a planned transfer of responsi-bility for European defense from American to European hands would be likely to include a rediscovery of vigor and initiative among Europeans as well as an increased cohesion and member-ship in EEC. Such potential benefits are good arguments for American troop reductions.

THE SOVIET PRESENCE

The reasons for the Soviet presence in such force in Eastern Europe are a rather complex mix of hard, pragmatic calculations with traditional, residual, and inertial concerns. Some of the essentials are, in order of importance:

1. The need to police the Eastern European satellites. (This function can, however, be served by troops on Soviet soil, and it is clearly in American interests to "assist" such a development.)

2. Inertia of the status quo. Military/bureaucratic establishments inevitably maintain and generate rationales for their existence and growth.

3. The competitive nature of the East-West and U.S.-Soviet relationships. It is likely that upon unilateral withdrawal of American forces from Europe, domestic economic pressure would start working for Soviet reductions in troops levels.

4. The view that the West does, in fact, constitute a military threat to the Soviet Union and to the Warsaw Pact, a view reinforced by John Foster Dulles' "roll-back" rhetoric and the current size of NATO forces.

Soviet goals in Europe are likely to include:

1. A desire to get Americans out--a mix of rational calculations of the balance of influence in Europe and fears

of a hostile capitalistic encirclement of the Soviet Union. Without American troops in Europe, the Soviet Union probably would have increased influence over Western European relations with its East European satellites, making inhibition of such "dangerous trends" as those in Czechoslovakia in 1968, and, later, in Rumania, somewhat easier for them.

At the same time, these trends might be perceived as less "dangerous" in light of a more relaxed military situation. No significant probability has been demonstrated that reductions in the U.S. presence would allow the Soviet Union to increase its influence in any way inimical to American interests or Western European freedoms. This apprehension, however, lies at the heart of the argument against modification of the American military posture in Europe.

2. Creation of conditions in Europe that would permit the Soviet Union to quietly cut its forces to police levels without a loss of control. This parallels the apparent American desire to maintain less influence in Europe while cutting back on troop levels and spending. Consequently, increasing domestic economic pressures coupled with favorable responses from NATO could well lead to substantial reductions of both Soviet and American troops in Europe over the next half decade or so.

3. Desires to gain benefits of easier trading relations with Western Europe and its technology while escaping the erosive effects, upon both Soviet society and the Warsaw Pact, of such increased contact. This is an attempt to get something for nothing and poses an insoluble dilemma for the Soviets as well as a primary source of instability in their behavior.

4. There is, no doubt, an element of expansionism in Soviet goals in Europe. The important question, however, concerns its relative priority for the Soviet leadership and their capacity to pursue it successfully.

AREAS OF CONCERN AND ALTERNATIVE COURSES OF ACTION

There appears to be an emerging consensus that the principal barriers to American troop reductions in the near future (mid-1971) are the potential resulting political problems in Western Europe and, currently, the possibility of upsetting the several rather delicate East-West negotiations under way (i.e., East-West German, Polish-West German, Soviet-West German, SALT, Four Power talks on Berlin). With reasonable

caution, however, such negotiations need not be hampered and
could well be helped by positive action on the part of the United
States.   A European Security Conference could prove useful.
If not, the dangers it poses, justifying American caution, need
to be more clearly delineated than they have been to date.
NATO/Warsaw Pact troop reduction talks could get under way
as a result of the U.S. initiative, even though chances of agreement are slim.

A number of hard questions to be asked of the Administration begin to emerge:

1.   What is the rationale for maintaining a rough conventional parity between the Warsaw Pact and NATO--

a.   in terms of maximum deterrence?   (A very
complicated question--the burden of proof and clarity should
rest with DOD.)

b.   in terms of a required ratio between the offense
and the defense?   (It has historically been 3:1 or greater; why
parity today?   Or is there not effective parity?)

c.   how small NATO conventional forces could be (in
light of a conservative but reasonable assessment of the Soviet
capabilities) and still do the same military/deterrence job?

2.   What is the rationale for the U.S. level of effort in
the face of unwillingness of nearly all other members to carry
a greater share of their own defense burden?   Is it that they
do not see the same threat that the United States does?

3.   What precisely could occur politically in Western
Europe as a result of the reduction of American forces?   Is it
sufficiently costly and probable to prevent our doing so?   How
can we prevent it?

4.   What do we want in Europe?   From NATO?   How do we
get NATO to do it, and how can it be done most economically?

5.   What is the significance, in terms of deterrence to
Soviet aggression, of the British Polaris submarines (four,
carrying some sixty-four missiles), of the French deployment
of twenty-seven MRBMs currently under way, and of the
British and French air forces (some ninety bombers), most of
which are adapted to low-level penetration and mounting several air-to-ground missiles or some half-dozen bombs each?
The total number of deliverable warheads is presently at least
500 and will grow to over 600 with a significant improvement
in their invulnerability over the next several years.

6.   What implications do assessments of contemporary
Soviet domestic economics have with regard to potentially
aggressive postures?   In the same vein, what are the implications of emerging economic relationships with Western Europe,

the degree of unity and cohesion within the Warsaw Pact, and
the possibilities of "pacifying" any large part of Western
Europe should the Soviets seek to capture it?

The alternatives for American action can be envisioned
in terms of roughly six distinct categories:

1. Increased American military presence.
2. Maintenance of present force levels and organization.
3. Limited, mutual, balanced reduction; limited reorganization, if any.
4. Limited unilateral reductions--in the event that mutual
reductions are not agreed upon (and this is a very distinct
possibility). Carefully done, with full consultation with
Europeans, substantial streamlining, NATO reorganization,
etc. Perhaps to under 100,000 American troops, over three
or four years, with a long-run commitment to whatever final
figure is chosen.
5. Immediate cut in U.S. forces to 100,000 (mid-1970)
without other actions--in the event of strong Congressional
action or strong resistance to change in Europe.
6. Immediate, unilateral, and total withdrawal.
It is probably clear from the preceding discussion that
options 1 and 2, increasing or maintaining present levels, have
been ruled out. Option 4, a gradual consultative reduction,
would appear the most desirable path even without the danger
of 5 being imposed by Congress in the absence of change by
the Administration.
Maintenance of present levels, in fact, is probably not
feasible in the longer run except in the unlikely event of a
major Soviet-instigated rise in tensions in Europe. Otherwise,
rising domestic difficulties in the United States are likely to
bring some increase in pressures for withdrawal and the reallocation of resources this implies. Even a repeat in Rumania
of the Soviet behavior in Czechoslovakia, for example, would
be unlikely to forestall such pressures from Congress just as
the Czech invasion itself did not.
Reciprocal reductions are as unlikely as maintenance of
the status quo. It is highly unlikely that significant progress
can be made while the Soviet Union fears any action that might
loosen its control over Eastern Europe. Additionally, there
are large technical difficulties involved in negotiating the
balance in any mutual withdrawal plan. The resulting drawn-
out and fruitless negotiations are unlikely to forestall domestic
pressures to reduce force levels for very long.
The United States is probably left with a situation in which
what is subject to choice is the "when" and "how" of force

reductions. Under such circumstances, the powerful arguments are on the side of reasonable prudence, full consultation,
and consideration of all possible trade-offs. Without substantial guarantees, West Berlin ought not be included in such
modifications.

RECOMMENDATIONS

1.   Limited reductions could be made in U.S. forces in
Europe, perhaps to under 100,000 men over three or four
years. Both the size and timing of the reduction, however,
should be determined through a process of full consultation
with Europeans as part of a program of streamlining and reorganization of NATO. Large manpower reductions are possible without change in the U.S. combat contribution if the
Europeans could assume a greater role in logistical support.
The withdrawals ideally would be coupled with a multi-year
commitment of U.S. forces at the lower manpower level. A
reduction of 100,000 would, at minimum, save approximately
$1 billion in budgetary outlays annually. Coupled with sub-
stantial streamlining and consolidation of headquarters, the
budgetary savings could be much larger.
2.   Transfer of Supreme Allied Commander Europe
(SACEUR) to the Europeans and substantial reorganization of
NATO to coincide with the increased role of Europeans in their
own defense.

NOTES

1.   Elliot L. Richardson, Speech before the Chicago
Council on Foreign Relations, January 20, 1970, Sheridan-
Blackstone Hotel, Chicago, Illinois.

23

**LAND
FORCES IN
ASIA**

Even beyond the American forces fighting in various parts of Indochina, the U.S. commitment in all of Asia is substantial. Aside from the over 450,000 troops in Viet-Nam, Laos, Cambodia, and Thailand, the Pacific fleet carries approximately 390,000 men, and there are support and other forces in large numbers in Japan, Korea, Okinawa, Taiwan, and the Philippines.

The key question focusing on the factors responsible for this massive presence is relatively simple: What is the vital interest of the United States in the Pacific Basin?

Unless vital interest is at stake, the United States should be extremely careful before undertaking further interventions. That condition should be maintained even when interventions involve only military aid, equipment, and training.

The final clause of the Nixon Doctrine expounded at Guam deserves close examination. The President stated that "we shall look to the nation directly threatened to assume the primary responsibility of providing the manpower for its defense."[1] The catch phrase is "primary responsibility." The history of American involvement with Viet-Nam began largely under similar conditions.

Hopefully, in Southeast Asia and the Pacific Basin, American defense commitments can be safely reduced by a careful application of the Nixon Doctrine--mainly by limiting its utilization strictly to areas where U.S. vital security interests are immediately and primarily at stake.

There is not room in this overall analysis for a detailed study of current American troop allocations and the potential

for future reductions in those levels in each Asian country.
Instead, as a case in point, we will examine just one contro-
versial nation--Korea. It should be recognized that the analysis
of the Korean situation is done under the unique conditions of
that country but is not uncharacteristic of general manpower
problems applicable world-wide.

DESCRIPTION OF U.S. COMMITMENT
IN SOUTH KOREA

    South Korea provides an excellent example of an Asian
nation in which President Nixon's Guam Doctrine could be immediately implemented.

    Some 55,000 U.S. troops were stationed in Korea during
1970, principally organized into two divisions. At least one
of these U.S. divisions could be withdrawn, saving $250 mil-
lion, without significantly weakening either the defenses of
South Korea or the ability to deter a possible attack on the
South from North Korea or China.

    First, South Korea today, without the assistance of any
U.S. ground forces, possesses the military manpower and
resources to handle any invasion threat North Korea could
pose in the foreseeable future, providing U.S. air support is
continued.

    The South has a population of 31 million compared to a
population in the North of only 13 million. In 1968, the most
recent year for which data is available, South Korea recorded
a gross national product of $5.2 billion; the North Korean GNP
was only $2.8 billion. Based on a projection of current growth
rates, this disparity in the economic capacity of the two Koreas
will increase in the decade ahead.

    In 1969, the South Korean economy grew at 13 per cent,
more than three times the growth rate of the U.S. economy.
At the same time, available evidence suggests that the North
Korean economy is stagnating. When General Earle G.
Wheeler, Chairman of the Joint Chiefs of Staff, was asked by
a House Appropriations Subcommittee in June, 1969, to compare the two Korean economies, he replied, "As you know,
the South Korean economy has burgeoned over the past several
years. On the contrary, the North Korean economy is prac-
tically dead."

    This economic superiority of the South is increasingly
being reflected in the military balance sheet for the two Koreas.

South Korea now boasts a total armed force of 620,000 men--
the third largest army in the non-communist world. North
Korea, on the other hand, has total armed forces of about
384,000 men.

Of greater long-term military significance is the fact that
the South supports this larger force with a defense budget that
consumes only 6 per cent of its GNP. By contrast, the North
Koreans must devote 25 per cent of their smaller GNP to field
a force which is only 60 per cent as large as that of the South.
In other words, if necessary, the South could expand its own
forces considerably without assuming the relative economic
burden the North has already incurred.

Therefore, given the greater size, growth rate, and
industrial capacity of the South Korean economy, and the current advantage the South holds over the North with respect to
military manpower, there is every reason to believe the government in Seoul currently can defend its borders against a North
Korean attack without the assistance of U.S. ground forces.

Certainly, the South possesses the military personnel to
fill with existing Republic of Korea forces any gaps the removal
of one U.S. division might create. And given the excellent
training and fighting ability of the South Korean troops, the
Americans could be replaced without any significant sacrifice
in combat effectiveness--particularly if some American weapons
assistance were to be maintained.

If Seoul is reluctant to draw on South Korean forces currently deployed in Korea to replace departing American troops,
it has several other options. There were 2 1/3 South Korean
divisions--50,000 men--stationed in Viet-Nam in 1970. Just
as Vietnamization is expected to permit the total withdrawal
of U.S. ground forces from Viet-Nam in the coming year, this
policy should permit the withdrawal of South Korean troops.
One of these 2 1/3 crack divisions could be used to assume
the positions of a departing American division in Korea. Additionally, if really necessary, South Korea has the economic
resources and manpower pool to create and equip one new
division. Of the 305,373 men eligible for the South Korean
draft in 1969, only 180,000, or 58 per cent, were inducted.

North Korea has been able to meet its armed forces
needs with a much smaller manpower potential than the South
and without recourse to Chinese or Soviet troops. It appears
probable that the South, with its economic and manpower superiority, could do likewise in the face of a decreasing American
troop commitment.

It should be noted here that North Korea does enjoy marked

air superiority over the South.   Therefore, any American troop
withdrawals from Korea at this time should not include a reduction in U. S. tactical air power in the Pacific.

An effective defense against a massive Chinese invasion--
a highly unlikely event given the risks Peking would run of
nuclear war with the United States--would require a far larger
U. S. force than is currently deployed in Korea.

In summary, the size of the American troop deployment
in South Korea can be modified within rather wide limits without changing the role or the effectiveness of the American
presence. It is important to point out that this role does not
include a conventional capability against a massive Chinese-
North Korean attack.

THE STRATEGIC ROLE

The withdrawal of one U. S. division from Korea would
not diminish the deterrent to a North Korean or Chinese attack provided by America's commitment to defend South Korea
from external aggression.

U. S. ground troops in South Korea are not essential to the
actual conventional defense of that nation; they could be replaced by South Korean forces with no significant decrease of
South Korea's defense capability. If there is a case to be made
for the continued deployment of U. S. troops in Korea, it is in
terms of their role as a deterrent.

There is no question that the stationing of U. S. ground
forces in South Korea is a very direct way of warning Pyong-
yang and Peking that an attack on South Korea necessarily
means war with the United States. However, one U. S. division
can convey the U. S. commitment as effectively as two; the
function the American deployment serves is to demonstrate
the high probability of U. S. involvement in any attack against
South Korea.

The presence of U. S. troops in South Korea has not been
the only basis of our deterrent since the United States-Republic
of Korea Mutual Defense Treaty was signed in 1953.   Article
III of that treaty commits the United States to take appropriate
action if South Korea is the victim of an "armed attack. " In
addition, the United States has a commitment under the United
Nations to defend South Korea from an attack by North Korea
or China. In August of 1953, after the armistice concluding
the Korean War was signed, the sixteen nations that had fur-
nished military forces to the U. N. command during the war

issued a statement pledging themselves to renew the war if communist aggression recurred.

Another factor serving to reinforce the credibility of the U.S. commitment as a deterrent to an attack on South Korea-- the ability of the U.S. tactical air force in the Pacific to strike North Korea--would in no way be diminished by the withdrawal of ground troops.

American sealift and airlift capability, sizable in the past and steadily increasing, is an additional factor, permitting a gradual decrease in the number of American ground troops based overseas.

In 1969, the United States airlifted a sizable force of combat-ready troops from North Carolina to South Korea in thirty-one hours. This capability, coupled with the growing capacity of surveillance and intelligence to detect large troop movements, preserves a conventional deterrent even in the face of substantial decrease in an overseas conventional presence.

A surprise attack such as that launched by the Chinese in 1950 in the mountainous terrain of North Korea would not be possible today, for the demilitarization zone dividing the Koreas does not afford adequate cover. Any large concentration of Chinese troops would be spotted well in advance of an invasion of the South.

In short, the facts strongly suggest that the continued presence of both U.S. ground divisions on Korean soil is not a prerequisite to the preservation of a credible U.S. deterrent to a major enemy attack on South Korea.

STRATEGIC RISKS

The present deployment of one American division on the front line in South Korea entails dangerous and unnecessary risks and costs to the United States.

The U.S.-South Korean security treaty stipulates that the manner in which the United States fulfills its commitment must be determined "in accordance with U.S. constitutional purposes." In other words, the President and the Congress retain the power to determine the form of U.S. action in response to a threat to the security of South Korea or any other nation with which we have a reciprocal defense agreement.

This American determination of the nature and magnitude of a response to a threat is endangered in South Korea. By stationing an American division on the front line in Korea,

the power to decide how the United States will fulfill its treaty
obligations has been effectively removed from Washington and
shifted to Seoul and Pyong-yang. The one U.S. division now
positioned along the demilitarized zone--the other is held back
in reserve--serves as a "trip-wire"; that is, it operates as
a deterrent by ensuring that any North Korean invasion of the
South will necessarily involve U.S. troops.

Given Korean geography, it is the American presence itself which is essential to deterrence, and the deployment of
the forces is not as important.

Furthermore, the employment of this division as a trip-
wire vitiates the critical "constitutional processes" clause in
our mutual defense treaty with Seoul, for should the North
Koreans invade across the demilitarized zone, our front-line
division would automatically trigger U.S. participation in a
ground war in Korea.

A more serious potential problem is the situation that
would arise should the aggression be initiated by South Korea.
The United States-Republic of Korea Mutual Defense Treaty
of 1953 contains an understanding, insisted upon by the U.S.
Senate, that releases the United States from any obligation to
aid South Korea in an attack against the North.

The presence of an American division in the demilitarized
zone, however, renders that understanding meaningless. For
the North Korean reaction to an attack from the South would
necessarily subject those U.S. troops to enemy fire; fired
against, they would be forced to defend themselves. The President and the Congress would then be under great pressure to
send additional troops and materials to help defend the involved
American forces.

COSTS INVOLVED

In addition, the maintenance of U.S. troops along what is
generally considered the most vulnerable and dangerous
eighteen-mile stretch of the demilitarized zone is being paid
for at the cost of American blood as well as dollars. These
troops, along with those in Viet-Nam and Laos, are the only
American military personnel in the world today judged in
sufficient danger to warrant combat pay. During the last two
years for which figures are available, 1967-68, thirty-one
American soldiers have been killed and 118 wounded by enemy
fire in Korea.

Seventeen years have elapsed since the Korean armistice
was signed. The United States has invested $8 billion in South
Korea over that period to build a vigorous economy and an effective armed force in that nation. Based on the evidence,
this effort has been a success.

Replacing one U.S. division in Korea with a South Korean
division from Viet-Nam would result in a substantial budgetary
savings for the United States if the withdrawn American division
were demobilized.

Conservative estimates of the annual price tag for American military presence in Korea put the amount at somewhat in
excess of $1.1 billion. Of this sum, roughly half--or about
$500 million--is directly related to the maintenance of the two
Army divisions.

It has been calculated that it costs only about one tenth as
much to keep a South Korean division in the field in Korea as
it costs to keep one U.S. division in Korea. This differential
is the result of higher U.S. salaries, a higher U.S. standard
of living, and the transportation costs of shipping U.S. forces
across the Pacific and back.

Therefore, replacing one American division--even if the
United States were to finance the latter--promises savings of
approximately $200 to $300 million a year and would also ease
the balance-of-payments problem. According to the Department of Defense, the United States incurred a balance-of-payments deficit of $269 million last year as the result of our
military presence in Korea. By way of contrast, Seoul has
been running surpluses in its foreign-exchange account in
recent years.

THE REPUBLIC OF KOREA:
READY TO STAND ALONE

Most importantly, the Republic of Korea has come of age
as a nation.

Its government is stable and appears to have the support
of the South Korean people. There is little question of their
will to defend themselves against an attack from North Korea.
Its Army is large and well trained. It appears quite capable
of dealing with any invasion threat North Korea can pose.

In 1953, the United States set out to provide the security
shield, resources, and know-how to enable South Korea to
become an economically and militarily self-sufficient nation.

This was the goal of all U.S. economic and military assistance over the past seventeen years.

As a result of $8 billion in U.S. aid and its own resourcefulness, South Korea today boasts one of the most vigorous economies in the world with a rapidly expanding base.

When a nation has reached that stage, it is hardly in American interests to serve as an obstacle to the expression of its full self-reliance. A lingering U.S. presence in South Korea can only be viewed, ultimately, by the Korean people as paternalistic.

The most widely stated objection to the removal of any U.S. troops from Korea at this time revolves around the question of nuclear weapons. The United States reportedly keeps nuclear weapons in South Korea to deter a combined Chinese-North Korean attack and possibly to defend against such an attack should deterrence fail.

Opponents of a troop withdrawal in Korea have argued that U.S. troops in adequate strength are needed to guard these nuclear weapons. Even the removal of one of the two U.S. divisions stationed there, it is contended, would leave these weapons vulnerable to North Korean seizure.

If the nuclear weapons in question are strategic, they can certainly be withdrawn from Korea with no diminution in U.S. strategic capabilities. There appears to be no compelling military reason for strategic weapons to be stored forward in Asia.

Tactical nuclear weapons present an entirely different set of variables. Putting aside for the purposes of argument the question of whether it is really possible to fight a limited nuclear war, the proponents of a U.S. tactical nuclear force readily concede that it makes sense to use this force only in certain situations.

If South Korean forces were either driving back an invading army or holding their own, the introduction of tactical nuclear weapons would clearly involve unjustifiable risks of widening the conflict and possibly triggering World War III. Presumably, the only situation in which the use of these weapons would be considered is one in which enemy troops were threatening to quickly overrun all of South Korea.

But a force of sufficient size and concentration to overrun South Korea, given the present strength of its ground forces, would certainly be detected by U.S. surveillance systems well in advance of the actual invasion. If such an invasion threat were to arise, tactical nuclear weapons could be brought forward along with additional conventional forces.

Could this be done rapidly enough? In June of 1950, it took North Korean forces with a troop superiority of roughly 2:1 three full days to reach Seoul, only sixty miles south of the demilitarized zone--and a long way from taking all of South Korea. And today, the manpower advantage belongs to the South Korean Army.

In short, Peking and Pyong-yang are aware that the United States can introduce tactical nuclear weapons into Korea very quickly. Pre-positioning these weapons is neither necessary for deterrence nor for their use in the defense of South Korea.

The other argument frequently offered in opposition to the withdrawal of U.S. troops rests on the contention that the United States pledged to maintain present troop levels in Korea as long as South Korean forces remained in Viet-Nam. However, according to Secretary of Defense Laird, no such agreement between Seoul and Washington was ever concluded.

RECOMMENDATIONS

1. The United States can withdraw one division (20,000 men) rather quickly. This can result in savings of some $200 million. Further reductions could also be negotiated in the land forces deployed in South Korea. This should not as yet include reduction in American tactical air support.

2. The United States should withdraw all nuclear weapons from South Korea.

3. The Nixon "Guam Doctrine" should be outlined in terms of troop commitments and contingencies for the Pacific Basin.

NOTES

1. Richard M. Nixon, Top O the Mar, Guam, July 26, 1969.

STATISTICAL APPENDIX
SUMMARY AND
BREAKDOWN OF MCPL
RECOMMENDATIONS FOR
FY 1971 MILITARY BUDGETS

Suggested Reductions in FY 1971 Military Budget

Budget Item	Suggested Reductions (in millions of dollars)	Current Estimate of Total Program* (in billions of dollars)
Strategic		
ABM	404-1,450	12
MM III MIRV	686	5.4
B-1	100	9.4
C-5A	200	5.3
Superhardening	77	6.0
Subtotal	1,467-2,513	38.1
Tactical Forces		
F-14	658.0	8.3
F-15	185.0	7.4
HARRIER	118.3	-
F-111A	515.1	9.2
MBT-70	77.0	8.0
Subtotal	1,553.4	32.9
Naval Forces		
CVAN-70	152.0	0.64
DD-963	100.0	3.35
Mark 48	46.8	3.57
	55.1, 8.7 delay	
DLGN-38	221.3	4.9
SSN-688	237.5	4.3
S-3A	309.5	2.9
Subtotal	1,130.9	19.66
Military Manpower		
General	15-20% overall reduction in land forces	4.0-8.0
Europe	100,000-man cut over 3-4 years ($1 billion minimum)	1.0 per year
Korea	20,000 men ($200 million)	0.20 per year
Subtotal		5.2-9.2
Total	4,351-5,397 (excluding manpower)	95.86-99.86

*Estimates of total program costs are tenuous at best. Existing data are not projected for equal time periods (cost of amortization), are unreliable due to cost overruns, and often do not include operation and maintenance costs. The data selected here usually reflect the lowest estimates available.

APPENDIX TABLE 2

Administration Requests and House Authorizations on Strategic Forces, FY 1971
(in millions of dollars)

Program	Description	Administration Request		House Authorization		Current Estimate Total Program	Proposed Program Action
		R&D	Procurement	R&D	Procurement		
Poseidon	submarine conversion & missile	122.7	921.6	122.7	371.1 (conversion of Polaris boats to Poseidon configuration) 550.5 (for missiles and other items)	5,555.2	continue, but not speed up
Minuteman III	strategic missile	211	475.7	slightly less than 211	475.7	5,375.8	cut 686
AMSA (B-1)	strategic bomber	100	0	100.2	0	9,377.0	cut 100
ULMS	submarine & strategic missile system	44	0	44	0	n.a.	low profile, no cut
Safeguard ABM	ABM system	365	660.4	365	661	12,000	range from 404-1,450
C-5A	transport	--	610.6		544.4 includes 200 contingency fund	at least 5,300.9	cut 200 contingency fund

APPENDIX TABLE 3

Administration Requests and House Authorizations for Tactical Aircraft, FY 1971

(in millions of dollars)

Program	Description	Administration Request		House Authorization		Current Estimate Total Program	Proposed Program Action
		R&D	Procurement	R&D	Procurement		
F-14	tactical fighter	274.0	658.0	324.2	658.0	8,279.1	cut 658 until DOD-GAO review of complete flight test program; retain full R&D.
F-15	air superiority fighter	370.0	0	370.0	0	7,355.2	cut R&D 370 total by half, to 185
A-X	counter-insurgency aircraft	27.9	0	27.9	0	in concept formulation	authorize full R&D request
F-111A	long-range fighter	48.2	515.1	48.2	515.1	6,380.8	cut all procurement 515.1; continue full R&D
A-7E	light bomber	0	252.9	0	133.0	1,397.5	defer procurement pending NSC review
HARRIER	British-made fighter	0	118.3	0	118.3	n.a.	delete pending Marine Corps-GAO review of complete flight testing

239

APPENDIX TABLE 4

Administration Requests and House Authorizations for Naval Forces, FY 1971
(in millions of dollars)

Program	Description	Administration Request		House Authorization		Current Estimate Total Program	Proposed Program Action
		R&D	Procurement	R&D	Procurement		
CVAN-70	nuclear carrier	0	152.0	0	152.0	640	cut 152.0
DD-963	anti-sub destroyer	0	459.5	0	506.8	3,350	cut 100.0
DLGN-38	nuclear missile frigate	0	221.3	0	213.8	4,875.4	cut 221.3
SSN-688	attack submarine	0	475.5	0	498.0	4,279.7	cut 237.5; shift 238.0 to R&D
Mark 48	anti-sub & ship torpedo	36.3	110.6	36.3	n.a.	Mod 0 3,570 Mod 1 185.4	cut 46.8 proc. Mod 0; delay 55.1 for Mod 1 and 8.7 for conversion of Mod 0 to Mod 2 pending justification
S-3A	anti-sub plane	207.8	101.7	207.8	101.7	2,931.7	cut 309.5

BIBLIOGRAPHY

BOOKS

Bator, Francis M. The Question of Government Spending.
New York: Harper, 1960.

Benoit, Emile (ed.). Disarmament and the Economy. New
York: Harper & Row, 1963.

Blackstock, Paul W. The Strategy of Subversion. Chicago:
Quadrangle Books, 1964.

Galbraith, John Kenneth. The Affluent Society. Boston:
Houghton Mifflin, 1969.

_____. A Theory of Price Control. Cambridge, Mass.:
Harvard University Press, 1952.

Harris, William R. Intelligence and National Security.
Cambridge, Mass.: Cambridge Press, 1968.

Hitch, Charles Johnston, and McKean, Roland N. Economics
of Defense in the Nuclear Age. Cambridge, Mass.:
Harvard University Press, 1960.

Jane's All the World's Aircraft, 1968-1969.

Kent, Sherman. Strategic Intelligence for American World
Policy. Princeton, N.J.: Princeton University Press,
1966.

Kim, Joung Hum. The Central Intelligence Agency: Problems
of Secrecy in a Democracy. Lexington, Mass.: Heath,
1968.

Kirkpatrick, Lyman B. The Real CIA. New York: Macmillan,
1968.

Knorr, Hans. Foreign Intelligence and the Social Sciences.
Princeton, N.J.: Princeton University Press, 1964.

243

Lapp, Ralph. Arms Beyond Doubt. New York: Cowles Book
    Co., 1970.

_____. The Weapons Culture. New York: W. W. Norton,
    1968.

Lincoln, George Arthur. Economics of National Security.
    New York: Prentice-Hall, 1954.

MacCloskey, Monro. The American Intelligence Community.
    New York: Rosen Press, 1967.

The Military Balance 1968-1969, 1969-1970. London: Institute
    of Strategic Studies.

Peck, Merton J., and Scherer, Frederic M. The Weapons
    Acquisition Process. Boston: Harvard University Press,
    1962.

Ransom, Harry Howe. Can American Democracy Survive
    Cold War? Garden City, N.Y.: Doubleday, 1963.

_____. Central Intelligence and National Security.
    Cambridge, Mass.: Harvard University Press, 1958.

Rathjens, George W. The Future of the Strategic Arms Race:
    Options for the 1970's. New York: Carnegie Endowment
    for International Peace, 1969.

Union of Concerned Scientists. MIRV. Cambridge, Mass.,
    June 20, 1969.

Wohlstetter, Roberta. Cuba and Pearl Harbor: Hindsight and
    Foresight. Santa Monica, Calif.: Rand Corporation, 1965.

_____. Pearl Harbor, Warning and Decision. Stanford,
    Calif.: Stanford University Press, 1962.

ARTICLES AND SPEECHES

"Air Force Studies Barges for Missiles," Washington Evening
    Star, April 14, 1970.

American Economic Review, Papers & Proceedings, May,
1969.

Ames, Capt. Lionel E., Jr. Speech before the Aviation Space
Writers Association, May, 1969, Dayton, Ohio.

Barnds, William J. "Intelligence and Foreign Policy: Dilemmas
of a Democracy," _Foreign Affairs,_ January, 1969, p. 281.

Benoit, Emile. "The Monetary and Real Costs of National
Defense," _American Economic Review, Papers & Proceedings,_ May, 1968.

Brown, Harold. "Air Power in Limited War," _Air University
Review,_ May-June, 1969, pp. 2-15.

_____. "Planning our Military Force," _Foreign Affairs,_
January, 1967, p. 277.

_____. "Security Through Limitations," _Foreign Affairs,_
April, 1969, pp. 422-32.

Coble, Donald W. "Destroyers Join the Jet Set," _Armed
Forces Management,_ Vol. 16, No. 3, December, 1969,
pp. 50-54.

Committee for Economic Development, "How Much Defense
Can the Economy Stand?," _The Problem of National
Security,_ July, 1958.

Cossaboom, Bruce. "F-15: Troubles at the 11th Hour,"
Armed Forces Journal, December 27, 1969, pp. 10-19.

CPR National Journal, March 14, 1970, pp. 544-47.

"Destroyers' Cost Soars; Navy to Cut Exotic Gear," _Washington
Post,_ February 23, 1970, pp. A1 and A8.

Foster, William C. "Prospects for Arms Control," _Foreign
Affairs,_ April, 1969.

Garwin, Richard, and Bethe, Hans. "Anti-Ballistic Missile
Systems," _Scientific American,_ March, 1958, p. 21.

Getler, Michael. "Arms Control and the SS-9," _Space/
Aeronautics,_ November, 1969.

Hamilton, Andrew. "Air Force, Navy Request for New Fighter Planes Spur Cost Controversy," National Journal, September 22, 1969.

Hilsman, Roger. "Intelligence and Policy Making in Foreign Affairs," World Politics, Vol. V, No. 1 (October, 1952).

Leary, Frank. "ULMS: Will All the Targets Go to Sea?," Armed Forces Management, May, 1970, pp. 36-40.

Leontief, Wassily W. "The Economic Effects of Disarmament," Scientific American, April, 1961.

Murphy, Charles J. V. "Decision Time for Tactical Air Power," Fortune, December, 1968.

New York Times, March 21, 1969; March 22, 1969; April 9, 1969, p. 1; April 27, 1969, p. 2E; June 9, 1969, p. 1.

"The Northrop F-5-21: Study of a Fighter in Evolution," Interavia, July, 1969, pp. 912-15.

Paolucci, Capt. Dominic A. "Poseidon and Minuteman," U.S. Naval Institute Proceedings, August, 1968.

"Partial Modernization Due for Tactical Air," Aviation Week and Space Technology, March 9, 1970, p. 12.

"Russians Seen Deploying MIRV in 1970," Washington Post, August 6, 1969.

"Ships - DD-963 Class," DMS Market Intelligence Report, October, 1969, pp. 1-9.

"Soviet Anti-Missile Systems Spur New U.S. Weapons," The New York Times, February 5, 1967.

"Soviet Missile Deployment Puzzles Top U.S. Analysts," The New York Times, April 14, 1969.

"Soviets Reported Stressing Multiple Warhead Missile," The New York Times, September 10, 1967.

Space/Aeronautics, L, November, 1968, 49-77.

"SS-9 Helps Administration Score Points in Missile Debate,"
   New York Times, March 24, 1969.

Stone, Jeremy. "When and How to Use Salt," Foreign Affairs,
   January, 1970, pp. 262-73.

"Study Backs Foes of Missile Shield," New York Times,
   April 9, 1969.

Tobin, James. "Defense, Dollars, and Doctrines," Yale
   Review, Spring, 1958.

Ulsamer, E. "A-X, Lethal, Accurate, Agile and Cheap,"
   Air Force and Space Digest, January, 1970, p. 33.

Washington Post, April 13, 1969, p. B-1; June 12, 1969, p. 1;
   June 21, 1969; June 25, 1969.

OFFICIAL RECORDS AND DOCUMENTS

Authorization for Military Procurement, Research and Development Fiscal Year 1970, and Reserve Strength. Hearings
   before the Committee on Armed Services, U.S. Senate,
   Part 2, 91st Cong., 1st Sess. (1969).

Brown, George. Congressional Record, H 1473-1475, March
   3, 1970.

Cannon, Howard W. "Report on Tactical Aircraft and Tactical
   Air-to-Ground Missiles," Congressional Record, July 10,
   1969, pp. S 7859-7863.

Clifford, Clark M. The 1970 Defense Budget and Defense
   Program for Fiscal Years 1970-74.

Competition in Defense Procurement--1969. Hearing before
   the Subcommittee on Antitrust and Monopoly of the Committee on the Judiciary, U.S. Senate, 91st Cong., 1st
   Sess. (1970).

Department of Defense Appropriation Bill, 1969. Report
   Submitted by George H. Mahon, 90th Cong., 2d Sess.,
   Report Number 90 S 1735, submitted July 18, 1968.

Department of Defense Appropriation Bill, 1970. Report Submitted by George H. Mahon, 91st Cong., 2d Sess., Report Number 91-698, submitted December 3, 1969.

Department of Defense Appropriations for 1969. Hearings before a Subcommittee of the Committee on Appropriations, House of Representatives, 90th Cong., 2d Sess. (1968).

Department of Defense Appropriations for 1970. Hearings before the Committee on Appropriations of the U.S. Senate, Part 6, 91st Cong., 1st Sess. (1969).

Department of Defense Appropriations for 1970. Hearings held by the House Committee on Appropriations.

Department of Defense Appropriations for 1970. Hearings before a Subcommittee of the Committee on Appropriations, House of Representatives, Part 3, Procurement, and Part 7, 91st Cong., 1st Sess. (1969).

Diplomatic and Strategic Impact of Multiple Missiles. Hearings before the Subcommittee on National Security Policy and Scientific Developments, 91st Cong., 1st Sess.

DMS Market Intelligence Report on Advanced ICBM, September, 1968.

Ferguson, General James. Statement to Subcommittee of the House Armed Services Committee on Budget Estimates for FY 1971, March, 1970.

Foreign Broadcast Information Service, U.S. National Archives.

Glasser, Lieutenant General Otto J. Statement to the House Armed Services Committee on Budget Estimates for FY 1971, March 11, 1970.

Goldwater, Barry. "The F-14 Program, Comments on MCPL 1969 Report on Military Spending," Congressional Record, August 11, 1969, pp. S 9664-9667.

Hartke, Vance. "Doubts About the F-14 at the Pentagon," address in Senate Chamber, September 5, 1969.

_____. "F-14: A $25 Billion Monument to the Past?," address in Senate Chamber, August 13, 1969.

Intelligence and the ABM. Hearings before the Committee on Foreign Relations, 91st Cong., 1st Sess. (June 23, 1969).

Keller, Robert F., Assistant Comptroller General of the United States. Statement before the Subcommittee on Economy in Government, Joint Economic Committee, December 29, 1969.

Laird, Melvin R. Defense Report. Washington, D.C.: Government Printing Office, March 19, 1969.

_____. Defense Program and Budget for FY 1971 Statement before a Joint Session of the Senate Armed Services and Appropriations Committees, February 20, 1970.

"New Plane Seen More Costly, Little Better Than F-111," Congressional Quarterly Special Report, May 3, 1968, pp. 1007-1009.

Office of the Chief of Naval Operations. "The F-14 Fighter Program," Memorandum, September 6, 1969. Inserted in the Congressional Record by Senator Charles Goodell, September 18, 1969, pp. S 10858-10864.

Permanent Subcommittee on Investigations of the Senate Government Operations Committee. Hearings on the F-11 Program. Spring, 1970.

Preparedness Investigating Subcommittee of the Committee on Armed Services. "Status of U.S. Strategic Power," 90th Cong., 2d Sess.

"Pro and Con on New MIRV Advanced Weapons System," Congressional Quarterly, June 20, 1969.

"Report on Adverse Effects of Procuring the Drone Anti-Submarine Helicopter Before Completion of Development and Tests," GAO Report, February 20, 1970.

"Report on Adverse Effects of Producing the AN-SQS-26 Surface Ship Sonar System Before Completion of Development and Tests," GAO Report, May 12, 1970.

Safeguard ABM System. Hearings before the Subcommittee
of the Committee on Appropriations, House of Representatives, 91st Cong., 1st Sess.

Strategic and Foreign Policy Implications of ABM Systems.
Hearings before the Subcommittee on International Organ-
ization and Disarmament Affairs of the Committee on
Foreign Relations, Parts I, II, III, 91st Cong., 1st Sess.

Unclassified Navy ULMS Fact Sheet, U. S. Department of the
Navy.

U. S. Commission on Organization of the Executive Branch of
the Government. Washington, D. C.: Government Printing
Office, 1955.

U. S. Tactical Air Power Program. Hearings before the Preparedness Investigating Subcommittee of the Committee
on Armed Services of the U. S. Senate. 91st Cong., 2d
Sess. (1968).

U. S. Tactical Air Power Program. Report by the Preparedness
Investigating Subcommittee of the Committee on Armed
Services of the U. S. Senate. 91st Cong., 2d Sess. (1968).

INDEX

A-4 Skyhawk, 122
A-6 Intruder, 115, 121, 122, 125, 126-27
A-7 Corsair, 115, 118, 125, 126, 128
A-X aircraft, 121-22, 128
Adams, Brock, vi
Advanced ICBM (WS 120-A), 103-5, 107
   Self-Aligning Boost and Re-entry Program (SABRE), 104
   Survivable Radio Guidance System (SRGS), 104
AEGIS, 173, 174
Agent Blue, 133, 134, 136
Agent Orange, 133, 134, 136, 137
Agent Purple, 134
Agent White, 133, 134, 137
AGILE, 123
AID, 35
Aircraft carriers, 5, 118, 155-65, 174
   CVA attack aircraft carrier, 151-52
   CVAN-70, 156, 175
   CVS anti-submarine carrier, 150, 151
Anthony, Robert, 24
Anti-Ballistic Missile System (ABM)
   new concepts of, 40
   Safeguard, 4, 5, 40, 41, 42, 44, 45, 48, 50, 51-62, 65-66, 67, 99, 100-101, 106, 107, 180
   Soviet ABM, 45, 63, 64-65, 67, 69, 74-75
Anti-submarine warfare, 151-52, 153-54
   aircraft carriers, 155-65
   anti-submarine rocket (ASROC), 174
   DD-963 destroyer, 166-71
   DLGN-38 nuclear frigate, 172-76
   Mark-48 torpedo, 182-89
   S-3A airplane, 190-93
   Soviet submarine threat, 167-68, 169-70
   SSN-688 attack submarine, 177-81
Appropriations Committees, 6, 7
   House, 125, 132, 208, 226
Armed Services Committees, 7, 33, 34, 211
   House, 73, 150, 175, 184, 188, 199-201
   Senate, 68, 125, 200
Atomic Energy Commission (AEC), 31

B-1 (Advanced Manned Strategic Aircraft), 40, 47, 50, 71-81
   compared to Boeing 747, 78-80
B-52 bomber, 50, 72-73, 74, 75, 78, 99, 100
Balance of Terror, 45
Ballistic Missile Early Warning Systems (BMEWS), 44
Bare Base Support Program, 158
Bay of Pigs, 32
Bisplinghoff Committee, 93
Blackout, 53, 54
Blue water option, 102
Board of National Estimates, 31, 35
Boland, Edward P., vi
Bourguiba, Habib, President of Tunisia, 3
Brookings Institution, 24, 41
Brown, George E., Jr., vi
Bulgaria, 115, 216
Burns, Arthur, 27

C-5A transport, 77, 79, 86-96
Cambodia, defoliation of, 139-42
Center for Naval Analysis (CNA), 160
Central Intelligence Agency (CIA), 16, 29, 30, 31-32, 34-35
Chaff, 53, 68
Chemical warfare, 5-6, 133-42
China (CPR), 16
   contingency planning against, 113-14, 116, 150, 152-53, 154
   deterring of, 101
   ICBM attack on U.S., 57-58
   and Korea, 227-28
   military manpower level of, 197-99
   U.S.-China Committee (MCPL), 4
   U.S.-China relations, 4
Civilianization, program of, 206-7, 211
Clark, Joseph S., 3, 4, 7
Clevite Corporation, 185-86
Clifford, Clark, 24
Cohelan, Jeffery, vi
Consumer Price Index (CPI), as gauge of inflation, 13
Contingency planning, 113-14
   2 1/2 - 1 1/2 wars, 203, 210
Cost-benefit curves, 22
Cost estimates
   See individual weapon systems
Cuban missile crisis, 6
Czechoslovakia, 115, 216, 218, 221, 223

DD-963 destroyer, 166-71
Decoys, 53, 54, 68
Defense Intelligence Agency (DIA), 30, 31, 35, 203

253

254

ABOUT THE COMMITTEE

The Military Spending Committee of Members of Congress for Peace Through Law is composed of Members of both the House and Senate. Their association is voluntary and bi-partisan. Unencumbered by seniority and party or ideological labels, these men have undertaken a continuing study of U.S. military policies and programs. This alliance of common interest and dedication is unique to Congressional politics.

Under the chairmanship of Senator Mark O. Hatfield of Oregon, the Committee has energetically challenged basic military assumptions and has called for a re-evaluation of U.S. policies in light of changing international conditions and domestic concerns.